Go Programming Blueprints

Second Edition

Build real-world, production-ready solutions in Go using cutting-edge technology and techniques

Mat Ryer

BIRMINGHAM - MUMBAI

Go Programming Blueprints

Second Edition

First published: January 2015

Second edition: October 2016

Production reference: 1211016

Published by Packt Publishing Ltd.
Livery Place
35 Livery Street
Birmingham
B3 2PB, UK.

ISBN 978-1-78646-894-9

www.packtpub.com

Credits

Author

Mat Ryer

Reviewers

Michael Hamrah
David Hernandez

Commissioning Editor

Kunal Parikh

Acquisition Editor

Sonali Vernekar

Content Development Editor

Siddhi Chavan

Technical Editors

Bhavin Savalia
Dhiraj Chandanshive

Copy Editor

Stuti Srivastava

Project Coordinator

Suzanne Coutinho

Proofreader

SAFIS Editing

Indexer

Tejal Daruwale Soni

Graphics

Abhinash Sahu

Production Coordinator

Aparna Bhagat

About the Author

Mat Ryer has been programming computers since he was 6 years old; he and his father would build games and programs, first in BASIC on a ZX Spectrum and then in AmigaBASIC and AMOS on Commodore Amiga. Many hours were spent on manually copying the code from Amiga Format magazine and tweaking variables or moving GOTO statements around to see what might happen. The same spirit of exploration and obsession with programming led Mat to start work with a local agency in Mansfield, England, when he was 18, where he started to build websites and services.

In 2006, Mat left rural Nottinghamshire for London, where he took a job at BT. It was here that he worked with a talented group of developers and managers on honing his agile development skills and developing the light flavor that he still uses today.

After being contracted around London for a few years, coding everything from C# and Objective-C to Ruby and JavaScript, Mat noticed a new systems language called Go that Google was pioneering. Since it addressed very pertinent and relevant modern technical challenges, Mat started using it to solve problems while the language was still in the beta stage and he has used it ever since.

In 2012, Mat moved to Boulder, Colorado, where he worked on a variety of projects, from big data web services and highly available systems to small side projects and charitable endeavors. He returned home, to London, in 2015 after the company he was working in was sold. Mat, to this day, continues to use Go to build a variety of products, services, and open-source projects. He writes articles about Go on his blog at `matryer.com` and tweets about Go with the handle *@matryer*.

Mat is a regular speaker at Go conferences around the world and encourages people to come up and introduce themselves if their paths ever cross.

Acknowledgments

I wouldn't have been able to write this book, or the second edition, without the help of the wonderful Laurie Edwards, who, while working on her own projects took the time to keep me organized and focused. Without her continuous and undying support, I dare say this book (along with every other project I have embarked on) would never have happened. Development heroes of mine include David Hernández (@dahernan on GitHub), who delights in telling me that my ideas are "terrible" before later falling in love with them; Ernesto Jiménez, who works extremely hard and extremely effectively on private and public projects alike; Tyler Bunnell (@tylerb on GitHub), who I learned Go with; and Ryan Quinn (@mazondo on GitHub), who seems to build an app a day and is living proof of how building something, however simple, is always better than building nothing. Thanks also goes out to Tim Schreiner for engaging in debates with me over the good and bad bits of Go as well as being my go-to guy on matters close to and beyond the fringes of computer science. Thanks go to the core Go team for building such a fun language and to the entire Go community, who have saved me months of development with their contributions. A special shout out to the Women Who Go and Go Bridge (@golangbridge on Twitter) groups, who are working increasingly hard to help us reach and maintain a rich and diversely populated community. Special thanks also goes to everyone who has supported me in my life and helped me in developing what I love into a career, including, but not limited to, Nick and Maggie Ryer, Chris Ryer, Glenn and Tracey Wilson, Phil Jackson, Aaron Edell, Sek Chai, David Hernández, Ernesto Jiménez, Blaine Garst, Tim and Stacey Stockhaus, Tom Szabo, Steve Davis, Mark Gray, John Motz, Rory Donnelly, Piotr Rojek, Corey Prak, Peter Bourgon, Andrew Gerrand, Dave Cheney, William (Bill) Kennedy, Matt Heath, Carlisia Campos, Tiffany Jernigan, Natalie Pistunovich, Simon Howard, Sean Thompson, Jeff Cavins, Edd Grant, Alan Meade, Steve Cart, Andy Jackson, Aditya Pradana, Andy Joslin, Kal Chottai, Tim Ryer, Emma Payne, Corey and Ashton Ryer, Clair Ryer, Gareth and Dylan Evans, Holly Smitheman, Phil Edwards, Tracey Edwards, Kirsten, Megan and Paul Krawczyk, Alex, Adriénne and Ethan Edwards, Chantelle and Greg Rosson, and all my other great friends and family. In the loving memory of Maggie Ryer, 1961 - 2015.

About the Reviewer

Michael Hamrah is a software engineer from Brooklyn, New York, specializing in scalable and distributed systems with more than a decade of development experience. He is currently working as a Senior Software Engineer at Uber focusing on metrics and monitoring systems, which handles billions of low-latency events per day across multiple data centers. He works primarily with Go and has an extensive experience with all levels of the software stack . He can be reached on LinkedIn at `https://www.linkedin.com/in/ham rah`.

David Hernandez is an independent software engineer from London. He helps companies improve their software. He has worked in different countries, such as Spain, UK, and Australia. He has participated in projects such as the BBC London Olympics 2012. Additionally, he has also helped to achieve Continuous Delivery at Atlassian, and he has delivered services to citizens at UK Government Digital Services.

You can find David speaking and collaborating at the Go London User Group, as Go is his favorite programming language.

www.PacktPub.com

For support files and downloads related to your book, please visit www.PacktPub.com. For support files and downloads related to your book, please visit www.PacktPub.com.

Did you know that Packt offers eBook versions of every book published, with PDF and ePub files available? You can upgrade to the eBook version at www.PacktPub.com and as a print book customer, you are entitled to a discount on the eBook copy. Get in touch with us at service@packtpub.com for more details.

At www.PacktPub.com, you can also read a collection of free technical articles, sign up for a range of free newsletters and receive exclusive discounts and offers on Packt books and eBooks.

https://www.packtpub.com/mapt

Get the most in-demand software skills with Mapt. Mapt gives you full access to all Packt books and video courses, as well as industry-leading tools to help you plan your personal development and advance your career.

Why subscribe?

- Fully searchable across every book published by Packt
- Copy and paste, print, and bookmark content
- On demand and accessible via a web browser

Table of Contents

Preface

I have been blown away by the response *Go Programming Blueprints* has received, both from newcomers to Go, as well as well-respected titans of the community. The positive feedback has inspired me to do this second edition, where the code has been updated to the latest thinking and three new chapters have been added. Thanks to the contributions and questions from readers on the GitHub repository (`https://github.com/matryer/gobluep rints`), I have been able to address some errors, fix some bugs, and clear some things up. See the `README` file on GitHub for a complete list of their names.

I decided to write *Go Programming Blueprints* because I wanted to expel the myth that Go, being a relatively young language and community, is a bad choice to write and iterate on software quickly. I have a friend who knocks out complete Ruby on Rails apps in a weekend by mashing up pre-existing gems and libraries; Rails as a platform has become known for enabling rapid development. As I do the same with Go and the ever-growing buffet of open source packages, I wanted to share some real-world examples of how we can quickly build and release software that performs well from day one and is ready to scale when our projects take off in a way that Rails cannot compete with. Of course, most scalability happens outside the language, but features such as Go's built-in concurrency mean you can get some very impressive results from even the most basic hardware, giving you a head start when things start to get real.

This book explores some very different projects, any of which can form the basis of a genuine startup. Whether it's a low-latency chat application, a domain name suggestion tool, a social polling and election service built on Twitter, or a random night out generator powered by Google Places, each chapter touches upon a variety of problems that most products or services written in Go will need to address. The solutions I present in this book are just one of many ways to tackle each project, and I will encourage you to make up your own mind about how I approached them. The concepts are more important than the code itself, but you'll hopefully pick up a few tips and tricks here and there that can go into your Go toolbelt.

New to this second edition, we will explore some practical modern architectural thinking, such as how to build for Google App Engine, what a microservice looks like, and how to package up our code with Docker and deploy to anywhere.

The process by which I wrote this book may be interesting because it represents something about the philosophies adopted by many agile developers. I started by giving myself the challenge of building a real deployable product (albeit a simple one; a minimum viable product, if you will) before getting stuck into it and writing a version 1. Once I got it working, I would rewrite it from scratch. It is said many times by novelists and journalists that the art of writing is rewriting; I have found this to be true for software as well. The first time we write a piece of code, all we are really doing is learning about the problem and how it might be tackled, as well as getting some of our thinking out of our heads and onto paper, or into a text editor. The second time we write it, we are applying our new knowledge to actually solve the problem. If you've never tried this, give it a shot—you might find that the quality of your code shoots up quite dramatically as I did. It doesn't mean the second time will be the last time—software evolves and we should try to keep it as cheap and disposable as possible so we don't mind throwing pieces away if they go stale or start to get in the way.

I write all of my code following **Test-driven development** (TDD) practices, some of which we will do together throughout the book and some you'll just see the result of in the final code. All of the test code can be found in the GitHub repositories for this book, even if it's not included in print.

Once I had my test-driven second versions completed, I started writing the chapter describing how and why I did what I did. In most cases, the iterative approach I took is left out of the book because it would just add pages of tweaks and edits, which would probably just become frustrating for the reader. However, on a couple of occasions, we will iterate together to get a feel of how a process of gradual improvements and small iterations (starting and keeping it simple and introducing complexity only when absolutely necessary) can be applied when writing Go packages and programs.

I moved to the United States from England in 2012, but that is not why the chapters are authored in American English; it was a requirement from the publisher. I suppose this book is aimed at an American audience, or perhaps it's because American English is the standard language of computing (in British code, properties that deal with color are spelled without the U). Either way, I apologize in advance for any trans-Atlantic slips; I know how pedantic programmers can be.

Any questions, improvements, suggestions, or debates (I love how opinionated the Go community—as well as the core team and the language itself—is) are more than welcome. These should probably take place in the GitHub issues for the book setup, specifically at `https://github.com/matryer/goblueprints`, so that everybody can take part.

Finally, I would be thrilled if somebody forms a start-up based on any of these projects, or makes use of them in other places. I would love to hear about it; you can tweet me at *@matryer*.

What this book covers

Chapter 1, *Chat Application with Web Sockets*, shows how to build a complete web application that allows multiple people to have a real-time conversation right in their web browser. We will see how the NET/HTTP package let us serve HTML pages as well as connect to the client's browser with web sockets.

Chapter 2, *Adding User Accounts*, shows how to add OAuth to our chat application so that we can keep track of who is saying what, but let them log in using Google, Facebook, or GitHub.

Chapter 3, *Three Ways to Implement Profile Pictures*, explains how to add profile pictures to the chat application taken from either the authentication service, the Gravitar.com web service, or by allowing users to upload their own picture from their hard drive.

Chapter 4, *Command-Line Tools to Find Domain Names*, explores how easy building command-line tools is in Go and puts those skills to use to tackle the problem of finding the perfect domain name for our chat application. It also explores how easy Go makes it to utilize the standard-in and standard-out pipes to produce some pretty powerful composable tools.

Chapter 5, *Building Distributed Systems and Working with Flexible Data*, explains how to prepare for the future of democracy by building a highly-scalable Twitter polling and vote counting engine powered by NSQ and MongoDB.

Chapter 6, *Exposing Data and Functionality through a RESTful Data Web Service API*, looks at how to expose the capabilities we built in Chapter 5, *Building Distributed Systems and Working with Flexible Data*, through a JSON web service, specifically how the wrapping `http.HandlerFunc` functions give us a powerful pipeline pattern.

Chapter 7, *Random Recommendations Web Service*, shows how to consume the Google Places API to generate a location-based random recommendations API that represents a fun way to explore any area. It also explores why it's important to keep internal data structures private, controlling the public view into the same data, as well as how to implement enumerators in Go.

Chapter 8, *Filesystem Backup,* helps to build a simple but powerful filesystem backup tool for our code projects and explore interacting with the filesystem using the OS package from the Go standard library. It also looks at how Go's interfaces allow simple abstractions to yield powerful results.

Chapter 9, *Building a Q&A Application for Google App Engine,* shows how to build applications that can be deployed to Google's infrastructure and run at high scale with little to no operational duties for us. The project we build utilizes some of the cloud services available on Google App Engine, including the Google Cloud Datastore—a highly available and extremely fast schema-less data storage option.

Chapter 10, *Micro-services in Go with the Go Kit Framework,* explores a modern software architecture paradigm whereby large monolithic applications are broken down into discrete services with a singular focus. The services run independently of each other, allowing them to be individually scaled to meet demand. Go Kit is a software framework that addresses some of the challenges of a microservice architecture while remaining agnostic to the implementation details.

Chapter 11, *Deploying Go Applications Using Docker,* looks at how simple it is to build Docker images to package and deploy the application we built in Chapter 9, *Building a Q&A Application for Google App Engine.* We will write a Dockerfile that describes the image, and use the Docker tools to build the image, which we will then deploy to the Digital Ocean cloud.

Appendix, *Good Practices for a Stable Go Environment,* shows how to install Go from scratch on a new machine and discusses some of the environmental options we have and the impact they might have in the future. We will look at a few code editor (or IDE—Integrated Developer Environment) options and also consider how collaboration might influence some of our decisions as well as the impact open sourcing our packages might have.

What you need for this book

To compile and run the code from this book, you will need a computer capable of running an operating system that supports the Go toolset, a list of which can be found at https://g olang.org/doc/install#requirements.

Appendix, *Good Practices for a Stable Go Environment,* has some useful tips to install Go and set up your development environment, including how to work with the GOPATH environment variable.

Who this book is for

This book is for all Go programmers, ranging from beginners looking to explore the language by building real projects to expert gophers with an interest in how the language can be applied in interesting ways.

Conventions

In this book, you will find a number of text styles that distinguish between different kinds of information. Here are some examples of these styles and an explanation of their meaning. Code words in text, database table names, folder names, filenames, file extensions, pathnames, dummy URLs, user input, and Twitter handles are shown as follows: "You will notice that the deployable artifact for your application is the `webApp.war` file."

A block of code is set as follows:

```
package meander
type Cost int8
const (
  _ Cost = iota
  Cost1
  Cost2
  Cost3
  Cost4
  Cost5
)
```

Any command-line input or output is written as follows:

```
go build -o project && ./project
```

New terms and important words are shown in bold. Words that you see on the screen, for example, in menus or dialog boxes, appear in the text like this: "Once you install Xcode, you open Preferences and navigate to the **Downloads** section"

 Warnings or important notes appear in a box like this.

 Tips and tricks appear like this.

Reader feedback

Feedback from our readers is always welcome. Let us know what you think about this book—what you liked or disliked. Reader feedback is important for us as it helps us develop titles that you will really get the most out of.

To send us general feedback, simply e-mail feedback@packtpub.com, and mention the book's title in the subject of your message.

If there is a topic that you have expertise in and you are interested in either writing or contributing to a book, see our author guide at www.packtpub.com/authors.

Customer support

Now that you are the proud owner of a Packt book, we have a number of things to help you to get the most from your purchase.

Downloading the example code

You can download the example code files for this book from your account at http://www.packtpub.com. If you purchased this book elsewhere, you can visit http://www.packtpub.com/support and register to have the files e-mailed directly to you.

You can download the code files by following these steps:

1. Log in or register to our website using your e-mail address and password.
2. Hover the mouse pointer on the **SUPPORT** tab at the top.
3. Click on **Code Downloads & Errata**.
4. Enter the name of the book in the **Search** box.
5. Select the book for which you're looking to download the code files.
6. Choose from the drop-down menu where you purchased this book from.
7. Click on **Code Download**.

You can also download the code files by clicking on the **Code Files** button on the book's webpage at the Packt Publishing website. This page can be accessed by entering the book's name in the Search box. Please note that you need to be logged in to your Packt account.

Once the file is downloaded, please make sure that you unzip or extract the folder using the latest version of:

- WinRAR / 7-Zip for Windows
- Zipeg / iZip / UnRarX for Mac
- 7-Zip / PeaZip for Linux

The code bundle for the book is also hosted on GitHub at `https://github.com/PacktPubl ishing/Go-Programming-Blueprints`. We also have other code bundles from our rich catalog of books and videos available at `https://github.com/PacktPublishing/`. Check them out!

Errata

Although we have taken every care to ensure the accuracy of our content, mistakes do happen. If you find a mistake in one of our books—maybe a mistake in the text or the code—we would be grateful if you could report this to us. By doing so, you can save other readers from frustration and help us improve subsequent versions of this book. If you find any errata, please report them by visiting `http://www.packtpub.com/submit-errata`, selecting your book, clicking on the Errata Submission Form link, and entering the details of your errata. Once your errata are verified, your submission will be accepted and the errata will be uploaded to our website or added to any list of existing errata under the Errata section of that title.

To view the previously submitted errata, go to `https://www.packtpub.com/books/conten t/support` and enter the name of the book in the search field. The required information will appear under the Errata section.

Piracy

Piracy of copyrighted material on the Internet is an ongoing problem across all media. At Packt, we take the protection of our copyright and licenses very seriously. If you come across any illegal copies of our works in any form on the Internet, please provide us with the location address or website name immediately so that we can pursue a remedy.

Please contact us at `copyright@packtpub.com` with a link to the suspected pirated material.

We appreciate your help in protecting our authors and our ability to bring you valuable content.

Questions

If you have a problem with any aspect of this book, you can contact us at `questions@packtpub.com`, and we will do our best to address the problem.

1
Chat Application with Web Sockets

Go is great for writing high-performance, concurrent server applications and tools, and the Web is the perfect medium over which to deliver them. It would be difficult these days to find a gadget that is not web-enabled and this allows us to build a single application that targets almost all platforms and devices.

Our first project will be a web-based chat application that allows multiple users to have a real-time conversation right in their web browser. Idiomatic Go applications are often composed of many packages, which are organized by having code in different folders, and this is also true of the Go standard library. We will start by building a simple web server using the net/http package, which will serve the HTML files. We will then go on to add support for web sockets through which our messages will flow.

In languages such as C#, Java, or Node.js, complex threading code and clever use of locks need to be employed in order to keep all clients in sync. As we will see, Go helps us enormously with its built-in channels and concurrency paradigms.

In this chapter, you will learn how to:

- Use the net/http package to serve HTTP requests
- Deliver template-driven content to users' browsers
- Satisfy a Go interface to build our own http.Handler types
- Use Go's goroutines to allow an application to perform multiple tasks concurrently
- Use channels to share information between running goroutines
- Upgrade HTTP requests to use modern features such as web sockets
- Add tracing to the application to better understand its inner working

- Write a complete Go package using test-driven development practices
- Return unexported types through exported interfaces

 Complete source code for this project can be found at `https://github.co` `m/matryer/goblueprints/tree/master/chapter1/chat`. The source code was periodically committed so the history in GitHub actually follows the flow of this chapter too.

A simple web server

The first thing our chat application needs is a web server that has two main responsibilities:

- Serving the HTML and JavaScript chat clients that run in the user's browser
- Accepting web socket connections to allow the clients to communicate

 The `GOPATH` environment variable is covered in detail in `Appendix`, *Good Practices for a Stable Go environment*. Be sure to read that first if you need help getting set up.

Create a `main.go` file inside a new folder called `chat` in your `GOPATH` and add the following code:

```
package main
import (
  "log"
  "net/http"
)
func main() {
  http.HandleFunc("/", func(w http.ResponseWriter, r  *http.Request) {
    w.Write([]byte(`
      <html>
        <head>
          <title>Chat</title>
        </head>
        <body>
          Let's chat!
        </body>
      </html>
    `))
  })
  // start the web server
  if err := http.ListenAndServe(":8080", nil); err != nil {
```

```
        log.Fatal("ListenAndServe:", err)
    }
}
```

This is a complete, albeit simple, Go program that will:

- Listen to the root path using the `net/http` package
- Write out the hardcoded HTML when a request is made
- Start a web server on port `:8080` using the `ListenAndServe` method

The `http.HandleFunc` function maps the path pattern `/` to the function we pass as the second argument, so when the user hits `http://localhost:8080/`, the function will be executed. The function signature of `func(w http.ResponseWriter, r *http.Request)` is a common way of handling HTTP requests throughout the Go standard library.

We are using `package main` because we want to build and run our program from the command line. However, if we were building a reusable chatting package, we might choose to use something different, such as `package chat`.

In a terminal, run the program by navigating to the `main.go` file you just created and execute the following command:

```
go run main.go
```

The `go run` command is a helpful shortcut for running simple Go programs. It builds and executes a binary in one go. In the real world, you usually use `go build` yourself to create and distribute binaries. We will explore this later.

Open the browser and type `http://localhost:8080` to see the **Let's chat!** message.

Having the HTML code embedded within our Go code like this works, but it is pretty ugly and will only get worse as our projects grow. Next, we will see how templates can help us clean this up.

Separating views from logic using templates

Templates allow us to blend generic text with specific text, for instance, injecting a user's name into a welcome message. For example, consider the following template:

```
Hello {{name}}, how are you?
```

We are able to replace the {{name}} text in the preceding template with the real name of a person. So if Bruce signs in, he might see:

```
Hello Bruce, how are you?
```

The Go standard library has two main template packages: one called text/template for text and one called html/template for HTML. The html/template package does the same as the text version except that it understands the context in which data will be injected into the template. This is useful because it avoids script injection attacks and resolves common issues such as having to encode special characters for URLs.

Initially, we just want to move the HTML code from inside our Go code to its own file, but won't blend any text just yet. The template packages make loading external files very easy, so it's a good choice for us.

Create a new folder under our chat folder called templates and create a chat.html file inside it. We will move the HTML from main.go to this file, but we will make a minor change to ensure our changes have taken effect:

```html
<html>
  <head>
    <title>Chat</title>
  </head>
  <body>
    Let's chat (from template)
  </body>
</html>
```

Now, we have our external HTML file ready to go, but we need a way to compile the template and serve it to the user's browser.

 Compiling a template is a process by which the source template is interpreted and prepared for blending with various data, which must happen before a template can be used but only needs to happen once.

We are going to write our own `struct` type that is responsible for loading, compiling, and delivering our template. We will define a new type that will take a `filename` string, compile the template once (using the `sync.Once` type), keep the reference to the compiled template, and then respond to HTTP requests. You will need to import the `text/template`, `path/filepath`, and `sync` packages in order to build your code.

In `main.go`, insert the following code above the `func main()` line:

```
// templ represents a single template
type templateHandler struct {
  once     sync.Once
  filename string
  templ    *template.Template
}
// ServeHTTP handles the HTTP request.
func (t *templateHandler) ServeHTTP(w http.ResponseWriter, r
*http.Request) {
  t.once.Do(func() {
    t.templ = template.Must(template.ParseFiles(filepath.Join("templates",
      t.filename)))
  })
  t.templ.Execute(w, nil)
}
```

 Did you know that you could automate the adding and removing of imported packages? See `Appendix`, *Good Practices for a Stable Go Environment*, on how to do this.

The `templateHandler` type has a single method called `ServeHTTP` whose signature looks suspiciously like the method we passed to `http.HandleFunc` earlier. This method will load the source file, compile the template and execute it, and write the output to the specified `http.ResponseWriter` method. Because the `ServeHTTP` method satisfies the `http.Handler` interface, we can actually pass it directly to `http.Handle`.

 A quick look at the Go standard library source code, which is located at `http://golang.org/pkg/net/http/#Handler`, will reveal that the interface definition for `http.Handler` specifies that only the `ServeHTTP` method need be present in order for a type to be used to serve HTTP requests by the `net/http` package.

Doing things once

We only need to compile the template once, and there are a few different ways to approach this in Go. The most obvious is to have a `NewTemplateHandler` function that creates the type and calls some initialization code to compile the template. If we were sure the function would be called by only one goroutine (probably the main one during the setup in the `main` function), this would be a perfectly acceptable approach. An alternative, which we have employed in the preceding section, is to compile the template once inside the `ServeHTTP` method. The `sync.Once` type guarantees that the function we pass as an argument will only be executed once, regardless of how many goroutines are calling `ServeHTTP`. This is helpful because web servers in Go are automatically concurrent and once our chat application takes the world by storm, we could very well expect to have many concurrent calls to the `ServeHTTP` method.

Compiling the template inside the `ServeHTTP` method also ensures that our code does not waste time doing work before it is definitely needed. This lazy initialization approach doesn't save us much in our present case, but in cases where the setup tasks are time- and resource-intensive and where the functionality is used less frequently, it's easy to see how this approach would come in handy.

Using your own handlers

To implement our `templateHandler` type, we need to update the `main` body function so that it looks like this:

```
func main() {
  // root
  http.Handle("/", &templateHandler{filename: "chat.html"})
  // start the web server
  if err := http.ListenAndServe(":8080", nil); err != nil {
    log.Fatal("ListenAndServe:", err)
  }
}
```

The `templateHandler` structure is a valid `http.Handler` type so we can pass it directly to the `http.Handle` function and ask it to handle requests that match the specified pattern. In the preceding code, we created a new object of the type `templateHandler`, specifying the filename as `chat.html` that we then take the address of (using the `&` address of the operator) and pass it to the `http.Handle` function. We do not store a reference to our newly created `templateHandler` type, but that's OK because we don't need to refer to it again.

In your terminal, exit the program by pressing *Ctrl + C* and re-run it, then refresh your browser and notice the addition of the (from template) text. Now our code is much simpler than an HTML code and free from its ugly blocks.

Properly building and executing Go programs

Running Go programs using a `go run` command is great when our code is made up of a single `main.go` file. However, often we might quickly need to add other files. This requires us to properly build the whole package into an executable binary before running it. This is simple enough, and from now on, this is how you will build and run your programs in a terminal:

```
go build -o {name}
./{name}
```

The `go build` command creates the output binary using all the `.go` files in the specified folder, and the `-o` flag indicates the name of the generated binary. You can then just run the program directly by calling it by name.

For example, in the case of our chat application, we could run:

```
go build -o chat
./chat
```

Since we are compiling templates the first time the page is served, we will need to restart your web server program every time anything changes in order to see the changes take effect.

Modeling a chat room and clients on the server

All users (clients) of our chat application will automatically be placed in one big public room where everyone can chat with everyone else. The `room` type will be responsible for managing client connections and routing messages in and out, while the `client` type represents the connection to a single client.

 Go refers to classes as types and instances of those classes as objects.

To manage our web sockets, we are going to use one of the most powerful aspects of the Go community open source third-party packages. Every day, new packages solving real-world problems are released, ready for you to use in your own projects, and they even allow you to add features, report and fix bugs, and get support.

 It is often unwise to reinvent the wheel unless you have a very good reason. So before embarking on building a new package, it is worth searching for any existing projects that might have already solved your very problem. If you find one similar project that doesn't quite satisfy your needs, consider contributing to the project and adding features. Go has a particularly active open source community (remember that Go itself is open source) that is always ready to welcome new faces or avatars.

We are going to use Gorilla Project's `websocket` package to handle our server-side sockets rather than write our own. If you're curious about how it works, head over to the project home page on GitHub, `https://github.com/gorilla/websocket`, and browse the open source code.

Modeling the client

Create a new file called `client.go` alongside `main.go` in the `chat` folder and add the following code:

```
package main
import (
  "github.com/gorilla/websocket"
)
// client represents a single chatting user.
type client struct {
  // socket is the web socket for this client.
  socket *websocket.Conn
  // send is a channel on which messages are sent.
  send chan []byte
  // room is the room this client is chatting in.
  room *room
}
```

In the preceding code, `socket` will hold a reference to the web socket that will allow us to communicate with the client, and the `send` field is a buffered channel through which received messages are queued ready to be forwarded to the user's browser (via the socket). The `room` field will keep a reference to the room that the client is chatting in this is required so that we can forward messages to everyone else in the room.

If you try to build this code, you will notice a few errors. You must ensure that you have called `go get` to retrieve the `websocket` package, which is as easy as opening a terminal and typing the following:

```
go get github.com/gorilla/websocket
```

Building the code again will yield another error:

```
./client.go:17 undefined: room
```

The problem is that we have referred to a `room` type without defining it anywhere. To make the compiler happy, create a file called `room.go` and insert the following placeholder code:

```
package main
type room struct {
  // forward is a channel that holds incoming messages
  // that should be forwarded to the other clients.
  forward chan []byte
}
```

We will improve this definition later once we know a little more about what our room needs to do, but for now, this will allow us to proceed. Later, the `forward` channel is what we will use to send the incoming messages to all other clients.

 You can think of channels as an in-memory thread-safe message queue where senders pass data and receivers read data in a non-blocking, thread-safe way.

In order for a client to do any work, we must define some methods that will do the actual reading and writing to and from the web socket. Adding the following code to `client.go` outside (underneath) the `client` struct will add two methods called `read` and `write` to the `client` type:

```
func (c *client) read() {
  defer c.socket.Close()
  for {
    _, msg, err := c.socket.ReadMessage()
    if err != nil {
```

```
            return
        }
        c.room.forward <- msg
    }
}
func (c *client) write() {
    defer c.socket.Close()
    for msg := range c.send {
        err := c.socket.WriteMessage(websocket.TextMessage, msg)
        if err != nil {
            return
        }
    }
}
```

The `read` method allows our client to read from the socket via the `ReadMessage` method, continually sending any received messages to the `forward` channel on the `room` type. If it encounters an error (such as `'the socket has died'`), the loop will break and the socket will be closed. Similarly, the `write` method continually accepts messages from the `send` channel writing everything out of the socket via the `WriteMessage` method. If writing to the socket fails, the `for` loop is broken and the socket is closed. Build the package again to ensure everything compiles.

In the preceding code, we introduced the `defer` keyword, which is worth exploring a little. We are asking Go to run `c.socket.Close()` when the function exits. It's extremely useful for when you need to do some tidying up in a function (such as closing a file or, as in our case, a socket) but aren't sure where the function will exit. As our code grows, if this function has multiple `return` statements, we won't need to add any more calls to close the socket, because this single `defer` statement will catch them all.

Some people complain about the performance of using the `defer` keyword, since it doesn't perform as well as typing the `close` statement before every exit point in the function. You must weigh up the runtime performance cost against the code maintenance cost and potential bugs that may get introduced if you decide not to use defer. As a general rule of thumb, writing clean and clear code wins; after all, we can always come back and optimize any bits of code we feel is slowing our product down if we are lucky enough to have such success.

Modeling a room

We need a way for clients to join and leave rooms in order to ensure that
the c.room.forward <- msg code in the preceding section actually forwards the message
to all the clients. To ensure that we are not trying to access the same data at the same time, a
sensible approach is to use two channels: one that will add a client to the room and another
that will remove it. Let's update our room.go code to look like this:

```
package main
type room struct {
  // forward is a channel that holds incoming messages
  // that should be forwarded to the other clients.
  forward chan []byte
  // join is a channel for clients wishing to join the room.
  join chan *client
  // leave is a channel for clients wishing to leave the room.
  leave chan *client
  // clients holds all current clients in this room.
  clients map[*client]bool
}
```

We have added three fields: two channels and a map. The join and leave channels exist
simply to allow us to safely add and remove clients from the clients map. If we were to
access the map directly, it is possible that two goroutines running concurrently might try to
modify the map at the same time, resulting in corrupt memory or unpredictable state.

Concurrency programming using idiomatic Go

Now we get to use an extremely powerful feature of Go's concurrency offerings the select
statement. We can use select statements whenever we need to synchronize or modify
shared memory, or take different actions depending on the various activities within our
channels.

Beneath the room structure, add the following run method that contains three select
cases:

```
func (r *room) run() {
  for {
    select {
    case client := <-r.join:
      // joining
      r.clients[client] = true
    case client := <-r.leave:
      // leaving
```

```
        delete(r.clients, client)
        close(client.send)
      case msg := <-r.forward:
        // forward message to all clients
        for client := range r.clients {
          client.send <- msg
        }
      }
    }
  }
}
```

Although this might seem like a lot of code to digest, once we break it down a little, we will see that it is fairly simple, although extremely powerful. The top `for` loop indicates that this method will run forever, until the program is terminated. This might seem like a mistake, but remember, if we run this code as a goroutine, it will run in the background, which won't block the rest of our application. The preceding code will keep watching the three channels inside our room: `join`, `leave`, and `forward`. If a message is received on any of those channels, the `select` statement will run the code for that particular case.

 It is important to remember that it will only run one block of case code at a time. This is how we are able to synchronize to ensure that our `r.clients` map is only ever modified by one thing at a time.

If we receive a message on the `join` channel, we simply update the `r.clients` map to keep a reference of the client that has joined the room. Notice that we are setting the value to `true`. We are using the map more like a slice, but do not have to worry about shrinking the slice as clients come and go through time setting the value to `true` is just a handy, low-memory way of storing the reference.

If we receive a message on the `leave` channel, we simply delete the `client` type from the map, and close its `send` channel. If we receive a message on the `forward` channel, we iterate over all the clients and add the message to each client's `send` channel. Then, the `write` method of our client type will pick it up and send it down the socket to the browser.

Turning a room into an HTTP handler

Now we are going to turn our `room` type into an `http.Handler` type like we did with the template handler earlier. As you will recall, to do this, we must simply add a method called `ServeHTTP` with the appropriate signature.

Add the following code to the bottom of the `room.go` file:

```
const (
  socketBufferSize  = 1024
  messageBufferSize = 256
)
var upgrader = &websocket.Upgrader{ReadBufferSize:  socketBufferSize,
  WriteBufferSize: socketBufferSize}
func (r *room) ServeHTTP(w http.ResponseWriter, req *http.Request) {
  socket, err := upgrader.Upgrade(w, req, nil)
  if err != nil {
    log.Fatal("ServeHTTP:", err)
    return
  }
  client := &client{
    socket: socket,
    send:   make(chan []byte, messageBufferSize),
    room:   r,
  }
  r.join <- client
  defer func() { r.leave <- client }()
  go client.write()
  client.read()
}
```

The `ServeHTTP` method means a room can now act as a handler. We will implement it shortly, but first let's have a look at what is going on in this snippet of code.

 If you accessed the chat endpoint in a web browser, you would likely crash the program and see an error like **ServeHTTPwebsocket: version != 13**. This is because it is intended to be accessed via a web socket rather than a web browser.

In order to use web sockets, we must upgrade the HTTP connection using the `websocket.Upgrader` type, which is reusable so we need only create one. Then, when a request comes in via the `ServeHTTP` method, we get the socket by calling the `upgrader.Upgrade` method. All being well, we then create our client and pass it into the `join` channel for the current room. We also defer the leaving operation for when the client is finished, which will ensure everything is tidied up after a user goes away.

The `write` method for the client is then called as a goroutine, as indicated by the three characters at the beginning of the line `go` (the word `go` followed by a space character). This tells Go to run the method in a different thread or goroutine.

Compare the amount of code needed to achieve multithreading or concurrency in other languages with the three key presses that achieve it in Go, and you will see why it has become a favorite among system developers.

Finally, we call the `read` method in the main thread, which will block operations (keeping the connection alive) until it's time to close it. Adding constants at the top of the snippet is a good practice for declaring values that would otherwise be hardcoded throughout the project. As these grow in number, you might consider putting them in a file of their own, or at least at the top of their respective files so they remain easy to read and modify.

Using helper functions to remove complexity

Our room is almost ready to go, although in order for it to be of any use, the channels and map need to be created. As it is, this could be achieved by asking the developer to use the following code to be sure to do this:

```
r := &room{
  forward: make(chan []byte),
  join:    make(chan *client),
  leave:   make(chan *client),
  clients: make(map[*client]bool),
}
```

Another, slightly more elegant, solution is to instead provide a `newRoom` function that does this for us. This removes the need for others to know about exactly what needs to be done in order for our room to be useful. Underneath the `type room struct` definition, add this function:

```
// newRoom makes a new room.
func newRoom() *room {
  return &room{
    forward: make(chan []byte),
    join:    make(chan *client),
    leave:   make(chan *client),
    clients: make(map[*client]bool),
  }
}
```

Now the users of our code need only call the `newRoom` function instead of the more verbose six lines of code.

Creating and using rooms

Let's update our `main` function in `main.go` to first create and then run a room for everybody to connect to:

```
func main() {
  r := newRoom()
  http.Handle("/", &templateHandler{filename: "chat.html"})
  http.Handle("/room", r)
  // get the room going
  go r.run()
  // start the web server
  if err := http.ListenAndServe(":8080", nil); err != nil {
    log.Fatal("ListenAndServe:", err)
  }
}
```

We are running the room in a separate goroutine (notice the `go` keyword again) so that the chatting operations occur in the background, allowing our main goroutine to run the web server. Our server is now finished and successfully built, but remains useless without clients to interact with.

Building an HTML and JavaScript chat client

In order for the users of our chat application to interact with the server and therefore other users, we need to write some client-side code that makes use of the web sockets found in modern browsers. We are already delivering HTML content via the template when users hit the root of our application, so we can enhance that.

Update the `chat.html` file in the `templates` folder with the following markup:

```
<html>
  <head>
    <title>Chat</title>
    <style>
      input { display: block; }
      ul    { list-style: none; }
    </style>
  </head>
  <body>
    <ul id="messages"></ul>
    <form id="chatbox">
      <textarea></textarea>
      <input type="submit" value="Send" />
```

```
        </form>    </body>
    </html>
```

The preceding HTML will render a simple web form on the page containing a text area and a **Send** button this is how our users will submit messages to the server. The messages element in the preceding code will contain the text of the chat messages so that all the users can see what is being said. Next, we need to add some JavaScript to add some functionality to our page. Underneath the form tag, above the closing </body> tag, insert the following code:

```
<script  src="//ajax.googleapis.com/ajax/libs/jquery/1.11.1/jquery.min.js">
</script>
    <script>
      $(function(){
        var socket = null;
        var msgBox = $("#chatbox textarea");
        var messages = $("#messages");
        $("#chatbox").submit(function(){
          if (!msgBox.val()) return false;
          if (!socket) {
            alert("Error: There is no socket connection.");
            return false;
          }
          socket.send(msgBox.val());
          msgBox.val("");
          return false;
        });
        if (!window["WebSocket"]) {
          alert("Error: Your browser does not support web  sockets.")
        } else {
          socket = new WebSocket("ws://localhost:8080/room");
          socket.onclose = function() {
            alert("Connection has been closed.");
          }
          socket.onmessage = function(e) {
            messages.append($("<li>").text(e.data));
          }
        }
      });
    </script>
```

The socket = new WebSocket("ws://localhost:8080/room") line is where we open the socket and add event handlers for two key events: onclose and onmessage. When the socket receives a message, we use jQuery to append the message to the list element and thus present it to the user.

Submitting the HTML form triggers a call to `socket.send`, which is how we send messages to the server.

Build and run the program again to ensure the templates recompile so these changes are represented.

Navigate to `http://localhost:8080/` in two separate browsers (or two tabs of the same browser) and play with the application. You will notice that messages sent from one client appear instantly in the other clients:

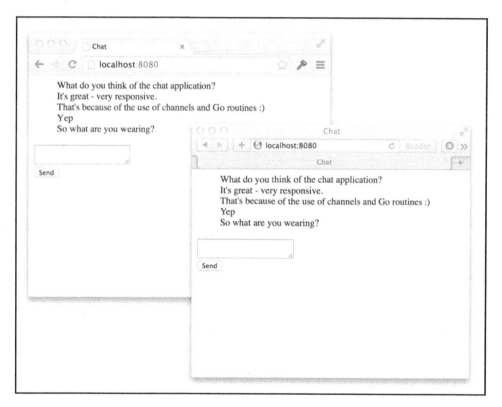

Getting more out of templates

Currently, we are using templates to deliver static HTML, which is nice because it gives us a clean and simple way to separate the client code from the server code. However, templates are actually much more powerful, and we are going to tweak our application to make some more realistic use of them.

The host address of our application (`:8080`) is hardcoded at two places at the moment. The first instance is in `main.go` where we start the web server:

```
if err := http.ListenAndServe(":8080", nil); err != nil {
  log.Fatal("ListenAndServe:", err)
}
```

The second time it is hardcoded in the JavaScript when we open the socket:

```
socket = new WebSocket("ws://localhost:8080/room");
```

Our chat application is pretty stubborn if it insists on only running locally on port `8080`, so we are going to use command-line flags to make it configurable and then use the injection capabilities of templates to make sure our JavaScript knows the right host.

Update your `main` function in `main.go`:

```
func main() {
  var addr = flag.String("addr", ":8080", "The addr of the  application.")
  flag.Parse() // parse the flags
  r := newRoom()
  http.Handle("/", &templateHandler{filename: "chat.html"})
  http.Handle("/room", r)
  // get the room going
  go r.run()
  // start the web server
  log.Println("Starting web server on", *addr)
  if err := http.ListenAndServe(*addr, nil); err != nil {
    log.Fatal("ListenAndServe:", err)
  }
}
```

You will need to import the `flag` package in order for this code to build. The definition for the `addr` variable sets up our flag as a string that defaults to `:8080` (with a short description of what the value is intended for). We must call `flag.Parse()` that parses the arguments and extracts the appropriate information. Then, we can reference the value of the host flag by using `*addr`.

 The call to `flag.String` returns a type of `*string`, which is to say it returns the address of a string variable where the value of the flag is stored. To get the value itself (and not the address of the value), we must use the pointer indirection operator, `*`.

We also added a `log.Println` call to output the address in the terminal so we can be sure that our changes have taken effect.

We are going to modify the `templateHandler` type we wrote so that it passes the details of the request as data into the template's `Execute` method. In `main.go`, update the `ServeHTTP` function to pass the request `r` as the `data` argument to the `Execute` method:

```
func (t *templateHandler) ServeHTTP(w http.ResponseWriter, r
*http.Request) {
  t.once.Do(func() {
    t.templ =  template.Must(template.ParseFiles(filepath.Join("templates",
      t.filename)))
  })
  t.templ.Execute(w, r)
}
```

This tells the template to render itself using data that can be extracted from `http.Request`, which happens to include the host address that we need.

To use the `Host` value of `http.Request`, we can then make use of the special template syntax that allows us to inject data. Update the line where we create our socket in the `chat.html` file:

```
socket = new WebSocket("ws://{{.Host}}/room");
```

The double curly braces represent an annotation and the way we tell our template source to inject data. The `{{.Host}}` is essentially equivalent of telling it to replace the annotation with the value from `request.Host` (since we passed the request `r` object in as data).

> We have only scratched the surface of the power of the templates built into Go's standard library. The `text/template` package documentation is a great place to learn more about what you can achieve. You can find more about it at `http://golang.org/pkg/text/template`.

Rebuild and run the chat program again, but this time notice that the chatting operations no longer produce an error, whichever host we specify:

```
go build -o chat
./chat -addr=":3000"
```

View the source of the page in the browser and notice that `{{.Host}}` has been replaced with the actual host of the application. Valid hosts aren't just port numbers; you can also specify the IP addresses or other hostnames provided they are allowed in your environment, for example, `-addr="192.168.0.1:3000"`.

Tracing code to get a look under the hood

The only way we will know that our application is working is by opening two or more browsers and using our UI to send messages. In other words, we are manually testing our code. This is fine for experimental projects such as our chat application or small projects that aren't expected to grow, but if our code is to have a longer life or be worked on by more than one person, manual testing of this kind becomes a liability. We are not going to tackle **Test-driven Development (TDD)** for our chat program, but we should explore another useful debugging technique called**tracing**.

Tracing is a practice by which we log or print key steps in the flow of a program to make what is going on under the covers visible. In the previous section, we added a `log.Println` call to output the address that the chat program was binding to. In this section, we are going to formalize this and write our own complete tracing package.

We are going to explore TDD practices when writing our tracing code because TDD is a perfect example of a package that we are likely to reuse, add to, share, and hopefully, even open source.

Writing a package using TDD

Packages in Go are organized into folders, with one package per folder. It is a build error to have differing package declarations within the same folder because all sibling files are expected to contribute to a single package. Go has no concept of subpackages, which means nested packages (in nested folders) exist only for aesthetic or informational reasons but do not inherit any functionality or visibility from super packages. In our chat application, all of our files contributed to the `main` package because we wanted to build an executable tool. Our tracing package will never be run directly, so it can and should use a different package name. We will also need to think about the **Application Programming Interface (API)** of our package, considering how to model a package so that it remains as extensible and flexible as possible for users. This includes the fields, functions, methods, and types that should be exported (visible to the user) and remain hidden for simplicity's sake.

 Go uses capitalization of names to denote which items are exported such that names that begin with a capital letter (for example, `Tracer`) are visible to users of a package, and names that begin with a lowercase letter (for example, `templateHandler`) are hidden or private.

Create a new folder called `trace`, which will be the name of our tracing package, alongside the `chat` folder so that the folder structure now looks like this:

```
/chat
  client.go
  main.go
  room.go
/trace
```

Before we jump into code, let's agree on some design goals for our package by which we can measure success:

- The package should be easy to use
- Unit tests should cover the functionality
- Users should have the flexibility to replace the tracer with their own implementation

Interfaces

Interfaces in Go are an extremely powerful language feature that allows us to define an API without being strict or specific on the implementation details. Wherever possible, describing the basic building blocks of your packages using interfaces usually ends up paying dividends down the road, and this is where we will start for our tracing package.

Create a new file called `tracer.go` inside the `trace` folder and write the following code:

```
package trace
// Tracer is the interface that describes an object capable of
// tracing events throughout code.
type Tracer interface {
  Trace(...interface{})
}
```

The first thing to notice is that we have defined our package as `trace`.

While it is a good practice to have the folder name match the package name, Go tools do not enforce it, which means you are free to name them differently if it makes sense. Remember, when people import your package, they will type the name of the folder, and if suddenly a package with a different name is imported, it could get confusing.

Our `Tracer` type (the capital `T` means we intend this to be a publicly visible type) is an interface that describes a single method called `Trace`. The `. . . interface{}` argument type states that our `Trace` method will accept zero or more arguments of any type. You might think that this is a redundant provision as the method should just take a single string (we want to just trace out some string of characters, don't we?). However, consider functions such as `fmt.Sprint` and `log.Fatal`, both of which follow a pattern littered throughout Go's standard library that provides a helpful shortcut when trying to communicate multiple things in one go. Wherever possible, we should follow such patterns and practices because we want our own APIs to be familiar and clear to the Go community.

Unit tests

We promised ourselves that we would follow test-driven practices, but interfaces are simply definitions that do not provide any implementation and so cannot be directly tested. But we are about to write a real implementation of a `Tracer` method, and we will indeed write the tests first.

Create a new file called `tracer_test.go` in the `trace` folder and insert the following scaffold code:

```
package trace
import (
  "testing"
)
func TestNew(t *testing.T) {
  t.Error("We haven't written our test yet")
}
```

Testing was built into the Go tool chain from the very beginning, making writing automatable tests a first-class citizen. The test code lives alongside the production code in files suffixed with `_test.go`. The Go tools will treat any function that starts with `Test` (taking a single `*testing.T` argument) as a unit test, and it will be executed when we run our tests. To run them for this package, navigate to the `trace` folder in a terminal and do the following:

```
go test
```

You will see that our tests fail because of our call to `t.Error` in the body of our `TestNew` function:

```
--- FAIL: TestNew (0.00 seconds)
    tracer_test.go:8: We haven't written our test yet
FAIL
exit status 1
FAIL    trace 0.011s
```

 Clearing the terminal before each test run is a great way to make sure you aren't confusing previous runs with the most recent one. On Windows, you can use the `cls` command; on Unix machines, the `clear` command does the same thing.

Obviously, we haven't properly written our test and we don't expect it to pass yet, so let's update the `TestNew` function:

```go
func TestNew(t *testing.T) {
  var buf bytes.Buffer
  tracer := New(&buf)
  if tracer == nil {
    t.Error("Return from New should not be nil")
  } else {
    tracer.Trace("Hello trace package.")
    if buf.String() != "Hello trace package.\n" {
      t.Errorf("Trace should not write '%s'.", buf.String())
    }
  }

}
```

Most packages throughout the book are available from the Go standard library, so you can add an `import` statement for the appropriate package in order to access the package. Others are external, and that's when you need to use `go get` to download them before they can be imported. For this case, you'll need to add `import "bytes"` to the top of the file.

We have started designing our API by becoming the first user of it. We want to be able to capture the output of our tracer in a `bytes.Buffer` variable so that we can then ensure that the string in the buffer matches the expected value. If it does not, a call to `t.Errorf` will fail the test. Before that, we check to make sure the return from a made-up `New` function is not `nil`; again, if it is, the test will fail because of the call to `t.Error`.

Red-green testing

Running `go test` now actually produces an error; it complains that there is no `New` function. We haven't made a mistake here; we are following a practice known as red-green testing. Red-green testing proposes that we first write a unit test, see it fail (or produce an error), write the minimum amount of code possible to make that test pass, and rinse and repeat it again. The key point here being that we want to make sure the code we add is actually doing something as well as ensuring that the test code we write is testing something meaningful.

Consider a meaningless test for a minute:

```
if true == true {
  t.Error("True should be true")
}
```

It is logically impossible for `true` to not be true (if `true` ever equals `false`, it's time to get a new computer), and so our test is pointless. If a test or claim cannot fail, there is no value whatsoever to be found in it.

Replacing `true` with a variable that you expect to be set to `true` under certain conditions would mean that such a test can indeed fail (like when the code being tested is misbehaving) at this point, you have a meaningful test that is worth contributing to the code base.

You can treat the output of `go test` like a to-do list, solving only one problem at a time. Right now, the complaint about the missing `New` function is all we will address. In the `trace.go` file, let's add the minimum amount of code possible to progress with things; add the following snippet underneath the interface type definition:

```
func New() {}
```

Running `go test` now shows us that things have indeed progressed, albeit not very far. We now have two errors:

```
./tracer_test.go:11: too many arguments in call to New
./tracer_test.go:11: New(&buf) used as value
```

The first error tells us that we are passing arguments to our New function, but the New function doesn't accept any. The second error says that we are using the return of the New function as a value, but that the New function doesn't return anything. You might have seen this coming, and indeed as you gain more experience writing test-driven code, you will most likely jump over such trivial details. However, to properly illustrate the method, we are going to be pedantic for a while. Let's address the first error by updating our New function to take in the expected argument:

```
func New(w io.Writer) {}
```

We are taking an argument that satisfies the io.Writer interface, which means that the specified object must have a suitable Write method.

Using existing interfaces, especially ones found in the Go standard library, is an extremely powerful and often necessary way to ensure that your code is as flexible and elegant as possible.

Accepting io.Writer means that the user can decide where the tracing output will be written. This output could be the standard output, a file, network socket, bytes.Buffer as in our test case, or even some custom-made object, provided it can act like an io.Writer interface.

Running go test again shows us that we have resolved the first error and we only need add a return type in order to progress past our second error:

```
func New(w io.Writer) Tracer {}
```

We are stating that our New function will return a Tracer, but we do not return anything, which go test happily complains about:

```
./tracer.go:13: missing return at end of function
```

Fixing this is easy; we can just return nil from the New function:

```
func New(w io.Writer) Tracer {
  return nil
}
```

Of course, our test code has asserted that the return should not be `nil`, so `go test` now gives us a failure message:

```
tracer_test.go:14: Return from New should not be nil
```

You can see how this hyper-strict adherence to the red-green principle can get a little tedious, but it is vital that we do not jump too far ahead. If we were to write a lot of implementation code in one go, we will very likely have code that is not covered by a unit test.

The ever-thoughtful core team has even solved this problem for us by providing code coverage statistics. The following command provides code statistics:

```
go test -cover
```

Provided that all tests pass, adding the `-cover` flag will tell us how much of our code was touched during the execution of the tests. Obviously, the closer we get to 100 percent the better.

Implementing the interface

To satisfy this test, we need something that we can properly return from the New method because Tracer is only an interface and we have to return something real. Let's add an implementation of a tracer to our `tracer.go` file:

```
type tracer struct {
  out io.Writer
}
func (t *tracer) Trace(a ...interface{}) {}
```

Our implementation is extremely simple: the `tracer` type has an `io.Writer` field called `out` which is where we will write the trace output to. And the Trace method exactly matches the method required by the Tracer interface, although it doesn't do anything yet.

Now we can finally fix the New method:

```
func New(w io.Writer) Tracer {
  return &tracer{out: w}
}
```

Running `go test` again shows us that our expectation was not met because nothing was written during our call to Trace:

```
tracer_test.go:18: Trace should not write ''.
```

Let's update our `Trace` method to write the blended arguments to the specified `io.Writer` field:

```
func (t *tracer) Trace(a ...interface{}) {
  fmt.Fprint(t.out, a...)
  fmt.Fprintln(t.out)
}
```

When the `Trace` method is called, we use `fmt.Fprint` (and `fmt.Fprintln`) to format and write the trace details to the `out` writer.

Have we finally satisfied our test?

```
go test -cover
PASS
coverage: 100.0% of statements
ok      trace 0.011s
```

Congratulations! We have successfully passed our test and have 100 percent test coverage. Once we have finished our glass of champagne, we can take a minute to consider something very interesting about our implementation.

Unexported types being returned to users

The `tracer` struct type we wrote is **unexported** because it begins with a lowercase `t`, so how is it that we are able to return it from the exported `New` function? After all, doesn't the user receive the returned object? This is perfectly acceptable and valid Go code; the user will only ever see an object that satisfies the `Tracer` interface and will never even know about our private `tracer` type. Since they only interact with the interface anyway, it wouldn't matter if our `tracer` implementation exposed other methods or fields; they would never be seen. This allows us to keep the public API of our package clean and simple.

This hidden implementation technique is used throughout the Go standard library; for example, the `ioutil.NopCloser` method is a function that turns a normal `io.Reader` interface into `io.ReadCloser` where the `Close` method does nothing (used for when `io.Reader` objects that don't need to be closed are passed into functions that require `io.ReadCloser` types). The method returns `io.ReadCloser` as far as the user is concerned, but under the hood, there is a secret `nopCloser` type hiding the implementation details.

To see this for yourself, browse the Go standard library source code at `http://golang.org/src/pkg/io/ioutil/ioutil.go` and search for the `nopCloser` struct.

Using our new trace package

Now that we have completed the first version of our `trace` package, we can use it in our chat application in order to better understand what is going on when users send messages through the user interface.

In `room.go`, let's import our new package and make some calls to the `Trace` method. The path to the `trace` package we just wrote will depend on your `GOPATH` environment variable because the import path is relative to the `$GOPATH/src` folder. So if you create your `trace` package in `$GOPATH/src/mycode/trace`, then you would need to import `mycode/trace`.

Update the `room` type and the `run()` method like this:

```
type room struct {
    // forward is a channel that holds incoming messages
    // that should be forwarded to the other clients.
    forward chan []byte
    // join is a channel for clients wishing to join the room.
    join chan *client
    // leave is a channel for clients wishing to leave the room.
    leave chan *client
    // clients holds all current clients in this room.
    clients map[*client]bool
    // tracer will receive trace information of activity
    // in the room.
    tracer trace.Tracer
}
func (r *room) run() {
    for {
        select {
        case client := <-r.join:
            // joining
            r.clients[client] = true
            r.tracer.Trace("New client joined")
        case client := <-r.leave:
            // leaving
            delete(r.clients, client)
            close(client.send)
            r.tracer.Trace("Client left")
        case msg := <-r.forward:
```

```
      r.tracer.Trace("Message received: ", string(msg))
      // forward message to all clients
      for client := range r.clients {
        client.send <- msg
        r.tracer.Trace(" -- sent to client")
      }
    }
  }
}
```

We added a `trace.Tracer` field to our `room` type and then made periodic calls to the `Trace` method peppered throughout the code. If we run our program and try to send messages, you'll notice that the application panics because the `tracer` field is `nil`. We can remedy this for now by making sure we create and assign an appropriate object when we create our `room` type. Update the `main.go` file to do this:

```
r := newRoom()
r.tracer = trace.New(os.Stdout)
```

We are using our `New` method to create an object that will send the output to the `os.Stdout` standard output pipe (this is a technical way of saying we want it to print the output to our terminal).

Rebuild and run the program and use two browsers to play with the application, and notice that the terminal now has some interesting trace information for us:

Now we are able to use the debug information to get an insight into what the application is doing, which will assist us when developing and supporting our project.

Making tracing optional

Once the application is released, the sort of tracing information we are generating will be pretty useless if it's just printed out to some terminal somewhere, or even worse, if it creates a lot of noise for our system administrators. Also, remember that when we don't set a tracer for our room type, our code panics, which isn't a very user-friendly situation. To resolve these two issues, we are going to enhance our trace package with a trace.Off() method that will return an object that satisfies the Tracer interface but will not do anything when the Trace method is called.

Let's add a test that calls the Off function to get a silent tracer before making a call to Trace to ensure the code doesn't panic. Since the tracing won't happen, that's all we can do in our test code. Add the following test function to the tracer_test.go file:

```
func TestOff(t *testing.T) {
  var silentTracer Tracer = Off()
  silentTracer.Trace("something")
}
```

To make it pass, add the following code to the tracer.go file:

```
type nilTracer struct{}

func (t *nilTracer) Trace(a ...interface{}) {}

// Off creates a Tracer that will ignore calls to Trace.
func Off() Tracer {
  return &nilTracer{}
}
```

Our nilTracer struct has defined a Trace method that does nothing, and a call to the Off() method will create a new nilTracer struct and return it. Notice that our nilTracer struct differs from our tracer struct in that it doesn't take an io.Writer interface; it doesn't need one because it isn't going to write anything.

Now let's solve our second problem by updating our `newRoom` method in the `room.go` file:

```
func newRoom() *room {
  return &room{
    forward: make(chan []byte),
    join:    make(chan *client),
    leave:   make(chan *client),
    clients: make(map[*client]bool),
    tracer:  trace.Off(),
  }
}
```

By default, our `room` type will be created with a `nilTracer` struct and any calls to `Trace` will just be ignored. You can try this out by removing the `r.tracer = trace.New(os.Stdout)` line from the `main.go` file: notice that nothing gets written to the terminal when you use the application and there is no panic.

Clean package APIs

A quick glance at the API (in this context, the exposed variables, methods, and types) for our `trace` package highlights that a simple and obvious design has emerged:

- The `New()` âøø method-creates a new instance of a Tracer
- The `Off()` âøø method-gets a Tracer that does nothing
- The `Tracer` interface âøø describes the methods Tracer objects will implement

I would be very confident to give this package to a Go programmer without any documentation or guidelines, and I'm pretty sure they would know what do to with it.

 In Go, adding documentation is as simple as adding comments to the line before each item. The blog post on the subject is a worthwhile read (`http://blog.golang.org/godoc-documenting-go-code`), where you can see a copy of the hosted source code for `tracer.go` that is an example of how you might annotate the `trace` package. For more information, refer to `https://github.com/matryer/goblueprints/blob/master/chapter1/trace/tracer.go`.

Summary

In this chapter, we developed a complete concurrent chat application and our own simple package to trace the flow of our programs to help us better understand what is going on under the hood.

We used the `net/http` package to quickly build what turned out to be a very powerful concurrent HTTP web server. In one particular case, we then upgraded the connection to open a web socket between the client and server. This means that we can easily and quickly communicate messages to the user's web browser without having to write messy polling code. We explored how templates are useful to separate the code from the content as well as to allow us to inject data into our template source, which let us make the host address configurable. Command-line flags helped us give simple configuration control to the people hosting our application while also letting us specify sensible defaults.

Our chat application made use of Go's powerful concurrency capabilities that allowed us to write clear *threaded* code in just a few lines of idiomatic Go. By controlling the coming and going of clients through channels, we were able to set synchronization points in our code that prevented us from corrupting memory by attempting to modify the same objects at the same time.

We learned how interfaces such as `http.Handler` and our own `trace.Tracer` interface allow us to provide disparate implementations without having to touch the code that makes use of them, and in some cases, without having to expose even the name of the implementation to our users. We saw how just by adding a `ServeHTTP` method to our `room` type, we turned our custom room concept into a valid HTTP handler object, which managed our web socket connections.

We aren't actually very far away from being able to properly release our application, except for one major oversight: you cannot see who sent each message. We have no concept of users or even usernames, and for a real chat application, this is not acceptable.

In the next chapter, we will add the names of the people responding to their messages in order to make them feel like they are having a real conversation with other humans.

2
Adding User Accounts

The chat application we built in the previous chapter focused on high performance transmission of messages from the clients to the server and back again. However, the way things stand, our users have no way of knowing who they would be talking to. One solution to this problem is building some kind of sign-up and login functionality and letting our users create accounts and authenticate themselves before they can open the chat page.

Whenever we are about to build something from scratch, we must ask ourselves how others have solved this problem before (it is extremely rare to encounter genuinely original problems) and whether any open solutions or standards already exist that we can make use of. Authorization and authentication can hardly be considered new problems, especially in the world of the Web, with many different protocols out there to choose from. So how do we decide the best option to pursue? As always, we must look at this question from the point of view of the user.

A lot of websites these days allow you to sign in using your accounts that exist elsewhere on a variety of social media or community websites. This saves users the tedious job of entering all of their account information over and over again as they decide to try out different products and services. It also has a positive effect on the conversion rates for new sites.

In this chapter, we will enhance our chat codebase to add authorization, which will allow our users to sign in using Google, Facebook, or GitHub, and you'll see how easy it is to add other sign-in portals too. In order to join the chat, users must first sign in. Following this, we will use the authorized data to augment our user experience so everyone knows who is in the room and who said what.

In this chapter, you will learn to:

- Use the decorator pattern to wrap `http.Handler` types in order to add additional functionality to handlers
- Serve HTTP endpoints with dynamic paths
- Use the `gomniauth` open source project to access authentication services
- Get and set cookies using the `http` package
- Encode objects as Base64 and back to normal again
- Send and receive JSON data over a web socket
- Give different types of data to templates
- Work with the channels of your own types

Handlers all the way down

For our chat application, we implemented our own `http.Handler` type (the room) in order to easily compile, execute, and deliver HTML content to browsers. Since this is a very simple but powerful interface, we are going to continue to use it wherever possible when adding functionality to our HTTP processing.

In order to determine whether a user is allowed to proceed, we will create an authorization wrapper handler that will perform the check and pass the execution on to the inner handler only if the user is authorized.

Our wrapper handler will satisfy the same `http.Handler` interface as the object inside it, allowing us to wrap any valid handler. In fact, even the authentication handler we are about to write could be later encapsulated inside a similar wrapper if required.

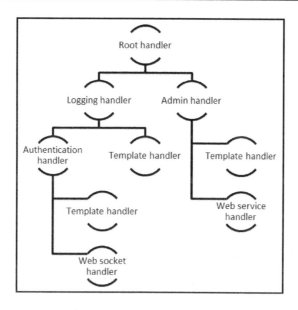

Chaining pattern when applied to HTTP handlers

The preceding diagram shows how this pattern could be applied in a more complicated HTTP handler scenario. Each object implements the `http.Handler` interface. This means that an object could be passed to the `http.Handle` method to directly handle a request, or it can be given to another object, which could add some kind of extra functionality. The `Logging` handler may write to a log file before and after the `ServeHTTP` method is called on the inner handler. Because the inner handler is just another `http.Handler`, any other handler can be wrapped in (or decorated with) the `Logging` handler.

It is also common for an object to contain logic that decides which inner handler should be executed. For example, our authentication handler will either pass the execution to the wrapped handler, or handle the request itself by issuing a redirect to the browser.

That's plenty of theory for now; let's write some code. Create a new file called `auth.go` in the `chat` folder:

```
package main
import ("net/http")
type authHandler struct {
  next http.Handler
}
func (h *authHandler) ServeHTTP(w http.ResponseWriter, r  *http.Request) {
  _, err := r.Cookie("auth")
  if err == http.ErrNoCookie {
    // not authenticated
```

```
      w.Header().Set("Location", "/login")
      w.WriteHeader(http.StatusTemporaryRedirect)
      return
  }
  if err != nil {
    // some other error
    http.Error(w, err.Error(), http.StatusInternalServerError)
    return
  }
  // success - call the next handler
  h.next.ServeHTTP(w, r)
}
func MustAuth(handler http.Handler) http.Handler {
  return &authHandler{next: handler}
}
```

The `authHandler` type not only implements the `ServeHTTP` method (which satisfies the `http.Handler` interface), but also stores (wraps) `http.Handler` in the `next` field. Our `MustAuth` helper function simply creates `authHandler` that wraps any other `http.Handler`. This is the pattern that allows us to easily add authorization to our code in `main.go`.

Let's tweak the following root mapping line:

```
http.Handle("/", &templateHandler{filename: "chat.html"})
```

Let's change the first argument to make it explicit about the page meant for chatting. Next, let's use the `MustAuth` function to wrap `templateHandler` for the second argument:

```
http.Handle("/chat", MustAuth(&templateHandler{filename:  "chat.html"}))
```

Wrapping `templateHandler` with the `MustAuth` function will cause the execution to run through `authHandler` first; it will run only to `templateHandler` if the request is authenticated.

The `ServeHTTP` method in `authHandler` will look for a special cookie called `auth`, and it will use the `Header` and `WriteHeader` methods on `http.ResponseWriter` to redirect the user to a login page if the cookie is missing. Notice that we discard the cookie itself using the underscore character and capture only the returning error; this is because we only care about whether the cookie is present at this point.

Build and run the chat application and try to hit `http://localhost:8080/chat`:

```
go build -o chat
./chat -host=":8080"
```

You need to delete your cookies to clear out previous authentication tokens or any other cookies that might be left over from other development projects served through the localhost.

If you look in the address bar of your browser, you will notice that you are immediately redirected to the /login page. Since we cannot handle that path yet, you'll just get a **404 page not found** error.

Making a pretty social sign-in page

So far, we haven't paid much attention to making our application look nice; after all, this book is about Go and not user interface development. However, there is no excuse for building ugly apps, and so we will build a social sign-in page that is as pretty as it is functional.

Bootstrap is a frontend framework for developing responsive projects on the Web. It provides CSS and JavaScript code that solve many user interface problems in a consistent and good-looking way. While sites built using Bootstrap tend to look the same (although there are a plenty of ways in which the UI can be customized), it is a great choice for early versions of apps or for developers who don't have access to designers.

 If you build your application using the semantic standards set forth by Bootstrap, it will become easy for you to make a Bootstrap theme for your site or application, and you know it will slot right into your code.

We will use the version of Bootstrap hosted on a CDN so we don't have to worry about downloading and serving our own version through our chat application. This means that in order to render our pages properly, we will need an active Internet connection even during development.

If you prefer to download and host your own copy of Bootstrap, you can do so. Keep the files in an `assets` folder and add the following call to your `main` function (it uses `http.Handle` to serve the assets via your application):

```
http.Handle("/assets/", http.StripPrefix("/assets",
http.FileServer(http.Dir("/path/to/assets/"))))
```

Notice how the `http.StripPrefix` and `http.FileServer` functions return objects that satisfy the `http.Handler` interface as per the decorator pattern that we implement with our `MustAuth` helper function.

In `main.go`, let's add an endpoint for the login page:

```
http.Handle("/chat", MustAuth(&templateHandler{filename: "chat.html"}))
http.Handle("/login", &templateHandler{filename: "login.html"})
http.Handle("/room", r)
```

Obviously, we do not want to use the `MustAuth` method for our login page because it will cause an infinite redirection loop.

Create a new file called `login.html` inside our `templates` folder and insert the following HTML code:

```html
<html>
  <head>
    <title>Login</title>
    <link rel="stylesheet" href="https://maxcdn.bootstrapcdn.com
    /bootstrap/3.3.6/css/bootstrap.min.css">
  </head>
  <body>
    <div class="container">
      <div class="page-header">
        <h1>Sign in</h1>
      </div>
      <div class="panel panel-danger">
        <div class="panel-heading">
          <h3 class="panel-title">In order to chat, you must be signed
          in</h3>
        </div>
        <div class="panel-body">
          <p>Select the service you would like to sign in with:</p>
          <ul>
            <li>
              <a href="/auth/login/facebook">Facebook</a>
            </li>
            <li>
              <a href="/auth/login/github">GitHub</a>
            </li>
            <li>
              <a href="/auth/login/google">Google</a>
            </li>
          </ul>
        </div>
```

```
        </div>
      </div>
    </body>
</html>
```

Restart the web server and navigate to `http://localhost:8080/login`. You will notice that it now displays our **Sign in** page:

Endpoints with dynamic paths

Pattern matching for the `http` package in the Go standard library isn't the most comprehensive and fully featured implementation out there. For example, Ruby on Rails makes it much easier to have dynamic segments inside the path. You could map the route like this:

```
"auth/:action/:provider_name"
```

Rails then provides a data map (or dictionary) containing the values that it automatically extracted from the matched path. So if you visit `auth/login/google`, then `params[:provider_name]` would equal `google` and `params[:action]` would equal `login`.

The most the `http` package lets us specify by default is a path prefix, which we can make use of by leaving a trailing slash at the end of the pattern:

```
"auth/"
```

We would then have to manually parse the remaining segments to extract the appropriate data. This is acceptable for relatively simple cases. This suits our needs for the time being since we only need to handle a few different paths, such as the following:

- `/auth/login/google`
- `/auth/login/facebook`
- `/auth/callback/google`
- `/auth/callback/facebook`

 If you need to handle more advanced routing situations, you may want to consider using dedicated packages, such as goweb, pat, routes, or mux. For extremely simple cases such as ours, built-in capabilities will do.

We are going to create a new handler that powers our login process. In `auth.go`, add the following `loginHandler` code:

```
// loginHandler handles the third-party login process.
// format: /auth/{action}/{provider}
func loginHandler(w http.ResponseWriter, r *http.Request) {
  segs := strings.Split(r.URL.Path, "/")
  action := segs[2]
  provider := segs[3]
  switch action {
  case "login":
    log.Println("TODO handle login for", provider)
      default:
        w.WriteHeader(http.StatusNotFound)
        fmt.Fprintf(w, "Auth action %s not supported", action)
  }
}
```

In the preceding code, we break the path into segments using `strings.Split` before pulling out the values for `action` and `provider`. If the action value is known, we will run the specific code; otherwise, we will write out an error message and return an `http.StatusNotFound` status code (which in the language of HTTP status code is `404`).

We will not bulletproof our code right now. But it's worth noticing that if someone hits `loginHandler` with few segments, our code will panic because it would expect `segs[2]` and `segs[3]` to exist.
For extra credit, see whether you can protect your code against this and return a nice error message instead of making it panic if someone hits `/auth/nonsense`.

Our `loginHandler` is only a function and not an object that implements the `http.Handler` interface. This is because, unlike other handlers, we don't need it to store any state. The Go standard library supports this, so we can use the `http.HandleFunc` function to map it in a way similar to how we used `http.Handle` earlier. In `main.go`, update the handlers:

```
http.Handle("/chat", MustAuth(&templateHandler{filename:  "chat.html"}))
http.Handle("/login", &templateHandler{filename: "login.html"})
http.HandleFunc("/auth/", loginHandler)
http.Handle("/room", r)
```

Rebuild and run the chat application:

```
go build -o chat
./chat -host=":8080"
```

Hit the following URLs and notice the output logged in the terminal:

- `http://localhost:8080/auth/login/google` outputs `TODO handle login for google`
- `http://localhost:8080/auth/login/facebook` outputs `TODO handle login for facebook`

We have successfully implemented a dynamic path-matching mechanism that just prints out `TODO` messages so far; we need to integrate it with authorization services in order to make our login process work.

Getting started with OAuth2

OAuth2 is an open authorization standard designed to allow resource owners to give clients delegated access to private data (such as wall posts or tweets) via an access token exchange handshake. Even if you do not wish to access the private data, OAuth2 is a great option that allows people to sign in using their existing credentials, without exposing those credentials to a third-party site. In this case, we are the third party, and we want to allow our users to sign in using services that support OAuth2.

From a user's point of view, the OAuth2 flow is as follows:

1. The user selects the provider with whom they wish to sign in to the client app.
2. The user is redirected to the provider's website (with a URL that includes the client app ID) where they are asked to give permission to the client app.
3. The user signs in from the OAuth2 service provider and accepts the permissions requested by the third-party application.
4. The user is redirected to the client app with a request code.
5. In the background, the client app sends the grant code to the provider, who sends back an authentication token.
6. The client app uses the access token to make authorized requests to the provider, such as to get user information or wall posts.

To avoid reinventing the wheel, we will look at a few open source projects that have already solved this problem for us.

Open source OAuth2 packages

Andrew Gerrand has been working on the core Go team since February 2010, that is, two years before Go 1.0 was officially released. His `goauth2` package (see `https://github.com/golang/oauth2`) is an elegant implementation of the OAuth2 protocol written entirely in Go.

Andrew's project inspired `gomniauth` (see `https://github.com/stretchr/gomniauth`). An open source Go alternative to Ruby's `omniauth` project, `gomniauth` provides a unified solution to access different OAuth2 services. In the future, when OAuth3 (or whatever the next-generation authorization protocol will be) comes out, in theory `gomniauth` could take on the pain of implementing the details, leaving the user code untouched.

For our application, we will use `gomniauth` to access OAuth services provided by Google, Facebook, and GitHub, so make sure you have it installed by running the following command:

go get github.com/stretchr/gomniauth

 Some of the project dependencies of `gomniauth` are kept in Bazaar repositories, so you'll need to head over to `http://wiki.bazaar.canonical.com` to download them.

Tell the authorization providers about your app

Before we ask an authorization provider to help our users sign in, we must tell them about our application. Most providers have some kind of web tool or console where you can create applications to kick this process off. Here's one from Google:

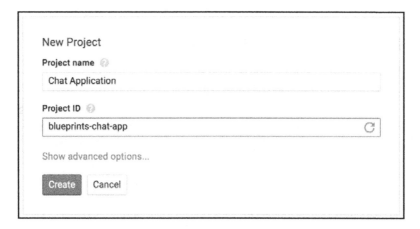

In order to identify the client application, we need to create a client ID and secret. Despite the fact that OAuth2 is an open standard, each provider has their own language and mechanism to set things up. Therefore, you will most likely have to play around with the user interface or the documentation to figure it out in each case.

At the time of writing, in **Google Cloud Console**, you navigate to **API Manager** and click on the **Credentials** section.

In most cases, for added security, you have to be explicit about the host URLs from where requests will come. For now, since we're hosting our app locally on `localhost:8080`, you should use it. You will also be asked for a redirect URI that is the endpoint in our chat application and to which the user will be redirected after they successfully sign in. The callback will be another action in `loginHandler`, so the redirect URL for the Google client will be `http://localhost:8080/auth/callback/google`.

Once you finish the authorization process for the providers you want to support, you will be given a client ID and secret for each provider. Make a note of these details because we will need them when we set up the providers in our chat application.

 If we host our application on a real domain, we have to create new client IDs and secrets or update the appropriate URL fields on our authorization providers to ensure that they point to the right place. Either way, it is good practice to have a different set of development and production keys for security.

Implementing external logging in

In order to make use of the projects, clients, or accounts that we created on the authorization provider sites, we have to tell gomniauth which providers we want to use and how we will interact with them. We do this by calling the WithProviders function on the primary gomniauth package. Add the following code snippet to main.go (just underneath the flag.Parse() line toward the top of the main function):

```
// setup gomniauth
gomniauth.SetSecurityKey("PUT YOUR AUTH KEY HERE")
gomniauth.WithProviders(
  facebook.New("key", "secret",
    "http://localhost:8080/auth/callback/facebook"),
  github.New("key", "secret",
    "http://localhost:8080/auth/callback/github"),
  google.New("key", "secret",
    "http://localhost:8080/auth/callback/google"),
)
```

You should replace the `key` and `secret` placeholders with the actual values you noted down earlier. The third argument represents the callback URL that should match the ones you provided when creating your clients on the provider's website. Notice the second path segment is `callback`; while we haven't implemented this yet, this is where we handle the response from the authorization process.

As usual, you will need to ensure all the appropriate packages are imported:

```
import (
  "github.com/stretchr/gomniauth/providers/facebook"
  "github.com/stretchr/gomniauth/providers/github"
  "github.com/stretchr/gomniauth/providers/google"
)
```

Gomniauth requires the `SetSecurityKey` call because it sends state data between the client and server along with a signature checksum, which ensures that the state values are not tempered with while being transmitted. The security key is used when creating the hash in a way that it is almost impossible to recreate the same hash without knowing the exact security key. You should replace `some long key` with a security hash or phrase of your choice.

Logging in

Now that we have configured Gomniauth, we need to redirect users to the provider's authorization page when they land on our `/auth/login/{provider}` path. We just have to update our `loginHandler` function in `auth.go`:

```
func loginHandler(w http.ResponseWriter, r *http.Request) {
  segs := strings.Split(r.URL.Path, "/")
  action := segs[2]
  provider := segs[3]
  switch action {
  case "login":
    provider, err := gomniauth.Provider(provider)
    if err != nil {
      http.Error(w, fmt.Sprintf("Error when trying to get provider
      %s: %s",provider, err), http.StatusBadRequest)
      return
    }
    loginUrl, err := provider.GetBeginAuthURL(nil, nil)
    if err != nil {
      http.Error(w, fmt.Sprintf("Error when trying to GetBeginAuthURL
      for %s:%s", provider, err), http. StatusInternalServerError)
```

```
            return
    }
    w.Header.Set("Location", loginUrl)
    w.WriteHeader(http.StatusTemporaryRedirect)
    default:
        w.WriteHeader(http.StatusNotFound)
        fmt.Fprintf(w, "Auth action %s not supported", action)
    }
}
```

We do two main things here. First, we use the `gomniauth.Provider` function to get the provider object that matches the object specified in the URL (such as `google` or `github`). Then, we use the `GetBeginAuthURL` method to get the location where we must send users to in order to start the authorization process.

The `GetBeginAuthURL(nil, nil)` arguments are for the state and options respectively, which we are not going to use for our chat application.

The first argument is a state map of data that is encoded and signed and sent to the authentication provider. The provider doesn't do anything with the state; it just sends it back to our callback endpoint. This is useful if, for example, we want to redirect the user back to the original page they were trying to access before the authentication process intervened. For our purpose, we have only the `/chat` endpoint, so we don't need to worry about sending any state.

The second argument is a map of additional options that will be sent to the authentication provider, which somehow modifies the behavior of the authentication process. For example, you can specify your own `scope` parameter, which allows you to make a request for permission to access additional information from the provider. For more information about the available options, search for OAuth2 on the Internet or read the documentation for each provider, as these values differ from service to service.

If our code gets no error from the `GetBeginAuthURL` call, we simply redirect the user's browser to the returned URL.

If errors occur, we use the `http.Error` function to write the error message out with a non-200 status code.

Rebuild and run the chat application:

```
go build -o chat
./chat -host=":8080"
```

We will continue to stop, rebuild, and run our projects manually throughout this book, but there are some tools that will take care of this for you by watching for changes and restarting Go applications automatically. If you're interested in such tools, check out `https://githu b.com/pilu/fresh` and `https://github.com/codegangsta/gin`.

Open the main chat page by accessing `http://localhost:8080/chat`. As we aren't logged in yet, we are redirected to our sign-in page. Click on the **Google** option to sign in using your Google account and you will notice that you are presented with a Google-specific sign-in page (if you are not already signed in to Google). Once you are signed in, you will be presented with a page asking you to give permission for our chat application before you can view basic information about your account:

This is the same flow that the users of our chat application will experience when signing in.

Click on **Accept** and you will notice that you are redirected to our application code but presented with an `Auth action callback not supported` error. This is because we haven't yet implemented the callback functionality in `loginHandler`.

Handling the response from the provider

Once the user clicks on **Accept** on the provider's website (or if they click on the equivalent of **Cancel**), they will be redirected to the callback endpoint in our application.

A quick glance at the complete URL that comes back shows us the grant code that the provider has given us:

```
http://localhost:8080/auth/callback/google?code=4/Q92xJ-
BQfoX6PHhzkjhgtyfLc0Ylm.QqV4u9AbA9sYguyfbjFEsNoJKMOjQI
```

We don't have to worry about what to do with this code because Gomniauth does it for us; we can simply jump to implementing our callback handler. However, it's worth knowing that this code will be exchanged by the authentication provider for a token that allows us to access private user data. For added security, this additional step happens behind the scenes, from server to server rather than in the browser.

In `auth.go`, we are ready to add another switch case to our action path segment. Insert the following code before the default case:

```
case "callback":
  provider, err := gomniauth.Provider(provider)
  if err != nil {
    http.Error(w, fmt.Sprintf("Error when trying to get provider %s: %s",
    provider, err), http.StatusBadRequest)
    return
  }
  creds, err :=
provider.CompleteAuth(objx.MustFromURLQuery(r.URL.RawQuery))
  if err != nil {
    http.Error(w, fmt.Sprintf("Error when trying to complete auth for
    %s: %s", provider, err), http.StatusInternalServerError)
    return
  }
  user, err := provider.GetUser(creds)
  if err != nil {
    http.Error(w, fmt.Sprintf("Error when trying to get user from %s: %s",
    provider, err), http.StatusInternalServerError)
    return
  }
  authCookieValue := objx.New(map[string]interface{}{
```

```
    "name": user.Name(),
  }).MustBase64()
  http.SetCookie(w, &http.Cookie{
    Name:   "auth",
    Value: authCookieValue,
    Path:   "/"})
  w.Header().Set("Location", "/chat")
  w.WriteHeader(http.StatusTemporaryRedirect)
```

When the authentication provider redirects the users after they have granted permission, the URL specifies that it is a callback action. We look up the authentication provider as we did before and call its CompleteAuth method. We parse RawQuery from the request into objx.Map (the multipurpose map type that Gomniauth uses), and the CompleteAuth method uses the values to complete the OAuth2 provider handshake with the provider. All being well, we will be given some authorized credentials with which we will be able to access our user's basic data. We then use the GetUser method for the provider, and Gomniauth will use the specified credentials to access some basic information about the user.

Once we have the user data, we **Base64-encode** the Name field in a JSON object and store it as a value for our auth cookie for later use.

> Base64-encoding data ensures it won't contain any special or unpredictable characters, which is useful for situations such as passing data to a URL or storing it in a cookie. Remember that although Base64-encoded data looks encrypted, it is not you can easily decode Base64-encoded data back to the original text with little effort. There are online tools that do this for you.

After setting the cookie, we redirect the user to the chat page, which we can safely assume was the original destination.

Once you build and run the code again and hit the /chat page, you will notice that the sign up flow works and we are finally allowed back to the chat page. Most browsers have an inspector or a consoleâ⊚⊚a tool that allows you to view the cookies that the server has sent you-that you can use to see whether the auth cookie has appeared:

```
go build -o chat
./chat -host=":8080"
```

In our case, the cookie value is `eyJuYW1lIjoiTWF0IFJ5ZXIifQ==`, which is a Base64-encoded version of `{"name":"Mat Ryer"}`. Remember, we never typed in a name in our chat application; instead, Gomniauth asked Google for a name when we opted to sign in with Google. Storing non-signed cookies like this is fine for incidental information, such as a user's name; however, you should avoid storing any sensitive information using non-signed cookies as it's easy for people to access and change the data.

Presenting the user data

Having the user data inside a cookie is a good start, but non-technical people will never even know it's there, so we must bring the data to the fore. We will do this by enhancing `templateHandler` that first passes the user data to the template's `Execute` method; this allows us to use template annotations in our HTML to display the user data to the users.

Update the `ServeHTTP` method of `templateHandler` in `main.go`:

```
func (t *templateHandler) ServeHTTP(w http.ResponseWriter, r
*http.Request) {
  t.once.Do(func() {
    t.templ = template.Must(template.ParseFiles(filepath.Join("templates",
    t.filename)))
  })
  data := map[string]interface{}{
    "Host": r.Host,
  }
  if authCookie, err := r.Cookie("auth"); err == nil {
    data["UserData"] = objx.MustFromBase64(authCookie.Value)
  }
  t.templ.Execute(w, data)
}
```

Instead of just passing the entire `http.Request` object to our template as data, we are creating a new `map[string]interface{}` definition for a data object that potentially has two fields: `Host` and `UserData` (the latter will only appear if an `auth` cookie is present). By specifying the map type followed by curly braces, we are able to add the `Host` entry at the same time as making our map while avoiding the `make` keyword altogether. We then pass this new `data` object as the second argument to the `Execute` method on our template.

Now we add an HTML file to our template source to display the name. Update the chatbox form in chat.html:

```
<form id="chatbox">
  {{.UserData.name}}:<br/>
  <textarea></textarea>
  <input type="submit" value="Send" />
</form>
```

The {{.UserData.name}} annotation tells the template engine to insert our user's name before the textarea control.

> Since we're using the objx package, don't forget to run go get
> http://github.com/stretchr/objx and import it. Additional
> dependencies add complexity to projects, so you may decide to copy and
> paste the appropriate functions from the package or even write your own
> code that marshals between Base64-encoded cookies and back.
> Alternatively, you can **vendor** the dependency by copying the whole
> source code to your project (inside a root-level folder called vendor). Go
> will, at build time, first check the vendor folder for any imported packages
> before checking them in $GOPATH (which were put there by go get). This
> allows you to fix the exact version of a dependency rather than rely on the
> fact that the source package hasn't changed since you wrote your code.
> For more information about using vendors in Go, check out Daniel
> Theophanes' post on the subject at
> https://blog.gopheracademy.com/advent-2015/vendor-folder/ or
> search for vendoring in Go.

Rebuild and run the chat application again and you will notice the addition of your name before the chat box:

```
go build -o chat
./chat -host=":8080"
```

Augmenting messages with additional data

So far, our chat application has only transmitted messages as slices of bytes or []byte types between the client and the server; therefore, the forward channel for our room has the chan []byte type. In order to send data (such as who sent it and when) in addition to the message itself, we enhance our forward channel and also how we interact with the web socket on both ends.

Define a new type that will replace the `[]byte` slice by creating a new file called `message.go` in the `chat` folder:

```
package main
import (
  "time"
)
// message represents a single message
type message struct {
  Name     string
  Message  string
  When     time.Time
}
```

The `message` type will encapsulate the message string itself, but we have also added the `Name` and `When` fields that respectively hold the user's name and a timestamp of when the message was sent.

Since the `client` type is responsible for communicating with the browser, it needs to transmit and receive more than just a single message string. As we are talking to a JavaScript application (that is, the chat client running in the browser) and the Go standard library has a great JSON implementation, this seems like the perfect choice to encode additional information in the messages. We will change the `read` and `write` methods in `client.go` to use the `ReadJSON` and `WriteJSON` methods on the socket, and we will encode and decode our new `message` type:

```
func (c *client) read() {
  defer c.socket.Close()
  for {
    var msg *message
    err := c.socket.ReadJSON(&msg)
    if err != nil {
      return
    }
    msg.When = time.Now()
    msg.Name = c.userData["name"].(string)
    c.room.forward <- msg
  }
}
func (c *client) write() {
  defer c.socket.Close()
  for msg := range c.send {
    err := c.socket.WriteJSON(msg)
    if err != nil {
      break
    }
```

```
    }
  }
```

When we receive a message from the browser, we will expect to populate only the `Message` field, which is why we set the `When` and `Name` fields ourselves in the preceding code.

You will notice that when you try to build the preceding code, it complains about a few things. The main reason is that we are trying to send a `*message` object down our `forward` and `send chan []byte` channels. This is not allowed until we change the type of the channel. In `room.go`, change the `forward` field to be of the type `chan *message`, and do the same for the `send chan` type in `client.go`.

We must update the code that initializes our channels since the types have now changed. Alternatively, you can wait for the compiler to raise these issues and fix them as you go. In `room.go`, you need to make the following changes:

- Change `forward: make(chan []byte)` to `forward: make(chan *message)`
- Change `r.tracer.Trace("Message received: ", string(msg))` to `r.tracer.Trace("Message received: ", msg.Message)`
- Change `send: make(chan []byte, messageBufferSize)` to `send: make(chan *message, messageBufferSize)`

The compiler will also complain about the lack of user data on the client, which is a fair point because the `client` type has no idea about the new user data we have added to the cookie. Update the `client` struct to include a new general-purpose `map[string]interface{}` called `userData`:

```
// client represents a single chatting user.
type client struct {
  // socket is the web socket for this client.
  socket *websocket.Conn
  // send is a channel on which messages are sent.
  send chan *message
  // room is the room this client is chatting in.
  room *room
  // userData holds information about the user
  userData map[string]interface{}
}
```

The user data comes from the client cookie that we access through the `http.Request` object's `Cookie` method. In `room.go`, update `ServeHTTP` with the following changes:

```go
func (r *room) ServeHTTP(w http.ResponseWriter, req *http.Request) {
  socket, err := upgrader.Upgrade(w, req, nil)
  if err != nil {
    log.Fatal("ServeHTTP:", err)
    return
  }
  authCookie, err := req.Cookie("auth")
  if err != nil {
    log.Fatal("Failed to get auth cookie:", err)
    return
  }
  client := &client{
    socket:   socket,
    send:     make(chan *message, messageBufferSize),
    room:     r,
    userData: objx.MustFromBase64(authCookie.Value),
  }
  r.join <- client
  defer func() { r.leave <- client }()
  go client.write()
  client.read()
}
```

We use the `Cookie` method on the `http.Request` type to get our user data before passing it to the client. We are using the `objx.MustFromBase64` method to convert our encoded cookie value back into a usable map object.

Now that we have changed the type being sent and received on the socket from `[]byte` to `*message`, we must tell our JavaScript client that we are sending JSON instead of just a plain string. Also, we must ask that it send JSON back to the server when a user submits a message. In `chat.html`, first update the `socket.send` call:

```javascript
socket.send(JSON.stringify({"Message": msgBox.val()}));
```

We are using `JSON.stringify` to serialize the specified JSON object (containing just the `Message` field) into a string, which is then sent to the server. Our Go code will decode (or unmarshal) the JSON string into a `message` object, matching the field names from the client JSON object with those of our `message` type.

Finally, update the `socket.onmessage` callback function to expect JSON, and also add the name of the sender to the page:

```
socket.onmessage = function(e) {
  var msg = JSON.parse(e.data);
  messages.append(
    $("<li>").append(
      $("<strong>").text(msg.Name + ": "),
      $("<span>").text(msg.Message)
    )
  );
}
```

In the preceding code snippet, we used JavaScript's `JSON.parse` function to turn the JSON string into a JavaScript object and then access the fields to build up the elements needed to properly display them.

Build and run the application, and if you can, log in with two different accounts in two different browsers (or invite a friend to help you test it):

```
go build -o chat
./chat -host=":8080"
```

The following screenshot shows the chat application's browser chat screens:

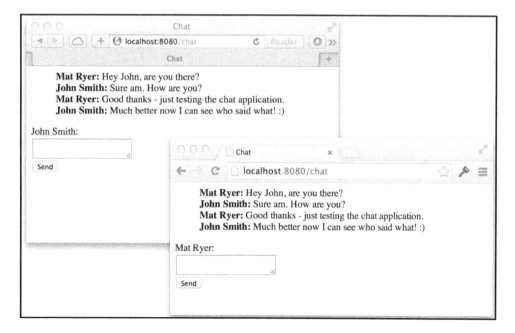

Summary

In this chapter, we added a useful and necessary feature to our chat application by asking users to authenticate themselves using OAuth2 service providers before we allow them to join the conversation. We made use of several open source packages, such as Gomniauth, which dramatically reduced the amount of multiserver complexity we would otherwise have dealt with.

We implemented a pattern when we wrapped http.Handler types to allow us to easily specify which paths require the user to be authenticated and which were available, even without an auth cookie. Our MustAuth helper function allowed us to generate the wrapper types in a fluent and simple way, without adding clutter and confusion to our code.

We saw how to use cookies and Base64-encoding to safely (although not securely) store the state of particular users in their respective browsers and to make use of that data over normal connections and through web sockets. We took more control of the data available to our templates in order to provide the name of the user to the UI and saw how to only provide certain data under specific conditions.

Since we needed to send and receive additional information over the web socket, we learned how easy it was to change the channels of native types into channels that work with types of our own, such as our message type. We also learned how to transmit JSON objects over the socket, rather than just slices of bytes. Thanks to the type safety of Go and the ability to specify types for channels, the compiler helps ensure that we do not send anything other than message objects through chan *message. Attempting to do so would result in a compiler error, alerting us to the fact right away.

From building a chat application to seeing the name of the person chatting is a great leap forward in terms of usability. But it's very formal and might not attract modern users of the Web, who are used to a much more visual experience. We are missing pictures of people chatting, and in the next chapter, we will explore different ways in which this could be done. We can allow users to better represent themselves in our application by pulling profile pictures (avatars) from the OAuth2 provider, the Gravatar web service, or the local disk after the users have uploaded them.

As an extra assignment, see whether you can make use of the time.Time field that we put into the message type to tell users when the messages were sent.

3
Three Ways to Implement Profile Pictures

So far, our chat application has made use of the **OAuth2** protocol to allow users to sign in to our application so that we know who is saying what. In this chapter, we are going to add profile pictures to make the chatting experience more engaging.

We will look at the following ways to add pictures or avatars alongside the messages in our application:

- Using the avatar picture provided by the auth service
- Using the `https://en.gravatar.com/` web service to look up a picture by the user's e-mail address
- Allowing the user to upload their own picture and host it themselves

The first two options allow us to delegate the hosting of pictures to a third party either an authorization service or `https://en.gravatar.com/` which is great because it reduces the cost of hosting our application (in terms of storage costs and bandwidth, since the user's browsers will actually download the pictures from the servers of the authenticating service, not ours). The third option requires us to host pictures ourselves at a location that is accessible on the Web.

These options aren't mutually exclusive; you will most likely use a combination of them in a real-world production application. Toward the end of the chapter, you will see how the flexible design that emerges allows us to try each implementation in turn until we find an appropriate avatar.

We are going to be agile with our design throughout this chapter, doing the minimum work needed to accomplish each milestone. This means that at the end of each section, we will have working implementations that are demonstrable in the browser. This also means that we will refactor code as and when we need to and discuss the rationale behind the decisions we make as we go.

Specifically, in this chapter, you will learn:

- What the good practices to get additional information from auth services are, even when there are no standards in place
- When it is appropriate to build abstractions into our code
- How Go's zero-initialization pattern can save time and memory
- How reusing an interface allows us to work with collections and individual objects in the same way as the existing interface did
- How to use the `https://en.gravatar.com/` web service
- How to do MD5 hashing in Go
- How to upload files over HTTP and store them on a server
- How to serve static files through a Go web server
- How to use unit tests to guide the refactoring of code
- How and when to abstract functionality from `struct` types into interfaces

Avatars from the OAuth2 server

It turns out that most auth servers already have images for their users, and they make them available through the protected user resource that we already used in order to get our user's names. To use this avatar picture, we need to get the URL from the provider, store it in the cookie for our user, and send it through a web socket so that every client can render the picture alongside the corresponding message.

Getting the avatar URL

The schema for user or profile resources is not part of the OAuth2 spec, which means that each provider is responsible for deciding how to represent that data. Indeed, providers do things differently; for example, the avatar URL in a GitHub user resource is stored in a field called `avatar_url`, whereas in Google, the same field is called `picture`. Facebook goes even further by nesting the avatar URL value in a `url` field inside an object called `picture`. Luckily, Gomniauth abstracts this for us; its `GetUser` call on a provider standardizes the interface to get common fields.

In order to make use of the avatar URL field, we need to go back and store that information in our cookie. In `auth.go`, look inside the `callback` action switch case and update the code that creates the `authCookieValue` object, as follows:

```
authCookieValue := objx.New(map[string]interface{}{
  "name":       user.Name(),
  "avatar_url": user.AvatarURL(),
}).MustBase64()
```

The `AvatarURL` field called in the preceding code will return the appropriate URL value and store it in our `avatar_url` field, which we then put into the cookie.

Gomniauth defines a `User` type of interface and each provider implements their own version. The generic `map[string]interface{}` data returned from the auth server is stored inside each object, and the method calls access the appropriate value using the right field name for that provider. This approach describing the way information is accessed without being strict about implementation details–is a great use of interfaces in Go.

Transmitting the avatar URL

We need to update our `message` type so that it can also carry the avatar URL with it. In `message.go`, add the `AvatarURL` string field:

```
type message struct {
  Name      string
  Message   string
  When      time.Time
  AvatarURL string
}
```

So far, we have not actually assigned a value to `AvatarURL` like we do for the `Name` field; so, we must update our `read` method in `client.go`:

```
func (c *client) read() {
  defer c.socket.Close()
  for {
    var msg *message
    err := c.socket.ReadJSON(&msg)
    if err != nil {
      return
    }
    msg.When = time.Now()
    msg.Name = c.userData["name"].(string)
```

```
        if avatarURL, ok := c.userData["avatar_url"]; ok {
            msg.AvatarURL = avatarURL.(string)
        }
        c.room.forward <- msg
    }
}
```

All we have done here is take the value from the `userData` field that represents what we put into the cookie and assigned it to the appropriate field in `message` if the value was present in the map. We now take the additional step of checking whether the value is present because we cannot guarantee that the auth service would provide a value for this field. And since it could be `nil`, it might cause panic to assign it to a `string` type if it's actually missing.

Adding the avatar to the user interface

Now that our JavaScript client gets an avatar URL value via the socket, we can use it to display the image alongside the messages. We do this by updating the `socket.onmessage` code in `chat.html`:

```
socket.onmessage = function(e) {
  var msg = JSON.parse(e.data);
  messages.append(
    $("<li>").append(
      $("<img>").css({
        width:50,
        verticalAlign:"middle"
      }).attr("src", msg.AvatarURL),
      $("<strong>").text(msg.Name + ": "),
      $("<span>").text(msg.Message)
    )
  );
}
```

When we receive a message, we will insert an `img` tag with the source set to the `AvatarURL` field. We will use jQuery's `css` method to force a width of 50 pixels. This protects us from massive pictures spoiling our interface and allows us to align the image to the middle of the surrounding text.

If we build and run our application having logged in with a previous version, you will find that the `auth` cookie that doesn't contain the avatar URL is still there. We are not asked to authenticate again (since we are already logged in), and the code that adds the `avatar_url` field never gets a chance to run. We could delete our cookie and refresh the page, but we would have to keep doing this whenever we make changes during development. Let's solve this problem properly by adding a logout feature.

Logging out

The simplest way to log out a user is to get rid of the `auth` cookie and redirect the user to the chat page, which will in turn cause a redirect to the login page (since we just removed the cookie). We do this by adding a new `HandleFunc` call to `main.go`:

```
http.HandleFunc("/logout", func(w http.ResponseWriter, r *http.Request) {
  http.SetCookie(w, &http.Cookie{
    Name:    "auth",
    Value:   "",
    Path:    "/",
    MaxAge: -1,
  })
  w.Header().Set("Location", "/chat")
  w.WriteHeader(http.StatusTemporaryRedirect)
})
```

The preceding handler function uses `http.SetCookie` to update the cookie setting `MaxAge` to `-1`, which indicates that it should be deleted immediately by the browser. Not all browsers are forced to delete the cookie, which is why we also provide a new `Value` setting of an empty string, thus removing the user data that would previously have been stored.

> As an additional assignment, you can bulletproof your app a little by updating the first line in `ServeHTTP` for your `authHandler` method in `auth.go` to make it cope with the empty value case as well as the missing cookie case:
> ```
> if cookie, err := r.Cookie("auth"); err ==
> http.ErrNoCookie || cookie.Value == ""
> ```
> Instead of ignoring the return of `r.Cookie`, we keep a reference to the returned cookie (if there was actually one) and also add an additional check to see whether the `Value` string of the cookie is empty or not.

Before we continue, let's add a `Sign Out` link to make it even easier to get rid of the cookie and also allow our end users to log out. In `chat.html`, update the `chatbox` form to insert a simple HTML link to the new `/logout` handler:

```
<form id="chatbox">
  {{.UserData.name}}:<br/>
  <textarea></textarea>
  <input type="submit" value="Send" />
  or <a href="/logout">sign out</a>
</form>
```

Now build and run the application and open a browser to `localhost:8080/chat`:

```
go build -o chat
./chat -host=:8080
```

Log out if you need to and log back in. When you click on **Send**, you will see your avatar picture appear next to your messages:

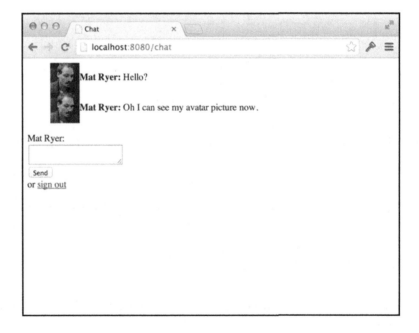

Making things prettier

Our application is starting to look a little ugly, and its time to do something about it. In the previous chapter, we implemented the Bootstrap library into our login page, and we are going to extend its use to our chat page now. We will make three changes in `chat.html`: include Bootstrap and tweak the CSS styles for our page, change the markup for our form, and tweak how we render messages on the page:

1. First, let's update the `style` tag at the top of the page and insert a `link` tag above it in order to include Bootstrap:

```
<link rel="stylesheet"href="//netdna.bootstrapcdn.com/bootstrap
   /3.3.6/css/bootstrap.min.css">
<style>
   ul#messages          { list-style: none; }
   ul#messages li       { margin-bottom: 2px; }
   ul#messages li img { margin-right: 10px; }
</style>
```

2. Next, let's replace the markup at the top of the `body` tag (before the `script` tags) with the following code:

```
<div class="container">
   <div class="panel panel-default">
     <div class="panel-body">
       <ul id="messages"></ul>
     </div>
   </div>
   <form id="chatbox" role="form">
     <div class="form-group">
       <label for="message">Send a message as {{.UserData.name}}
         </label> or <a href="/logout">Sign out</a>
       <textarea id="message" class="form-control"></textarea>
     </div>
     <input type="submit" value="Send" class="btn btn-default" />
   </form>
</div>
```

This markup follows Bootstrap standards of applying appropriate classes to various items; for example, the form-control class neatly formats elements within form (you can check out the Bootstrap documentation for more information on what these classes do).

3. Finally, let's update our `socket.onmessage` JavaScript code to put the sender's name as the title attribute for our image. This makes it display the image when you mouse over it rather than display it next to every message:

```
socket.onmessage = function(e) {
    var msg = JSON.parse(e.data);
    messages.append(
        $("<li>").append(
            $("<img>").attr("title", msg.Name).css({
                width:50,
                verticalAlign:"middle"
            }).attr("src", msg.AvatarURL),
            $("<span>").text(msg.Message)
        )
    );
}
```

Build and run the application and refresh your browser to see whether a new design appears:

```
go build -o chat
./chat -host=:8080
```

The preceding command shows the following output:

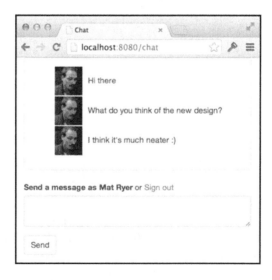

With relatively few changes to the code, we have dramatically improved the look and feel of our application.

Implementing Gravatar

Gravatar is a web service that allows users to upload a single profile picture and associate it with their e-mail address in order to make it available from any website. Developers, like us, can access these images for our application just by performing a GET operation on a specific API endpoint. In this section, we will look at how to implement Gravatar rather than use the picture provided by the auth service.

Abstracting the avatar URL process

Since we have three different ways of obtaining the avatar URL in our application, we have reached the point where it would be sensible to learn how to abstract the functionality in order to cleanly implement the options. Abstraction refers to a process in which we separate the idea of something from its specific implementation. The http.Handler method is a great example of how a handler will be used along with its ins and outs, without being specific about what action is taken by each handler.

In Go, we start to describe our idea of getting an avatar URL by defining an interface. Let's create a new file called avatar.go and insert the following code:

```
package main
import (
  "errors"
)
// ErrNoAvatar is the error that is returned when the
// Avatar instance is unable to provide an avatar URL.
var ErrNoAvatarURL = errors.New("chat: Unable to get an avatar  URL.")
// Avatar represents types capable of representing
// user profile pictures.
type Avatar interface {
  // GetAvatarURL gets the avatar URL for the specified client,
  // or returns an error if something goes wrong.
  // ErrNoAvatarURL is returned if the object is unable to get
  // a URL for the specified client.
  GetAvatarURL(c *client) (string, error)
}
```

The Avatar interface describes the GetAvatarURL method that a type must satisfy in order to be able to get avatar URLs. We took the client as an argument so that we know the user for which the URL to be returned. The method returns two arguments: a string (which will be the URL if things go well) and an error in case something goes wrong.

One of the things that could go wrong is simply that one of the specific implementations of Avatar is unable to get the URL. In that case, GetAvatarURL will return the ErrNoAvatarURL error as the second argument. The ErrNoAvatarURL error therefore becomes a part of the interface; it's one of the possible returns from the method and something that users of our code should probably explicitly handle. We mention this in the comments part of the code for the method, which is the only way to communicate such design decisions in Go.

Because the error is initialized immediately using errors.New and stored in the ErrNoAvatarURL variable, only one of these objects will ever be created; passing the pointer of the error as a return is inexpensive. This is unlike Java's checked exceptions which serve a similar purpose where expensive exception objects are created and used as part of the control flow.

The auth service and the avatar's implementation

The first implementation of Avatar we write will replace the existing functionality where we had hardcoded the avatar URL obtained from the auth service. Let's use a **Test-driven Development (TDD)** approach so that we can be sure our code works without having to manually test it. Let's create a new file called avatar_test.go in the chat folder:

```
package main
import "testing"
func TestAuthAvatar(t *testing.T) {
  var authAvatar AuthAvatar
  client := new(client)
  url, err := authAvatar.GetAvatarURL(client)
  if err != ErrNoAvatarURL {
    t.Error("AuthAvatar.GetAvatarURL should return ErrNoAvatarURL
    when no value present")
  }
  // set a value
  testUrl := "http://url-to-gravatar/"
  client.userData = map[string]interface{}{"avatar_url": testUrl}
  url, err = authAvatar.GetAvatarURL(client)
  if err != nil {
    t.Error("AuthAvatar.GetAvatarURL should return no error
    when value present")
  }
  if url != testUrl {
    t.Error("AuthAvatar.GetAvatarURL should return correct URL")
  }
}
```

This file contains a test for our as-of-yet, nonexistent `AuthAvatar` type's `GetAvatarURL` method. First, it uses a client with no user data and ensures that the `ErrNoAvatarURL` error is returned. After setting a suitable URL, our test calls the method again this time to assert that it returns the correct value. However, building this code fails because the `AuthAvatar` type doesn't exist, so we'll declare `authAvatar` next.

Before we write our implementation, it's worth noticing that we only declare the `authAvatar` variable as the `AuthAvatar` type but never actually assign anything to it so its value remains `nil`. This is not a mistake; we are actually making use of Go's zero-initialization (or default initialization) capabilities. Since there is no state needed for our object (we will pass `client` in as an argument), there is no need to waste time and memory on initializing an instance of it. In Go, it is acceptable to call a method on a `nil` object, provided that the method doesn't try to access a field. When we actually come to writing our implementation, we will look at a way in which we can ensure this is the case.

Let's head back over to `avatar.go` and make our test pass. Add the following code at the bottom of the file:

```
type AuthAvatar struct{}
var UseAuthAvatar AuthAvatar
func (AuthAvatar) GetAvatarURL(c *client) (string, error) {
   if url, ok := c.userData["avatar_url"]; ok {
     if urlStr, ok := url.(string); ok {
       return urlStr, nil
     }
   }
   return "", ErrNoAvatarURL
}
```

Here, we define our `AuthAvatar` type as an empty struct and define the implementation of the `GetAvatarURL` method. We also create a handy variable called `UseAuthAvatar` that has the `AuthAvatar` type but which remains of `nil` value. We can later assign the `UseAuthAvatar` variable to any field looking for an `Avatar` interface type.

The `GetAvatarURL` method we wrote earlier doesn't have a very nice **line of sight**; the happy return is buried within two `if` blocks. See if you can refactor it so that the last line is `return urlStr, nil` and the method exits early if the `avatar_url` field is missing. You can refactor with confidence, since this code is covered by a unit test.
For a little more on the rationale behind this kind of refactor, refer to the article at `http://bit.ly/lineofsightgolang`.

Normally, the receiver of a method (the type defined in parentheses before the name) will be assigned to a variable so that it can be accessed in the body of the method. Since, in our case, we assume the object can have `nil` value, we can omit a variable name to tell Go to throw away the reference. This serves as an added reminder to ourselves that we should avoid using it.

The body of our implementation is relatively simple otherwise: we are safely looking for the value of `avatar_url` and ensuring that it is a string before returning it. If anything fails, we return the `ErrNoAvatarURL` error, as defined in the interface.

Let's run the tests by opening a terminal and then navigating to the `chat` folder and typing the following:

```
go test
```

If all is well, our tests will pass and we will have successfully created our first `Avatar` implementation.

Using an implementation

When we use an implementation, we could refer to either the helper variables directly or create our own instance of the interface whenever we need the functionality. However, this would defeat the object of the abstraction. Instead, we use the `Avatar` interface type to indicate where we need the capability.

For our chat application, we will have a single way to obtain an avatar URL per chat room. So, let's update the `room` type so it can hold an `Avatar` object. In `room.go`, add the following field definition to the `room` `struct` type:

```
// avatar is how avatar information will be obtained.
avatar Avatar
```

Update the `newRoom` function so that we can pass in an `Avatar` implementation for use; we will just assign this implementation to the new field when we create our `room` instance:

```
// newRoom makes a new room that is ready to go.
func newRoom(avatar Avatar) *room {
  return &room{
    forward: make(chan *message),
    join:    make(chan *client),
    leave:   make(chan *client),
    clients: make(map[*client]bool),
    tracer:  trace.Off(),
    avatar:  avatar,
```

```
    }
  }
```

Building the project now will highlight the fact that the call to `newRoom` in `main.go` is broken because we have not provided an `Avatar` argument; let's update it by passing in our handy `UseAuthAvatar` variable, as follows:

```
r := newRoom(UseAuthAvatar)
```

We didn't have to create an instance of `AuthAvatar`, so no memory was allocated. In our case, this doesn't result in great saving (since we only have one room for our entire application), but imagine the size of the potential savings if our application has thousands of rooms. The way we named the `UseAuthAvatar` variable means that the preceding code is very easy to read and it also makes our intention obvious.

> Thinking about code readability is important when designing interfaces. Consider a method that takes a Boolean input just passing in true or false hides the real meaning if you don't know the argument names. Consider defining a couple of helper constants, as shown in the following short example:
> ```
> func move(animated bool) { /* ... */ }
> const Animate = true const
> DontAnimate = false
> ```
> Think about which of the following calls to move are easier to understand:
> ```
> move(true)
> move(false)
> move(Animate)
> move(DontAnimate)
> ```

All that is left now is to change `client` to use our new `Avatar` interface. In `client.go`, update the `read` method, as follows:

```
func (c *client) read() {
  defer c.socket.Close()
  for {
    var msg *message
    if err := c.socket.ReadJSON(&msg); err != nil {
      return
    }
    msg.When = time.Now()
    msg.Name = c.userData["name"].(string)
    msg.AvatarURL, _ = c.room.avatar.GetAvatarURL(c)
    c.room.forward <- msg
  }
}
```

Here, we are asking the `avatar` instance in `room` to get the avatar URL for us instead of extracting it from `userData` ourselves.

When you build and run the application, you will notice that (although we have refactored things a little) the behavior and user experience hasn't changed at all. This is because we told our room to use the `AuthAvatar` implementation.

Now let's add another implementation to the room.

The Gravatar implementation

The Gravatar implementation in `Avatar` will do the same job as the `AuthAvatar` implementation, except that it will generate a URL for a profile picture hosted on `https://en.gravatar.com/`. Let's start by adding a test to our `avatar_test.go` file:

```
func TestGravatarAvatar(t *testing.T) {
  var gravatarAvatar GravatarAvatar
  client := new(client)
  client.userData = map[string]interface{}{"email":
   "MyEmailAddress@example.com"}
  url, err := gravatarAvatar.GetAvatarURL(client)
  if err != nil {
    t.Error("GravatarAvatar.GetAvatarURL should not return an error")
  }
  if url != "//www.gravatar.com/avatar/0bc83cb571cd1c50ba6f3e8a78ef1346" {
    t.Errorf("GravatarAvatar.GetAvatarURL wrongly returned %s", url)
  }
}
```

Gravatar uses a hash of the e-mail address to generate a unique ID for each profile picture, so we set up a client and ensure `userData` contains an e-mail address. Next, we call the same `GetAvatarURL` method, but this time on an object that has the `GravatarAvatar` type. We then assert that a correct URL was returned. We already know this is the appropriate URL for the specified e-mail address because it is listed as an example in the Gravatar documentation a great strategy to ensure our code is doing what it should be doing.

Remember that all the source code for this book is available for download from the publishers and has also been published on GitHub. You can save time on building the preceding core by copying and pasting bits and pieces from `https://github.com/matryer/goblueprints`. Hardcoding things such as the base URL is not usually a good idea; we have hardcoded throughout the book to make the code snippets easier to read and more obvious, but you are welcome to extract them as you go along if you like.

Running these tests (with `go test`) obviously causes errors because we haven't defined our types yet. Let's head back to `avatar.go` and add the following code while being sure to import the `io` package:

```
type GravatarAvatar struct{}
var UseGravatar GravatarAvatar
func(GravatarAvatar) GetAvatarURL(c *client) (string, error) {
  if email, ok := c.userData["email"]; ok {
    if emailStr, ok := email.(string); ok {
      m := md5.New()
      io.WriteString(m, strings.ToLower(emailStr))
      return fmt.Sprintf("//www.gravatar.com/avatar/%x", m.Sum(nil)), nil
    }
  }
  return "", ErrNoAvatarURL
}
```

We used the same pattern as we did for `AuthAvatar`: we have an empty struct, a helpful `UseGravatar` variable, and the `GetAvatarURL` method implementation itself. In this method, we follow Gravatar's guidelines to generate an MD5 hash from the e-mail address (after we ensured it was lowercase) and append it to the hardcoded base URL using `fmt.Sprintf`.

The preceding method also suffers from a bad line of sight in code. Can you live with it, or would you want to improve the readability somehow?

It is very easy to achieve hashing in Go thanks to the hard work put in by the writers of the Go standard library. The `crypto` package has an impressive array of cryptography and hashing capabilities all very easy to use. In our case, we create a new `md5` hasher and because the hasher implements the `io.Writer` interface, we can use `io.WriteString` to write a string of bytes to it. Calling `Sum` returns the current hash for the bytes written.

 You might have noticed that we end up hashing the e-mail address every time we need the avatar URL. This is pretty inefficient, especially at scale, but we should prioritize getting stuff done over optimization. If we need to, we can always come back later and change the way this works.

Running the tests now shows us that our code is working, but we haven't yet included an e-mail address in the `auth` cookie. We do this by locating the code where we assign to the `authCookieValue` object in `auth.go` and updating it to grab the `Email` value from Gomniauth:

```
authCookieValue := objx.New(map[string]interface{}{
    "name":       user.Name(),
    "avatar_url": user.AvatarURL(),
    "email":       user.Email(),
}).MustBase64()
```

The final thing we must do is tell our room to use the Gravatar implementation instead of the `AuthAvatar` implementation. We do this by calling `newRoom` in `main.go` and making the following change:

```
r := newRoom(UseGravatar)
```

Build and run the chat program once again and head to the browser. Remember, since we have changed the information stored in the cookie, we must sign out and sign back in again in order to see our changes take effect.

Assuming you have a different image for your Gravatar account, you will notice that the system is now pulling the image from Gravatar instead of the auth provider. Using your browser's inspector or debug tool will show you that the `src` attribute of the `img` tag has indeed changed:

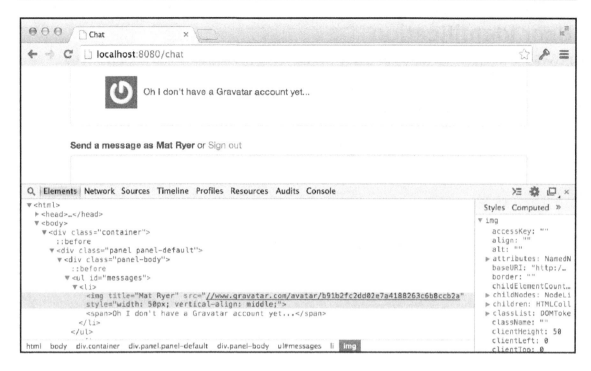

If you don't have a Gravatar account, you'll most likely see a default placeholder image in place of your profile picture.

Uploading an avatar picture

In the third and final approach of uploading a picture, we will look at how to allow users to upload an image from their local hard drive to use as their profile picture when chatting. The file will then be served to the browsers via a URL. We will need a way to associate a file with a particular user to ensure that we associate the right picture with the corresponding messages.

User identification

In order to uniquely identify our users, we are going to copy Gravatar's approach by hashing their e-mail address and using the resulting string as an identifier. We will store the user ID in the cookie along with the rest of the user-specific data. This will actually have the added benefit of removing the inefficiency associated with continuous hashing from `GravatarAuth`.

In `auth.go`, replace the code that creates the `authCookieValue` object with the following code:

```
m := md5.New()
io.WriteString(m, strings.ToLower(user.Email()))
userId := fmt.Sprintf("%x", m.Sum(nil))
authCookieValue := objx.New(map[string]interface{}{
  "userid":     userId,
  "name":       user.Name(),
  "avatar_url": user.AvatarURL(),
  "email":      user.Email(),
}).MustBase64()
```

Here, we have hashed the e-mail address and stored the resulting value in the `userid` field at the point at which the user logs in. From now on, we can use this value in our Gravatar code instead of hashing the e-mail address for every message. To do this, first, we update the test by removing the following line from `avatar_test.go`:

```
client.userData = map[string]interface{}{"email":
"MyEmailAddress@example.com"}
```

We then replace the preceding line with this line:

```
client.userData = map[string]interface{}{"userid":
"0bc83cb571cd1c50ba6f3e8a78ef1346"}
```

We no longer need to set the `email` field since it is not used; instead, we just have to set an appropriate value to the new `userid` field. However, if you run `go test` in a terminal, you will see this test fail.

To make the test pass, in `avatar.go`, update the `GetAvatarURL` method for the `GravatarAuth` type:

```
func(GravatarAvatar) GetAvatarURL(c *client) (string, error) {
  if userid, ok := c.userData["userid"]; ok {
    if useridStr, ok := userid.(string); ok {
      return "//www.gravatar.com/avatar/" + useridStr, nil
    }
```

```
    }
    return "", ErrNoAvatarURL
}
```

This won't change the behavior, but it allows us to make an unexpected optimization, which is a great example of why you shouldn't optimize code too early the inefficiencies that you spot early on may not last long enough to warrant the effort required to fix them.

An upload form

If our users are to upload a file as their avatar, they need a way to browse their local hard drive and submit the file to the server. We facilitate this by adding a new template-driven page. In the `chat/templates` folder, create a file called `upload.html`:

```html
<html>
  <head>
    <title>Upload</title>
    <link rel="stylesheet"
    href="//netdna.bootstrapcdn.com/bootstrap/3.6.6/css/bootstrap.min.css">
  </head>
  <body>
    <div class="container">
      <div class="page-header">
        <h1>Upload picture</h1>
      </div>
      <form role="form" action="/uploader" enctype="multipart/form-data"
       method="post">
        <input type="hidden" name="userid" value="{{.UserData.userid}}" />
        <div class="form-group">
          <label for="avatarFile">Select file</label>
          <input type="file" name="avatarFile" />
        </div>
        <input type="submit" value="Upload" class="btn" />
      </form>
    </div>
  </body>
</html>
```

We used Bootstrap again to make our page look nice and also to make it fit in with the other pages. However, the key point to note here is the HTML form that will provide the user interface required to upload files. The action points to /uploader, the handler for which we have yet to implement, and the enctype attribute must be multipart/form-data so that the browser can transmit binary data over HTTP. Then, there is an input element of the type file, which will contain a reference to the file we want to upload. Also, note that we have included the userid value from the UserData map as a hidden input this will tell us which user is uploading a file. It is important that the name attributes be correct, as this is how we will refer to the data when we implement our handler on the server.

Let's now map the new template to the /upload path in main.go:

```
http.Handle("/upload", &templateHandler{filename: "upload.html"})
```

Handling the upload

When the user clicks on **Upload** after selecting a file, the browser will send the data for the file as well as the user ID to /uploader, but right now, that data doesn't actually go anywhere. We will implement a new HandlerFunc interface that is capable of receiving the file, reading the bytes that are streamed through the connection, and saving it as a new file on the server. In the chat folder, let's create a new folder called avatars this is where we will save the avatar image files.

Next, create a new file called upload.go and insert the following code make sure that you add the appropriate package name and imports (which are ioutils, net/http, io, and path):

```
func uploaderHandler(w http.ResponseWriter, req *http.Request) {
  userId := req.FormValue("userid")
  file, header, err := req.FormFile("avatarFile")
  if err != nil {
    http.Error(w, err.Error(), http.StatusInternalServerError)
    return
  }
  data, err := ioutil.ReadAll(file)
  if err != nil {
    http.Error(w, err.Error(), http.StatusInternalServerError)
    return
  }
  filename := path.Join("avatars", userId+path.Ext(header.Filename))
  err = ioutil.WriteFile(filename, data, 0777)
  if err != nil {
    http.Error(w, err.Error(), http.StatusInternalServerError)
```

```
      return
   }
   io.WriteString(w, "Successful")
}
```

Here, first `uploaderHandler` uses the `FormValue` method in `http.Request` to get the user ID that we placed in the hidden input in our HTML form. Then, it gets an `io.Reader` type capable of reading the uploaded bytes by calling `req.FormFile`, which returns three arguments. The first argument represents the file itself with the `multipart.File` interface type, which is also `io.Reader`. The second is a `multipart.FileHeader` object that contains the metadata about the file, such as the filename. And finally, the third argument is an error that we hope will have a `nil` value.

What do we mean when we say that the `multipart.File` interface type is also `io.Reader`? Well, a quick glance at the documentation at `http://golang.org/pkg/mime/m ultipart/#File` makes it clear that the type is actually just a wrapper interface for a few other more general interfaces. This means that a `multipart.File` type can be passed to methods that require `io.Reader`, since any object that implements `multipart.File` must, therefore, implement `io.Reader`.

Embedding standard library interfaces, such as the wrapper, to describe new concepts is a great way to make sure your code works in as many contexts as possible. Similarly, you should try to write code that uses the simplest interface type you can find, ideally from the standard library. For example, if you wrote a method that needed you to read the contents of a file, you could ask the user to provide an argument of the type `multipart.File`. However, if you ask for `io.Reader` instead, your code will become significantly more flexible because any type that has the appropriate `Read` method can be passed in, which includes user-defined types as well.

The `ioutil.ReadAll` method will just keep reading from the specified `io.Reader` interface until all of the bytes have been received, so this is where we actually receive the stream of bytes from the client. We then use `path.Join` and `path.Ext` to build a new filename using `userid` and copy the extension from the original filename that we can get from `multipart.FileHeader`.

We then use the `ioutil.WriteFile` method to create a new file in the `avatars` folder. We use `userid` in the filename to associate the image with the correct user, much in the same way as Gravatar does. The `0777` value specifies that the new file we create should have complete file permissions, which is a good default setting if you're not sure what other permissions should be set.

If an error occurs at any stage, our code will write it out to the response along with a 500 status code (since we specify `http.StatusInternalServerError`), which will help us debug it, or it will write **Successful** if everything went well.

In order to map this new handler function to `/uploader`, we need to head back to `main.go` and add the following line to `func main`:

```
http.HandleFunc("/uploader", uploaderHandler)
```

Now build and run the application and remember to log out and log back in again in order to give our code a chance to upload the `auth` cookie:

```
go build -o chat
./chat -host=:8080
```

Open `http://localhost:8080/upload` and click on **Choose File**, and then select a file from your hard drive and click on **Upload**. Navigate to your `chat/avatars` folder and you will notice that the file was indeed uploaded and renamed to the value of your `userid` field.

Serving the images

Now that we have a place to keep our user's avatar images on the server, we need a way to make them accessible to the browser. We do this using the `net/http` package's built-in file server. In `main.go`, add the following code:

```
http.Handle("/avatars/",
    http.StripPrefix("/avatars/",
        http.FileServer(http.Dir("./avatars"))))
```

This is actually a single line of code that has been broken up to improve readability. The `http.Handle` call should feel familiar, as we are specifying that we want to map the `/avatars/` path with the specified handler this is where things get interesting. Both `http.StripPrefix` and `http.FileServer` return `http.Handler`, and they make use of the wrapping pattern we learned about in the previous chapter. The `StripPrefix` function takes `http.Handler` in, modifies the path by removing the specified prefix, and passes the functionality onto an inner handler. In our case, the inner handler is an `http.FileServer` handler that will simply serve static files, provide index listings, and generate the `404 Not Found` error if it cannot find the file. The `http.Dir` function allows us to specify which folder we want to expose publicly.

If we didn't strip the `/avatars/` prefix from the requests with `http.StripPrefix`, the file server would look for another folder called `avatars` inside the actual `avatars` folder, that is, `/avatars/avatars/filename` instead of `/avatars/filename`.

Let's build the program and run it before opening `http://localhost:8080/avatars/` in a browser. You'll notice that the file server has generated a listing of the files inside our `avatars` folder. Clicking on a file will either download the file, or in the case of an image, simply display it. If you haven't done this already, go to `http://localhost:8080/upload` and upload a picture, and then head back to the listing page and click on it to see it in the browser.

The Avatar implementation for local files

The final step in making filesystem avatars work is writing an implementation of our `Avatar` interface that generates URLs that point to the filesystem endpoint we created in the previous section.

Let's add a test function to our `avatar_test.go` file:

```
func TestFileSystemAvatar(t *testing.T) {
  filename := filepath.Join("avatars", "abc.jpg")
  ioutil.WriteFile(filename, []byte{}, 0777)
  defer os.Remove(filename)
  var fileSystemAvatar FileSystemAvatar
  client := new(client)
  client.userData = map[string]interface{}{"userid": "abc"}
  url, err := fileSystemAvatar.GetAvatarURL(client)
  if err != nil {
    t.Error("FileSystemAvatar.GetAvatarURL should not return an error")
  }
  if url != "/avatars/abc.jpg" {
    t.Errorf("FileSystemAvatar.GetAvatarURL wrongly returned %s", url)
  }
}
```

This test is similar to, but slightly more involved than, the `GravatarAvatar` test because we are also creating a test file in our `avatars` folder and deleting it afterwards.

 Even if our test code panics, the deferred functions will still be called. So regardless of what happens, our test code will clean up after itself.

The rest of the test is simple: we set a `userid` field in `client.userData` and call `GetAvatarURL` to ensure we get the right value back. Of course, running this test will fail, so let's go and add the following code in order to make it pass in `avatar.go`:

```
type FileSystemAvatar struct{}
var UseFileSystemAvatar FileSystemAvatar
func (FileSystemAvatar) GetAvatarURL(c *client) (string, error) {
  if userid, ok := c.userData["userid"]; ok {
    if useridStr, ok := userid.(string); ok {
      return "/avatars/" + useridStr + ".jpg", nil
    }
  }
  return "", ErrNoAvatarURL
}
```

As you can see here, in order to generate the correct URL, we simply get the `userid` value and build the final string by adding the appropriate segments together. You may have noticed that we have hardcoded the file extension to `.jpg`, which means that the initial version of our chat application will only support JPEGs.

Supporting only JPEGs might seem like a half-baked solution, but following Agile methodologies, this is perfectly fine; after all, custom JPEG profile pictures are better than no custom profile pictures at all.

Let's look at our new code in action by updating `main.go` to use our new `Avatar` implementation:

```
r := newRoom(UseFileSystemAvatar)
```

Now build and run the application as usual and go to `http://localhost:8080/upload` and use a web form to upload a JPEG image to use as your profile picture. To make sure it's working correctly, choose a unique image that isn't your Gravatar picture or the image from the auth service. Once you see the successful message after clicking on **Upload**, go to `http://localhost:8080/chat` and post a message. You will notice that the application has indeed used the profile picture that you uploaded.

To change your profile picture, go back to the `/upload` page and upload a different picture, and then jump back to the `/chat` page and post more messages.

Supporting different file types

To support different file types, we have to make our GetAvatarURL method for the FileSystemAvatar type a little smarter.

Instead of just blindly building the string, we will use the very important ioutil.ReadDir method to get a listing of the files. The listing also includes directories so we will use the IsDir method to determine whether we should skip it or not.

We will then check whether each file matches the userid field (remember that we named our files in this way) by a call to path.Match. If the filename matches the userid field, then we have found the file for that user and we return the path. If anything goes wrong or if we can't find the file, we return the ErrNoAvatarURL error as usual.

Update the appropriate method in avatar.go with the following code:

```
func (FileSystemAvatar) GetAvatarURL(c *client) (string, error) {
  if userid, ok := c.userData["userid"]; ok {
    if useridStr, ok := userid.(string); ok {
      files, err := ioutil.ReadDir("avatars")
      if err != nil {
        return "", ErrNoAvatarURL
      }
      for _, file := range files {
        if file.IsDir() {
```

```
            continue
        }
        if match, _ := path.Match(useridStr+"*", file.Name());
        match {
          return "/avatars/" + file.Name(), nil
        }
      }
    }
  }
  return "", ErrNoAvatarURL
}
```

Delete all the files in the `avatar` folder to prevent confusion and rebuild the program. This time, upload an image of a different type and note that our application has no difficulty handling it.

Refactoring and optimizing our code

When we look back at how our `Avatar` type is used, you will notice that every time someone sends a message, the application makes a call to `GetAvatarURL`. In our latest implementation, each time the method is called, we iterate over all the files in the `avatars` folder. For a particularly chatty user, this could mean that we end up iterating over and over again many times a minute. This is an obvious waste of resources and would, at some point very soon, become a scaling problem.

Instead of getting the avatar URL for every message, we should get it only once when the user first logs in and cache it in the `auth` cookie. Unfortunately, our `Avatar` interface type requires that we pass in a `client` object to the `GetAvatarURL` method and we do not have such an object at the point at which we are authenticating the user.

 So did we make a mistake when we designed our `Avatar` interface? While this is a natural conclusion to come to, in fact we did the right thing. We designed the solution with the best information we had available at the time and therefore had a working chat application much sooner than if we'd tried to design for every possible future case. Software evolves and almost always changes during the development process and will definitely change throughout the lifetime of the code.

Replacing concrete types with interfaces

We have concluded that our GetAvatarURL method depends on a type that is not available to us at the point we need it, so what would be a good alternative? We could pass each required field as a separate argument, but this would make our interface brittle, since as soon as an Avatar implementation needs a new piece of information, we'd have to change the method signature. Instead, we will create a new type that will encapsulate the information our Avatar implementations need while conceptually remaining decoupled from our specific case.

In auth.go, add the following code to the top of the page (underneath the package keyword, of course):

```
import gomniauthcommon "github.com/stretchr/gomniauth/common"
type ChatUser interface {
  UniqueID() string
  AvatarURL() string
}
type chatUser struct {
  gomniauthcommon.User
  uniqueID string
}
func (u chatUser) UniqueID() string {
  return u.uniqueID
}
```

Here, the import statement imported the common package from Gomniauth and, at the same time, gave it a specific name through which it will be accessed: gomniauthcommon. This isn't entirely necessary since we have no package name conflicts. However, it makes the code easier to understand.

In the preceding code snippet, we also defined a new interface type called ChatUser, which exposes the information needed in order for our Avatar implementations to generate the correct URLs. Then, we defined an actual implementation called chatUser (notice the lowercase starting letter) that implements the interface. It also makes use of a very interesting feature in Go: type embedding. We actually embedded the gomniauth/common.User interface type, which means that our struct interface implements the interface automatically.

You may have noticed that we only actually implemented one of the two required methods to satisfy our `ChatUser` interface. We got away with this because the Gomniauth `User` interface happens to define the same `AvatarURL` method. In practice, when we instantiate our `chatUser` struct provided we set an appropriate value for the implied Gomniauth `User` field our object implements both Gomniauth's `User` interface and our own `ChatUser` interface at the same time.

Changing interfaces in a test-driven way

Before we can use our new type, we must update the `Avatar` interface and appropriate implementations to make use of it. As we will follow TDD practices, we are going to first make these changes in our test file, see the compiler errors when we try to build our code, and see failing tests once we fix those errors before finally making the tests pass.

Open `avatar_test.go` and replace `TestAuthAvatar` with the following code:

```go
func TestAuthAvatar(t *testing.T) {
  var authAvatar AuthAvatar
  testUser := &gomniauthtest.TestUser{}
  testUser.On("AvatarURL").Return("", ErrNoAvatarURL)
  testChatUser := &chatUser{User: testUser}
  url, err := authAvatar.GetAvatarURL(testChatUser)
  if err != ErrNoAvatarURL {
    t.Error("AuthAvatar.GetAvatarURL should return ErrNoAvatarURL
    when no value present")
  }
  testUrl := "http://url-to-gravatar/"
  testUser = &gomniauthtest.TestUser{}
  testChatUser.User = testUser
  testUser.On("AvatarURL").Return(testUrl, nil)
  url, err = authAvatar.GetAvatarURL(testChatUser)
  if err != nil {
    t.Error("AuthAvatar.GetAvatarURL should return no error
    when value present")
  }
  if url != testUrl {
    t.Error("AuthAvatar.GetAvatarURL should return correct URL")
  }
}
```

You will also need to import the `gomniauth/test` package as `gomniauthtest`, like we did in the last section.

Using our new interface before we have defined it is a good way to check the sanity of our thinking, which is another advantage of practicing TDD. In this new test, we create `TestUser` provided by Gomniauth and embed it into a `chatUser` type. We then pass the new `chatUser` type into our `GetAvatarURL` calls and make the same assertions about output as we always have done.

Gomniauth's `TestUser` type is interesting as it makes use of the `Testify` package's mocking capabilities. Refer to `https://github.com/stretchr/testify` for more information.

The `On` and `Return` methods allow us to tell `TestUser` what to do when specific methods are called. In the first case, we tell the `AvatarURL` method to return the error, and in the second case, we ask it to return the `testUrl` value, which simulates the two possible outcomes we are covering in this test.

Updating the other two tests is much simpler because they rely only on the `UniqueID` method, the value of which we can control directly.

Replace the other two tests in `avatar_test.go` with the following code:

```go
func TestGravatarAvatar(t *testing.T) {
  var gravatarAvatar GravatarAvatar
  user := &chatUser{uniqueID: "abc"}
  url, err := gravatarAvatar.GetAvatarURL(user)
  if err != nil {
    t.Error("GravatarAvatar.GetAvatarURL should not return an error")
  }
  if url != "//www.gravatar.com/avatar/abc" {
    t.Errorf("GravatarAvatar.GetAvatarURL wrongly returned %s", url)
  }
}
func TestFileSystemAvatar(t *testing.T) {
  // make a test avatar file
  filename := path.Join("avatars", "abc.jpg")
  ioutil.WriteFile(filename, []byte{}, 0777)
  defer func() { os.Remove(filename) }()
  var fileSystemAvatar FileSystemAvatar
  user := &chatUser{uniqueID: "abc"}
  url, err := fileSystemAvatar.GetAvatarURL(user)
  if err != nil {
    t.Error("FileSystemAvatar.GetAvatarURL should not return an error")
  }
  if url != "/avatars/abc.jpg" {
    t.Errorf("FileSystemAvatar.GetAvatarURL wrongly returned %s", url)
  }
```

```
}
```

Of course, this test code won't even compile because we are yet to update our `Avatar` interface. In `avatar.go`, update the `GetAvatarURL` signature in the `Avatar` interface type to take a `ChatUser` type rather than a `client` type:

```
GetAvatarURL(ChatUser) (string, error)
```

 Note that we are using the `ChatUser` interface (with the starting letter in uppercase) rather than our internal `chatUser` implementation struct after all, we want to be flexible about the types our `GetAvatarURL` methods accept.

Trying to build this will reveal that we now have broken implementations because all the `GetAvatarURL` methods are still asking for a `client` object.

Fixing the existing implementations

Changing an interface like the one we have is a good way to automatically find the parts of our code that have been affected because they will cause compiler errors. Of course, if we were writing a package that other people would use, we would have to be far stricter about changing the interfaces like this, but we haven't released our v1 yet, so it's fine.

We are now going to update the three implementation signatures to satisfy the new interface and change the method bodies to make use of the new type. Replace the implementation for `FileSystemAvatar` with the following:

```
func (FileSystemAvatar) GetAvatarURL(u ChatUser) (string, error) {
  if files, err := ioutil.ReadDir("avatars"); err == nil {
    for _, file := range files {
      if file.IsDir() {
        continue
      }
      if match, _ := path.Match(u.UniqueID()+"*", file.Name());
      match {
        return "/avatars/" + file.Name(), nil
      }
    }
  }
  return "", ErrNoAvatarURL
}
```

The key change here is that we no longer access the `userData` field on the client, and just call `UniqueID` directly on the `ChatUser` interface instead.

Next, we update the `AuthAvatar` implementation with the following code:

```
func (AuthAvatar) GetAvatarURL(u ChatUser) (string, error) {
  url := u.AvatarURL()
  if len(url) == 0 {
    return "", ErrNoAvatarURL
  }
  return url, nil
}
```

Our new design proves to be much simpler, it's always a good thing if we can reduce the amount of code required. The preceding code makes a call to get the `AvatarURL` value, and provided it isn't empty, we return it; otherwise, we return the `ErrNoAvatarURL` error.

 Note how the expected flow of the code is indented to one level, while error cases are nested inside `if` blocks. While you can't stick to this practice 100% of the time, it's a worthwhile endeavor. Being able to quickly scan the code (when reading it) to see the normal flow of execution down a single column allows you to understand the code much quicker. Compare this to code that has lots of `if...else` nested blocks, which takes a lot more unpicking to understand.

Finally, update the `GravatarAvatar` implementation:

```
func (GravatarAvatar) GetAvatarURL(u ChatUser) (string, error) {
  return "//www.gravatar.com/avatar/" + u.UniqueID(), nil
}
```

Global variables versus fields

So far, we have assigned the `Avatar` implementation to the `room` type, which enables us to use different avatars for different rooms. However, this has exposed an issue: when our users sign in, there is no concept of which room they are headed to so we cannot know which `Avatar` implementation to use. Because our application only supports a single room, we are going to look at another approach to select implementations: the use of global variables.

A global variable is simply a variable that is defined outside any type definition and is accessible from every part of the package (and from outside the package if it's exported). For a simple configuration, such as which type of Avatar implementation to use, global variables are an easy and simple solution. Underneath the import statements in main.go, add the following line:

```
// set the active Avatar implementation
var avatars Avatar = UseFileSystemAvatar
```

This defines avatars as a global variable that we can use when we need to get the avatar URL for a particular user.

Implementing our new design

We need to change the code that calls GetAvatarURL for every message to just access the value that we put into the userData cache (via the auth cookie). Change the line where msg.AvatarURL is assigned, as follows:

```
if avatarUrl, ok := c.userData["avatar_url"]; ok {
  msg.AvatarURL = avatarUrl.(string)
}
```

Find the code inside loginHandler in auth.go where we call provider.GetUser and replace it, down to where we set the authCookieValue object, with the following code:

```
user, err := provider.GetUser(creds)
if err != nil {
  log.Fatalln("Error when trying to get user from", provider, "-", err)
}
chatUser := &chatUser{User: user}
m := md5.New()
io.WriteString(m, strings.ToLower(user.Email()))
chatUser.uniqueID = fmt.Sprintf("%x", m.Sum(nil))
avatarURL, err := avatars.GetAvatarURL(chatUser)
if err != nil {
  log.Fatalln("Error when trying to GetAvatarURL", "-", err)
}
```

Here, we created a new chatUser variable while setting the User field (which represents the embedded interface) to the User value returned from Gomniauth. We then saved the userid MD5 hash to the uniqueID field.

The call to `avatars.GetAvatarURL` is where all of our hard work has paid off, as we now get the avatar URL for the user far earlier in the process. Update the `authCookieValue` line in `auth.go` to cache the avatar URL in the cookie and remove the e-mail address since it is no longer required:

```
authCookieValue := objx.New(map[string]interface{}{
  "userid":     chatUser.uniqueID,
  "name":       user.Name(),
  "avatar_url": avatarURL,
}).MustBase64()
```

However expensive the work the `Avatar` implementation needs to do, such as iterating over files on the filesystem, it is mitigated by the fact that the implementation only does so when the user first logs in and not every time they send a message.

Tidying up and testing

Finally, we get to snip away at some of the fat that has accumulated during our refactoring process.

Since we no longer store the `Avatar` implementation in `room`, let's remove the field and all references to it from the type. In `room.go`, delete the `avatar Avatar` definition from the `room` struct and update the `newRoom` method:

```
func newRoom() *room {
  return &room{
    forward: make(chan *message),
    join:    make(chan *client),
    leave:   make(chan *client),
    clients: make(map[*client]bool),
    tracer:  trace.Off(),
  }
}
```

> Remember to use the compiler as your to-do list where possible, and follow the errors to find where you have impacted other code.

In `main.go`, remove the parameter passed into the `newRoom` function call since we are using our global variable instead of this one.

After this exercise, the end user experience remains unchanged. Usually when refactoring the code, it is the internals that are modified while the public-facing interface remains stable and unchanged. As you go, remember to re-run the unit tests to make sure you don't break anything as you evolve the code.

 It's usually a good idea to run tools such as `golint` and `go vet` against your code as well in order to make sure it follows good practices and doesn't contain any Go faux pas, such as missing comments or badly named functions. There are a few deliberately left in for you to fix yourself.

Combining all three implementations

To close this chapter with a bang, we will implement a mechanism in which each `Avatar` implementation takes a turn in trying to get a URL for a user. If the first implementation returns the `ErrNoAvatarURL` error, we will try the next and so on until we find a useable value.

In `avatar.go`, underneath the `Avatar` type, add the following type definition:

```
type TryAvatars []Avatar
```

The `TryAvatars` type is simply a slice of `Avatar` objects that we are free to add methods to. Let's add the following `GetAvatarURL` method:

```
func (a TryAvatars) GetAvatarURL(u ChatUser) (string, error) {
  for _, avatar := range a {
    if url, err := avatar.GetAvatarURL(u); err == nil {
      return url, nil
    }
  }
  return "", ErrNoAvatarURL
}
```

This means that `TryAvatars` is now a valid `Avatar` implementation and can be used in place of any specific implementation. In the preceding method, we iterated over the slice of `Avatar` objects in an order, calling `GetAvatarURL` for each one. If no error is returned, we return the URL; otherwise, we carry on looking. Finally, if we are unable to find a value, we just return `ErrNoAvatarURL` as per the interface design.

Update the `avatars` global variable in `main.go` to use our new implementation:

```
var avatars Avatar = TryAvatars{
   UseFileSystemAvatar,
   UseAuthAvatar,
   UseGravatar}
```

Here, we created a new instance of our `TryAvatars` slice type while putting the other `Avatar` implementations inside it. The order matters since it iterates over the objects in the order in which they appear in the slice. So, first our code will check whether the user has uploaded a picture; if they haven't, the code will check whether the auth service has a picture for us to use. If the approaches fail, a Gravatar URL will be generated, which in the worst case (for example, if the user hasn't added a Gravatar picture) will render a default placeholder image.

To see our new functionality in action, perform the following steps:

1. Build and rerun the application:

   ```
   go build -o chat
   ./chat -host=:8080
   ```

2. Log out by visiting `http://localhost:8080/logout`.
3. Delete all the pictures from the `avatars` folder.
4. Log back in by navigating to `http://localhost:8080/chat`.
5. Send some messages and take note of your profile picture.
6. Visit `http://localhost:8080/upload` and upload a new profile picture.
7. Log out again and log back in as you did earlier.
8. Send some more messages and note that your profile picture has been updated.

Summary

In this chapter, we added three different implementations of profile pictures to our chat application. First, we asked the auth service to provide a URL for us to use. We did this using Gomniauth's abstraction of the user resource data, which we then included as part of the user interface every time a user would send a message. Using Go's zero (or default) initialization, we were able to refer to different implementations of our Avatar interface without actually creating any instances.

We stored data in a cookie for when the user would log in. Given the fact that cookies persist between builds of our code, we added a handy logout feature to help us validate our changes, which we also exposed to our users so that they could log out too. Other small changes to the code and the inclusion of Bootstrap on our chat page dramatically improved the look and feel of our application.

We used MD5 hashing in Go to implement the https://en.gravatar.com/ API by hashing the e-mail address that the auth service provided. If the e-mail address is not known to Gravatar, they will deliver a nice default placeholder image for us, which means our user interface will never be broken due to missing images.

We then built and completed an upload form and associated the server functionality that saved uploaded pictures in the avatars folder. We saw how to expose the saved uploaded pictures to users via the standard library's http.FileServer handler. As this introduced inefficiencies in our design by causing too much filesystem access, we refactored our solution with the help of our unit tests. By moving the GetAvatarURL call to the point at which users log in rather than every time a message is sent, we made our code significantly more scalable.

Our special ErrNoAvatarURL error type was used as part of our interface design in order to allow us to inform the calling code when it was not possible to obtain an appropriate URL this became particularly useful when we created our Avatars slice type. By implementing the Avatar interface on a slice of Avatar types, we were able to create a new implementation that took turns trying to get a valid URL from each of the different options available, starting with the filesystem, then the auth service, and finally Gravatar. We achieved this with zero impact on how the user would interact with the interface. If an implementation returned ErrNoAvatarURL, we tried the next one.

Our chat application is ready to go live, so we can invite our friends and have a real conversation. But first, we need to choose a domain name to host it at, something we will look at in the next chapter.

4
Command-Line Tools to Find Domain Names

The chat application we've built so far is ready to take the world by storm but not before we give it a home on the Internet. Before we invite our friends to join the conversation, we need to pick a valid, catchy, and available domain name, which we can point to the server running our Go code. Instead of sitting in front of our favorite domain name provider for hours on end trying different names, we are going to develop a few command-line tools that will help us find the right one. As we do so, we will see how the Go standard library allows us to interface with the terminal and other executing applications; we'll also explore some patterns and practices to build command-line programs.

In this chapter, you will learn:

- How to build complete command-line applications with as little as a single code file
- How to ensure that the tools we build can be composed with other tools using standard streams
- How to interact with a simple third-party JSON RESTful API
- How to utilize the standard in and out pipes in Go code
- How to read from a streaming source, one line at a time
- How to build a WHOIS client to look up domain information
- How to store and use sensitive or deployment-specific information in environment variables

Pipe design for command-line tools

We are going to build a series of command-line tools that use the standard streams (`stdin` and `stdout`) to communicate with the user and with other tools. Each tool will take an input line by line via the standard input pipe, process it in some way, and then print the output line by line to the standard out pipe for the next tool or user.

By default, the standard input is connected to the user's keyboard, and the standard output is printed to the terminal from where the command was run; however, both can be redirected using **redirection metacharacters**. It's possible to throw the output away by redirecting it to `NUL` on Windows or `/dev/null` on Unix machines, or redirecting it to a file that will cause the output to be saved to a disk. Alternatively, you can pipe (using the | pipe character) the output of one program to the input of another; it is this feature that we will make use of in order to connect our various tools together. For example, you could pipe the output from one program to the input of another program in a terminal using this code:

```
echo -n "Hello" | md5
```

The output of the `echo` command will be the string `Hello` (without the quotes), which is then **piped** to the `md5` command; this command will in turn calculate the MD5 hash of `Hello`:

```
8b1a9953c4611296a827abf8c47804d7
```

Our tools will work with lines of strings where each line (separated by a linefeed character) represents one string. When run without any pipe redirection, we will be able to interact directly with the programs using the default in and out, which will be useful when testing and debugging our code.

Five simple programs

In this chapter, we will build five small programs that we will combine at the end. The key features of the programs are as follows:

- **Sprinkle**: This program will add some web-friendly sprinkle words to increase the chances of finding the available domain names.
- **Domainify**: This program will ensure words are acceptable for a domain name by removing unacceptable characters. Once this is done, it will replace spaces with hyphens and add an appropriate top-level domain (such as `.com` and `.net`) to the end.

- **Coolify**: This program will change a boring old normal word to Web 2.0 by fiddling around with vowels.
- **Synonyms**: This pro will use a third-party API to find synonyms.
- **Available**: This gram will use a third-party API to find synonyms. Available: This program will check to see whether the domain is available or not using an appropriate**WHOIS** server.

Five programs might seem like a lot for one chapter, but don't forget how small entire programs can be in Go.

Sprinkle

Our first program augments the incoming words with some sugar terms in order to improve the odds of finding names that are available. Many companies use this approach to keep the core messaging consistent while being able to afford the .com domain. For example, if we pass in the word chat, it might pass out chatapp; alternatively, if we pass in talk, we may get back talk time.

Go's math/rand package allows us to break away from the predictability of computers. It gives our program the appearance of intelligence by introducing elements of chance into its decision making.

To make our Sprinkle program work, we will:

- Define an array of transformations, using a special constant to indicate where the original word will appear
- Use the bufio package to scan the input from stdin and fmt.Println in order to write the output to stdout
- Use the math/rand package to randomly select a transformation to apply

 All our programs will reside in the $GOPATH/src directory. For example, if your GOPATH is ~/Work/projects/go, you would create your program folders in the ~/Work/projects/go/src folder.

In the $GOPATH/src directory, create a new folder called sprinkle and add a main.go file containing the following code:

```
package main
import (
  "bufio"
```

```
        "fmt"
        "math/rand"
        "os"
        "strings"
        "time"
    )
    const otherWord = "*"
    var transforms = []string{
    otherWord,
        otherWord + "app",
        otherWord + "site",
        otherWord + "time",
        "get" + otherWord,
        "go" + otherWord,
        "lets " + otherWord,
        otherWord + "hq",
    }
    func main() {
        rand.Seed(time.Now().UTC().UnixNano())
        s := bufio.NewScanner(os.Stdin)
        for s.Scan() {
            t := transforms[rand.Intn(len(transforms))]
            fmt.Println(strings.Replace(t, otherWord, s.Text(), -1))
        }
    }
```

From now on, it is assumed that you will sort out the appropriate import statements yourself. If you need assistance, refer to the tips provided in Appendix, *Good Practices for a Stable Go Environment.*

The preceding code represents our complete Sprinkle program. It defines three things: a constant, a variable, and the obligatory main function, which serves as the entry point to Sprinkle. The otherWord constant string is a helpful token that allows us to specify where the original word should occur in each of our possible transformations. It lets us write code, such as otherWord+"extra", which makes it clear that in this particular case, we want to add the word "extra" to the end of the original word.

The possible transformations are stored in the transforms variable that we declare as a slice of strings. In the preceding code, we defined a few different transformations, such as adding app to the end of a word or lets before it. Feel free to add some more; the more creative, the better.

In the `main` function, the first thing we do is use the current time as a random seed. Computers can't actually generate random numbers, but changing the seed number of random algorithms gives the illusion that it can. We use the current time in nanoseconds because it's different each time the program is run (provided the system clock isn't being reset before each run). If we skip this step, the numbers generated by the `math/rand` package would be deterministic; they'd be the same every time we run the program.

We then create a `bufio.Scanner` object (by calling `bufio.NewScanner`) and tell it to read the input from `os.Stdin`, which represents the standard input stream. This will be a common pattern in our five programs since we are always going to read from the standard *in* and write to the standard *out*.

> The `bufio.Scanner` object actually takes `io.Reader` as its input source, so there is a wide range of types that we could use here. If you were writing unit tests for this code, you could specify your own `io.Reader` for the scanner to read from, removing the need for you to worry about simulating the standard input stream.

As the default case, the scanner allows us to read blocks of bytes separated by defined delimiters, such as carriage return and linefeed characters. We can specify our own split function for the scanner or use one of the options built in the standard library. For example, there is `bufio.ScanWords`, which scans individual words by breaking on whitespace rather than linefeeds. Since our design specifies that each line must contain a word (or a short phrase), the default line-by-line setting is ideal.

A call to the `Scan` method tells the scanner to read the next block of bytes (the next line) from the input, and then it returns a `bool` value indicating whether it found anything or not. This is how we are able to use it as the condition for the `for` loop. While there is content to work on, `Scan` returns `true` and the body of the `for` loop is executed; when `Scan` reaches the end of the input, it returns `false`, and the loop is broken. The bytes that are selected are stored in the `Bytes` method of the scanner, and the handy `Text` method that we use converts the `[]byte` slice into a string for us.

Inside the `for` loop (so for each line of input), we use `rand.Intn` to select a random item from the `transforms` slice and use `strings.Replace` to insert the original word where the `otherWord` string appears. Finally, we use `fmt.Println` to print the output to the default standard output stream.

The `math/rand` package provides insecure random numbers. If you want to write code that utilizes random numbers for security purposes, you must use the `crypto/rand` package instead.

Let's build our program and play with it:

```
go build -o sprinkle
./sprinkle
```

Once the program starts running, it will use the default behavior to read the user input from the terminal. It uses the default behavior because we haven't piped in any content or specified a source for it to read from. Type `chat` and hit return. The scanner in our code notices the linefeed character at the end of the word and runs the code that transforms it, outputting the result. For example, if you type `chat` a few times, you would see the following output:

```
chat
go chat
chat
lets chat
chat
chat app
```

Sprinkle never exits (meaning the `Scan` method never returns `false` to break the loop) because the terminal is still running; in normal execution, the in pipe will be closed by whatever program is generating the input. To stop the program, hit *Ctrl + C*.

Before we move on, let's try to run Sprinkle, specifying a different input source. We are going to use the `echo` command to generate some content and pipe it to our Sprinkle program using the pipe character:

```
echo "chat" | ./sprinkle
```

The program will randomly transform the word, print it out, and exit since the `echo` command generates only one line of input before terminating and closing the pipe.

We have successfully completed our first program, which has a very simple but useful function, as we will see.

As an extra assignment, rather than hardcoding the `transformations` array as we have done, see whether you can externalize it via flags or store them in a text file or database.

Domainify

Some of the words that output from Sprinkle contain spaces and perhaps other characters that are not allowed in domains. So we are going to write a program called Domainify; it converts a line of text into an acceptable domain segment and adds an appropriate **Top-level Domain (TLD)** to the end. Alongside the sprinkle folder, create a new one called domainify and add the main.go file with the following code:

```
package main
var tlds = []string{"com", "net"}
const allowedChars = "abcdefghijklmnopqrstuvwxyz0123456789_-"
func main() {
  rand.Seed(time.Now().UTC().UnixNano())
  s := bufio.NewScanner(os.Stdin)
  for s.Scan() {
    text := strings.ToLower(s.Text())
    var newText []rune
    for _, r := range text {
      if unicode.IsSpace(r) {
        r = '-'
      }
      if !strings.ContainsRune(allowedChars, r) {
        continue
      }
      newText = append(newText, r)
    }
    fmt.Println(string(newText) + "." +
              tlds[rand.Intn(len(tlds))])
  }
}
```

You will notice a few similarities between Domainify and the Sprinkle program: we set the random seed using rand.Seed, generate a NewScanner method wrapping the os.Stdin reader, and scan each line until there is no more input.

We then convert the text to lowercase and build up a new slice of rune types called newText. The rune types consist of only characters that appear in the allowedChars string, which strings.ContainsRune lets us know. If rune is a space that we determine by calling unicode.IsSpace, we replace it with a hyphen, which is an acceptable practice in domain names.

Ranging over a string returns the index of each character and a `rune` type, which is a numerical value (specifically, `int32`) representing the character itself. For more information about runes, characters, and strings, refer to h `ttp://blog.golang.org/strings`.

Finally, we convert `newText` from a `[]rune` slice into a string and add either `.com` or `.net` at the end, before printing it out using `fmt.Println`.

Let's build and run Domainify:

```
go build -o domainify
./domainify
```

Type in some of these options to see how `domainify` reacts:

- Monkey
- Hello Domainify
- "What's up?"
- One (two) three!

You can see that, for example, `One (two) three!` might yield `one-two-three.com`.

We are now going to compose Sprinkle and Domainify to see them work together. In your terminal, navigate to the parent folder (probably `$GOPATH/src`) of `sprinkle` and `domainify` and run the following command:

```
./sprinkle/sprinkle | ./domainify/domainify
```

Here, we ran the `sprinkle` program and piped the output to the `domainify` program. By default, `sprinkle` uses the terminal as the input and `domanify` outputs to the terminal. Try typing in `chat` a few times again and notice the output is similar to what Sprinkle was outputting previously, except now they are acceptable for domain names. It is this piping between programs that allows us to compose command-line tools together.

Only supporting `.com` and `.net` top-level domains is fairly limiting. As an additional assignment, see whether you can accept a list of TLDs via a command-line flag.

Coolify

Often, domain names for common words, such as chat, are already taken, and a common solution is to play around with the vowels in the words. For example, we might remove a and make it cht (which is actually less likely to be available) or add a to produce chaat. While this clearly has no actual effect on coolness, it has become a popular, albeit slightly dated, way to secure domain names that still sound like the original word.

Our third program, Coolify, will allow us to play with the vowels of words that come in via the input and write modified versions to the output.

Create a new folder called coolify alongside sprinkle and domainify, and create the main.go code file with the following code:

```go
package main
const (
  duplicateVowel bool   = true
  removeVowel    bool   = false
)
func randBool() bool {
  return rand.Intn(2) == 0
}
func main() {
  rand.Seed(time.Now().UTC().UnixNano())
  s := bufio.NewScanner(os.Stdin)
  for s.Scan() {
    word := []byte(s.Text())
    if randBool() {
      var vI int = -1
      for i, char := range word {
        switch char {
        case 'a', 'e', 'i', 'o', 'u', 'A', 'E', 'I', 'O', 'U':
          if randBool() {
            vI = i
          }
        }
      }
      if vI >= 0 {
        switch randBool() {
        case duplicateVowel:
          word = append(word[:vI+1], word[vI:]...)
        case removeVowel:
          word = append(word[:vI], word[vI+1:]...)
        }
      }
    }
  }
}
```

```
        fmt.Println(string(word))
    }
}
```

While the preceding Coolify code looks very similar to the code of Sprinkle and Domainify, it is slightly more complicated. At the very top of the code, we declare two constants, `duplicateVowel` and `removeVowel`, that help make the Coolify code more readable. The `switch` statement decides whether we duplicate or remove a vowel. Also, using these constants, we are able to express our intent very clearly, rather than use just `true` or `false`.

We then define the `randBool` helper function that just randomly returns either `true` or `false`. This is done by asking the `rand` package to generate a random number and confirming whether that number comes out as zero. It will be either 0 or 1, so there's a fifty-fifty chance of it being `true`.

The `main` function of Coolify starts the same way as that of Sprinkle and Domainify setting the `rand.Seed` method and creating a scanner of the standard input stream before executing the loop body for each line of input. We call `randBool` first to decide whether we are even going to mutate a word or not, so Coolify will only affect half the words passed through it.

We then iterate over each rune in the string and look for a vowel. If our `randBool` method returns `true`, we keep the index of the vowel character in the `vI` variable. If not, we keep looking through the string for another vowel, which allows us to randomly select a vowel from the words rather than always modify the same one.

Once we have selected a vowel, we use `randBool` again to randomly decide what action to take.

This is where the helpful constants come in; consider the following alternative switch statement:

```
switch randBool() {
  case true:
    word = append(word[:vI+1], word[vI:]...)
  case false:
    word = append(word[:vI], word[vI+1:]...) }
```

In the preceding code snippet, it's difficult to tell what is going on because `true` and `false` don't express any context. On the other hand, using `duplicateVowel` and `removeVowel` tells anyone reading the code what we mean by the result of `randBool`.

The three dots following the slices cause each item to pass as a separate argument to the `append` function. This is an idiomatic way of appending one slice to another. Inside the `switch` case, we do some slice manipulation to either duplicate the vowel or remove it altogether. We are slicing our `[]byte` slice again and using the `append` function to build a new one made up of sections of the original word. The following diagram shows which sections of the string we access in our code:

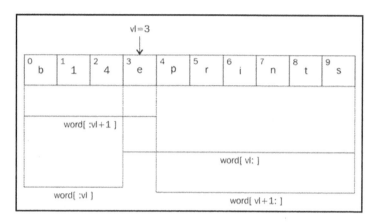

If we take the value `blueprints` as an example word and assume that our code has selected the first `e` character as the vowel (so that `vI` is 3), the following table will illustrate what each new slice of the word will represent:

Code	Value	Description
`word[:vI+1]`	blue	This describes the slice from the beginning of the word until the selected vowel. The +1 is required because the value following the colon does not include the specified index; rather, it slices up to that value.
`word[vI:]`	eprints	This describes the slice starting from and including the selected vowel to the end of the slice.
`word[:vI]`	blu	This describes the slice from the beginning of the word up to, but not including, the selected vowel.
`word[vI+1:]`	prints	This describes the slice from the item following the selected vowel to the end of the slice.

After we modify the word, we print it out using `fmt.Println`.

Let's build Coolify and play with it to see what it can do:

```
go build -o coolify
./coolify
```

When Coolify is running, try typing `blueprints` to see what sort of modifications it comes up with:

```
blueprnts
bleprints
bluepriints
blueprnts
blueprints
bluprints
```

Let's see how Coolify plays with Sprinkle and Domainify by adding their names to our pipe chain. In the terminal, navigate back (using the `cd` command) to the parent folder and run the following commands:

```
./coolify/coolify | ./sprinkle/sprinkle | ./domainify/domainify
```

We will first spice up a word with extra pieces and make it cooler by tweaking the vowels before finally transforming it into a valid domain name. Play around by typing in a few words and seeing what suggestions our code makes.

 Coolify only works on vowels; as an additional exercise, see whether you can make the code operate on every character it encounters just to see what happens.

Synonyms

So far, our programs have only modified words, but to really bring our solution to life, we need to be able to integrate a third-party API that provides word synonyms. This allows us to suggest different domain names while retaining the original meaning. Unlike Sprinkle and Domainify, Synonyms will write out more than one response for each word given to it. Our architecture of piping programs together means this won't be much of a problem; in fact, we do not even have to worry about it since each of the three programs is capable of reading multiple lines from the input source.

Big Huge Thesaurus, `http://bighugelabs.com/`, has a very clean and simple API that allows us to make a single HTTP `GET` request to look up synonyms.

In future, if the API we are using changes or disappears (after all, we're dealing with the Internet), you will find some options at `https://github.com/matryer/goblueprints`.

Before you can use Big Huge Thesaurus, you'll need an API key, which you can get by signing up to the service at `http://words.bighugelabs.com/`.

Using environment variables for configuration

Your API key is a sensitive piece of configuration information that you don't want to share with others. We could store it as `const` in our code. However, this would mean we will not be able to share our code without sharing our key (not good, especially if you love open source projects). Additionally, perhaps more importantly, you will have to recompile your entire project if the key expires or if you want to use a different one (you don't want to get into such a situation).

A better solution is using an environment variable to store the key, as this will allow you to easily change it if you need to. You could also have different keys for different deployments; perhaps you could have one key for development or testing and another for production. This way, you can set a specific key for a particular execution of code so you can easily switch between keys without having to change your system-level settings. Also, different operating systems deal with environment variables in similar ways, so they are a perfect choice if you are writing cross-platform code.

Create a new environment variable called `BHT_APIKEY` and set your API key as its value.

For machines running a bash shell, you can modify your `~/.bashrc` file or similar to include `export` commands, such as the following:
`export BHT_APIKEY=abc123def456ghi789jkl`
On Windows machines, you can navigate to the properties of your computer and look for **Environment Variables** in the **Advanced** section.

Consuming a web API

Making a request for in a web browser shows us what the structure of JSON response data looks like when finding synonyms for the word `love`:

```
{
    "noun":{
        "syn":[
            "passion",
```

```
      "beloved",
      "dear"
    ]
  },
  "verb":{
    "syn":[
      "love",
      "roll in the hay",
      "make out"
    ],
    "ant":[
      "hate"
    ]
  }
}
```

A real API will return a lot more actual words than what is printed here, but the structure is the important thing. It represents an object, where the keys describe the types of word (verbs, nouns, and so on). Also, values are objects that contain arrays of strings keyed on syn or ant (for the synonym and antonym, respectively); it is the synonyms we are interested in.

To turn this JSON string data into something we can use in our code, we must decode it into structures of our own using the capabilities found in the encoding/json package. Because we're writing something that could be useful outside the scope of our project, we will consume the API in a reusable package rather than directly in our program code. Create a new folder called thesaurus alongside your other program folders (in $GOPATH/src) and insert the following code into a new bighuge.go file:

```go
package thesaurus
import (
  "encoding/json"
  "errors"
  "net/http"
)
type BigHuge struct {
  APIKey string
}
type synonyms struct {
  Noun *words `json:"noun"`
  Verb *words `json:"verb"`
}
type words struct {
  Syn []string `json:"syn"`
}
func (b *BigHuge) Synonyms(term string) ([]string, error) {
```

```
  var syns []string
  response, err := http.Get("http://words.bighugelabs.com/api/2/" +
   b.APIKey + "/" + term + "/json")
  if err != nil {
    return syns, errors.New("bighuge: Failed when looking for  synonyms
     for "" + term + """ + err.Error())
  }
  var data synonyms
  defer response.Body.Close()
  if err := json.NewDecoder(response.Body).Decode(&data); err !=  nil {
    return syns, err
  }
  if data.Noun != nil {
    syns = append(syns, data.Noun.Syn...)
  }
  if data.Verb != nil {
    syns = append(syns, data.Verb.Syn...)
  }
  return syns, nil
}
```

In the preceding code, the BigHuge type we define houses the necessary API key and provides the Synonyms method that will be responsible for doing the work of accessing the endpoint, parsing the response, and returning the results. The most interesting parts of this code are the synonyms and words structures. They describe the JSON response format in Go terms, namely an object containing noun and verb objects, which in turn contain a slice of strings in a variable called Syn. The tags (strings in backticks following each field definition) tell the encoding/json package which fields to map to which variables; this is required since we have given them different names.

Typically in JSON, keys have lowercase names, but we have to use capitalized names in our structures so that the encoding/json package would also know that the fields exist. If we don't, the package would simply ignore the fields. However, the types themselves (synonyms and words) do not need to be exported.

The Synonyms method takes a term argument and uses http.Get to make a web request to the API endpoint in which the URL contains not only the API key value, but also the term value itself. If the web request fails for some reason, we will make a call to log.Fatalln, which will write the error to the standard error stream and exit the program with a non-zero exit code (actually an exit code of 1). This indicates that an error has occurred.

If the web request is successful, we pass the response body (another `io.Reader`) to the `json.NewDecoder` method and ask it to decode the bytes into the `data` variable that is of our `synonyms` type. We defer the closing of the response body in order to keep the memory clean before using Go's built-in `append` function to concatenate both `noun` and `verb` synonyms to the `syns` slice that we then return.

Although we have implemented the `BigHuge` thesaurus, it isn't the only option out there, and we can express this by adding a `Thesaurus` interface to our package. In the `thesaurus` folder, create a new file called `thesaurus.go` and add the following interface definition to the file:

```
package thesaurus
type Thesaurus interface {
  Synonyms(term string) ([]string, error)
}
```

This simple interface just describes a method that takes a `term` string and returns either a slice of strings containing the synonyms or an error (if something goes wrong). Our `BigHuge` structure already implements this interface, but now, other users could add interchangeable implementations for other services, such as `http://www.dictionary.com/` or the Merriam-Webster online service.

Next, we are going to use this new package in a program. Change the directory in the terminal back up a level to `$GOPATH/src`, create a new folder called `synonyms`, and insert the following code into a new `main.go` file you will place in this folder:

```
func main() {
  apiKey := os.Getenv("BHT_APIKEY")
  thesaurus := &thesaurus.BigHuge{APIKey: apiKey}
  s := bufio.NewScanner(os.Stdin)
  for s.Scan() {
    word := s.Text()
    syns, err := thesaurus.Synonyms(word)
    if err != nil {
      log.Fatalln("Failed when looking for synonyms for  "+word+", err)
    }
    if len(syns) == 0 {
      log.Fatalln("Couldn't find any synonyms for " + word +  ")
    }
    for _, syn := range syns {
      fmt.Println(syn)
    }
  }
}
```

Now when you manage your imports again, you will have written a complete program that is capable of looking up synonyms of words by integrating the Big Huge Thesaurus API.

In the preceding code, the first thing our `main` function does is that it gets the `BHT_APIKEY` environment variable value via the `os.Getenv` call. To protect your code, you might consider double-checking it to ensure the value is properly set; if not, report the error. For now, we will assume that everything is configured properly.

Next, the preceding code starts to look a little familiar since it scans each line of input again from `os.Stdin` and calls the `Synonyms` method to get a list of the replacement words.

Let's build a program and see what kind of synonyms the API comes back with when we input the word `chat`:

```
go build -o synonyms
./synonyms
chat
confab
confabulation
schmooze
New World chat
Old World chat
conversation
thrush
wood warbler
chew the fat
shoot the breeze
chitchat
chatter
```

The results you get will most likely differ from what we have listed here since we're hitting a live API. However, the important thing is that when we provide a word or term as an input to the program, it returns a list of synonyms as the output, one per line.

Getting domain suggestions

By composing the four programs we have built so far in this chapter, we already have a useful tool for suggesting domain names. All we have to do now is to run the programs while piping the output to the input in an appropriate way. In a terminal, navigate to the parent folder and run the following single line:

```
./synonyms/synonyms | ./sprinkle/sprinkle | ./coolify/coolify |
./domainify/domainify
```

Because the `synonyms` program is first in our list, it will receive the input from the terminal (whatever the user decides to type in). Similarly, because `domainify` is last in the chain, it will print its output to the terminal for the user to see. Along the way, the lines of words will be piped through other programs, giving each of them a chance to do their magic.

Type in a few words to see some domain suggestions; for example, when you type `chat` and hit return, you may see the following:

```
getcnfab.com
confabulationtim.com
getschmoozee.net
schmosee.com
neew-world-chatsite.net
oold-world-chatsite.com
conversatin.net
new-world-warblersit.com
gothrush.net
lets-wood-wrbler.com
chw-the-fat.com
```

The number of suggestions you get will actually depend on the number of synonyms. This is because it is the only program that generates more lines of output than what we input.

We still haven't solved our biggest problem: the fact that we have no idea whether the suggested domain names are actually available or not. So we still have to sit and type each one of them into a website. In the next section, we will address this issue.

Available

Our final program, Available, will connect to a WHOIS server to ask for details about the domains passed to it of course, if no details are returned, we can safely assume that the domain is available for purchase. Unfortunately, the WHOIS specification (see `http://tool s.ietf.org/html/rfc3912`) is very small and contains no information about how a WHOIS server should reply when you ask for details about a domain. This means programmatically parsing the response becomes a messy endeavor. To address this issue for now, we will integrate with only a single WHOIS server, which we can be sure will have `No match` somewhere in the response when it has no records for the domain.

A more robust solution is to have a WHOIS interface with a well-defined structure for the details and perhaps an error message for cases when the domain doesn't exist with different implementations for different WHOIS servers. As you can imagine, it's quite a project; it is perfect for an open source effort.

Create a new folder called `available` alongside others and add a `main.go` file to it containing the following function code:

```
func exists(domain string) (bool, error) {
  const whoisServer string = "com.whois-servers.net"
  conn, err := net.Dial("tcp", whoisServer+":43")
  if err != nil {
    return false, err
  }
  defer conn.Close()
  conn.Write([]byte(domain + "rn"))
  scanner := bufio.NewScanner(conn)
  for scanner.Scan() {
    if strings.Contains(strings.ToLower(scanner.Text()), "no match") {
      return false, nil
    }
  }
  return true, nil
}
```

The `exists` function implements what little there is in the WHOIS specification by opening a connection to port `43` on the specified `whoisServer` instance with a call to `net.Dial`. We then defer the closing of the connection, which means that no matter how the function exits (successful, with an error, or even a panic), `Close()` will still be called on the `conn` connection. Once the connection is open, we simply write the domain followed by `rn` (the carriage return and linefeed characters). This is all that the specification tells us, so we are on our own from now on.

Essentially, we are looking for some mention of "no match" in the response, and this is how we will decide whether a domain exists or not (`exists` in this case is actually just asking the WHOIS server whether it has a record for the domain we specified). We use our favorite `bufio.Scanner` method to help us iterate over the lines in the response. Passing the connection to `NewScanner` works because `net.Conn` is actually an `io.Reader` too. We use `strings.ToLower` so we don't have to worry about case sensitivity and `strings.Contains` to check whether any one of the lines contains the `no match` text. If it does, we return `false` (since the domain doesn't exist); otherwise, we return `true`.

The `com.whois-servers.net` WHOIS service supports domain names for `.com` and `.net`, which is why the Domainify program only adds these types of domains. If you had used a server that had WHOIS information for a wider selection of domains, you could have added support for additional TLDs.

Let's add a `main` function that uses our `exists` function to check whether the incoming domains are available or not. The check mark and cross mark symbols in the following code are optional if your terminal doesn't support them you are free to substitute them with simple`Yes` and `No` strings.

Add the following code to `main.go`:

```go
var marks = map[bool]string{true: "✓", false: "✗"}
func main() {
  s := bufio.NewScanner(os.Stdin)
  for s.Scan() {
    domain := s.Text()
    fmt.Print(domain, " ")
    exist, err := exists(domain)
    if err != nil {
      log.Fatalln(err)
    }
    fmt.Println(marks[!exist])
    time.Sleep(1 * time.Second)
  }
}
```

 We can use the check and cross characters in our code happily because all Go code files are UTF-8 compliant the best way to actually get these characters is to search the Web for them and use the copy and paste option to bring them into our code. Otherwise, there are platform-dependent ways to get such special characters.

In the preceding code for the `main` function, we simply iterate over each line coming in via `os.Stdin`. This process helps us print out the domain with `fmt.Print` (but not `fmt.Println`, as we do not want the linefeed yet), call our `exists` function to check whether the domain exists or not, and print out the result with `fmt.Println` (because we *do* want a linefeed at the end).

Finally, we use `time.Sleep` to tell the process to do nothing for a second in order to make sure we take it easy on the WHOIS server.

Most WHOIS servers will be limited in various ways in order to prevent you from taking up too much in terms of resources. So, slowing things down is a sensible way to make sure we don't make the remote servers angry.

Consider what this also means for unit tests. If a unit test were actually making real requests to a remote WHOIS server, every time your tests run, you will be clocking up statistics against your IP address. A much better approach would be to stub the WHOIS server to simulate responses.

The marks map at the top is a nice way to map the bool response from exists to human-readable text, allowing us to just print the response in a single line using fmt.Println(marks[!exist]). We are saying *not exist* because our program is checking whether the domain is available or not (logically, the opposite of whether it exists in the WHOIS server or not).

After fixing the import statements for the main.go file, we can try out Available to see whether the domain names are available or not by typing the following command:

```
go build -o available
./available
```

Once Available is running, type in some domain names and see the result appear on the next line:

```
2. go

packtpub.com
packtpub.com ✗
matryer.com
matryer.com ✗
made-up-domain-12345678.net
made-up-domain-12345678.net ✓
```

As you can see, for domains that are not available, we get a little cross mark next to them; however, when we make up a domain name using random numbers, we see that it is indeed available.

Composing all five programs

Now that we have completed all five programs, it's time to put them all together so that we can use our tool to find an available domain name for our chat application. The simplest way to do this is to use the technique we have been using throughout this chapter: using pipes in a terminal to connect the output and input.

In the terminal, navigate to the parent folder of the five programs and run the following single line of code:

```
./synonyms/synonyms | ./sprinkle/sprinkle | ./coolify/coolify |
./domainify/domainify | ./available/available
```

Once the programs are running, type in a starting word and see how it generates suggestions before checking their availability.

For example, typing in `chat` might cause the programs to take the following actions:

1. The word `chat` goes into `synonyms`, which results in a series of synonyms:

   - confab
   - confabulation
   - schmooze

2. The synonyms flow into `sprinkle`; here they are augmented with web-friendly prefixes and suffixes, such as the following:

   - confabapp
   - goconfabulation
   - schmooze time

3. These new words flow into `coolify`; here the vowels are potentially tweaked:

   - confabaapp
   - goconfabulatioon
   - schmoooze time

4. The modified words then flow into `domainify`; here they are turned into valid domain names:

- confabaapp.com
- goconfabulatioon.net
- schmooze-time.com

5. Finally, the domain names flow into `available`; here they are checked against the WHOIS server to see whether somebody has already taken the domain or not:

- confabaapp.com ✗
- goconfabulatioon.net ✓
- schmooze-time.com ✓

One program to rule them all

Running our solution by piping programs together is an elegant form of architecture, but it doesn't have a very elegant interface. Specifically, whenever we want to run our solution, we have to type the long, messy line where each program is listed and separated by pipe characters. In this section, we are going to write a Go program that uses the `os/exec` package to run each subprogram while piping the output from one to the input of the next, as per our design.

Create a new folder called `domainfinder` alongside the other five programs and create another new folder called `lib` inside this folder. The `lib` folder is where we will keep builds of our subprograms, but we don't want to copy and paste them every time we make a change. Instead, we will write a script that builds the subprograms and copies the binaries to the `lib` folder for us.

Create a new file called `build.sh` on Unix machines or `build.bat` for Windows and insert into it the following code:

```
#!/bin/bash
echo Building domainfinder...
go build -o domainfinder
echo Building synonyms...
cd ../synonyms
go build -o ../domainfinder/lib/synonyms
echo Building available...
cd ../available
go build -o ../domainfinder/lib/available
```

```
cd ../build
echo Building sprinkle...
cd ../sprinkle
go build -o ../domainfinder/lib/sprinkle
cd ../build
echo Building coolify...
cd ../coolify
go build -o ../domainfinder/lib/coolify
cd ../build
echo Building domainify...
cd ../domainify
go build -o ../domainfinder/lib/domainify
cd ../build
echo Done.
```

The preceding script simply builds all our subprograms (including `domainfinder`, which we are yet to write), telling `go build` to place them in our `lib` folder. Be sure to give execution rights to the new script by doing `chmod +x build.sh` or something similar. Run this script from a terminal and look inside the `lib` folder to ensure that it has indeed placed the binaries for our subprograms.

Don't worry about the `no buildable Go source files` error for now; it's just Go telling us that the `domainfinder` program doesn't have any `.go` files to build.

Create a new file called `main.go` inside `domainfinder` and insert the following code into the file:

```go
package main
var cmdChain = []*exec.Cmd{
  exec.Command("lib/synonyms"),
  exec.Command("lib/sprinkle"),
  exec.Command("lib/coolify"),
  exec.Command("lib/domainify"),
  exec.Command("lib/available"),
}
func main() {
  cmdChain[0].Stdin = os.Stdin
  cmdChain[len(cmdChain)-1].Stdout = os.Stdout
  for i := 0; i < len(cmdChain)-1; i++ {
    thisCmd := cmdChain[i]
    nextCmd := cmdChain[i+1]
    stdout, err := thisCmd.StdoutPipe()
    if err != nil {
      log.Fatalln(err)
    }
```

```
        nextCmd.Stdin = stdout
    }
    for _, cmd := range cmdChain {
        if err := cmd.Start(); err != nil {
            log.Fatalln(err)
        } else {
            defer cmd.Process.Kill()
        }
    }
    for _, cmd := range cmdChain {
        if err := cmd.Wait(); err != nil {
            log.Fatalln(err)
        }
    }
}
```

The os/exec package gives us everything we need to work with to run external programs or commands from within Go programs. First, our cmdChain slice contains *exec.Cmd commands in the order in which we want to join them together.

At the top of the main function, we tie the Stdin (standard in stream) of the first program with the os.Stdin stream of this program and the Stdout (standard out stream) of the last program with the os.Stdout stream of this program. This means that, like before, we will be taking input through the standard input stream and writing output to the standard output stream.

Our next block of code is where we join the subprograms together by iterating over each item and setting its Stdin to the Stdout stream of the program before it.

The following table shows each program with a description of where it gets its input from and where its output goes:

Program	Input (Stdin)	Output (Stdout)
synonyms	The same Stdin as domainfinder	sprinkle
sprinkle	synonyms	coolify
coolify	sprinkle	domainify
domainify	coolify	available
available	domainify	The same Stdout as domainfinder

We then iterate over each command calling the `Start` method, which runs the program in the background (as opposed to the `Run` method, which will block our code until the subprogram exists which would be no good since we will have to run five programs at the same time). If anything goes wrong, we bail with `log.Fatalln`; however, if the program starts successfully, we defer a call to kill the process. This helps us ensure the subprograms exit when our `main` function exits, which will be when the `domainfinder` program ends.

Once all the programs start running, we iterate over every command again and wait for it to finish. This is to ensure that `domainfinder` doesn't exit early and kill off all the subprograms too soon.

Run the `build.sh` or `build.bat` script again and notice that the `domainfinder` program has the same behavior as we have seen before, with a much more elegant interface.

The following screenshot shows the output from our programs when we type `clouds`; we have found quite a few available domain name options:

```
● ● ●                         1. bash
clouds
swarm.net ✗
lets-animal-group.com ✓
atmospheric-phenmenon.net ✓
getgloom.net ✓
gloominss.net ✓
getglumneess.com ✓
irreality.com ✗
physical-phenomenon.net ✓
suspicion.net ✗
getunreeality.net ✓
overcast.net ✗
getobscure.net ✓
befgapp.com ✓
beclod.com ✓
obnubilatesite.net ✓
haze-over.com ✓
fog.com ✗
mist.com ✗
getdefil.net ✓
sullyapp.net ✓
corruptapp.com ✓
^C
echo:domainfinder matryer$ 
```

Summary

In this chapter, we learned how five small command-line programs can, when composed together, produce powerful results while remaining modular. We avoided tightly coupling our programs so they could still be useful in their own right. For example, we can use our Available program just to check whether the domain names we manually enter are available or not, or we can use our `synonyms` program just as a command-line thesaurus.

We learned how standard streams could be used to build different flows of these types of programs and how the redirection of standard input and standard output lets us play around with different flows very easily.

We learned how simple it is in Go to consume a JSON RESTful API web service when we wanted to get the synonyms from Big Huge Thesaurus. We also consumed a non-HTTP API when we opened a connection to the WHOIS server and wrote data over raw TCP.

We saw how the `math/rand` package can bring a little variety and unpredictability by allowing us to use pseudo random numbers and decisions in our code, which means that each time we run our program, we will get different results.

Finally, we built our `domainfinder` super program that composes all the subprograms together, giving our solution a simple, clean, and elegant interface.

In the next chapter, we will take some ideas we have learned so far one step further by exploring how to connect programs using messaging queue technologies allowing them to distributed across many machines to achieve large scale.

5
Building Distributed Systems and Working with Flexible Data

In this chapter, we will explore transferrable skills that allow us to use schemaless data and distributed technologies to solve big data problems. The system we will build in this chapter will prepare us for a future where all democratic elections happen online on Twitter, of course. Our solution will collect and count votes by querying Twitter's streaming API for mentions of specific hash tags, and each component will be capable of horizontally scaling to meet demand. Our use case is a fun and interesting one, but the core concepts we'll learn and the specific technology choices we'll make are the real focus of this chapter. The ideas discussed here are directly applicable to any system that needs true-scale capabilities.

 Horizontal scaling refers to adding nodes, such as physical machines, to a system in order to improve its availability, performance, and/or capacity. Big data companies such as Google can scale by adding affordable and easy-to-obtain hardware (commonly referred to as commodity hardware) due to the way they write their software and architect their solutions. **Vertical scaling** is synonymous to increasing the resource available to a single node, such as adding additional RAM to a box or a processor with more cores.

In this chapter, you will:

- Learn about distributed **NoSQL** datastores, specifically how to interact with MongoDB
- Learn about **distributed messaging queues**, in our case, Bit.ly's NSQ and how to use the `go-nsq` package to easily publish and subscribe to events

- Stream live tweet data through Twitter's streaming APIs and manage long running net connections
- Learn how to properly stop programs with many internal goroutines
- Learn how to use low memory channels for signaling

The system design

Having a basic design sketched out is often useful, especially in distributed systems where many components will be communicating with each other in different ways. We don't want to spend too long on this stage because our design is likely to evolve as we get stuck into the details, but we will look at a high-level outline so that we can discuss the constituents and how they fit together:

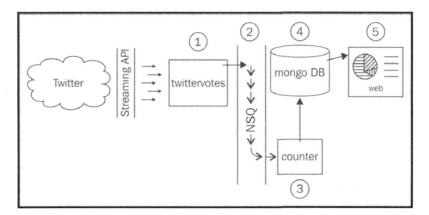

The preceding diagram shows the basic overview of the system we are going to build:

- Twitter is the social media network we all know and love.
- Twitter's streaming API allows long-running connections where tweet data is streamed as quickly as possible.
- twittervotes is a program we will write that pulls the relevant tweet data via the Twitter API, decides what is being voted for (rather, which options are mentioned in the tweet body), and then pushes the vote into NSQ.
- NSQ is an open source, real-time distributed messaging platform designed to operate at scale, built and maintained by Bit.ly. NSQ carries the message across its instances, making it available to anyone who has expressed an interest in the vote data.

- `counter` is a program we will write that listens out for votes on the messaging queue and periodically saves the results in the MongoDB database. It receives the vote messages from NSQ and keeps an in-memory tally of the results, periodically pushing an update to persist the data.
- MongoDB is an open source document database designed to operate at scale.
- `web` is a web server program that will expose the live results that we will write in the next chapter.

It could be argued that a single Go program could be written that reads the tweets, counts the votes, and pushes them to a user interface, but such a solution, while being a great proof of concept, would be very limited in scale. In our design, any one of the components can be horizontally scaled as the demand for that particular capability increases. If we have relatively few polls but lots of people viewing the data, we can keep the `twittervotes` and `counter` instances down and add more `web` and MongoDB nodes or vice versa if the situation is reversed.

Another key advantage to our design is redundancy; since we can have many instances of our components working at the same time, if one of our boxes disappears (due to a system crash or a power cut, for example), the others can pick up the slack. Modern architectures often distribute such a system over the geographical expanse in order to protect from local natural disasters too. All of these options are available for use if we build our solution in this way.

We chose specific technologies in this chapter because of their links to Go (NSQ, for example, is written entirely in Go) and the availability of well-tested drivers and packages. Conceptually, however, you can drop in a variety of alternatives as you see fit.

The database design

We will call our MongoDB database `ballots`. It will contain a single collection called `polls`, which is where we will store the poll details, such as the title, the options, and the results (in a single JSON document). The code for a poll will look something like this:

```
{
  "_id": "???",
  "title": "Poll title",
  "options": ["one", "two", "three"],
  "results": {
    "one": 100,
    "two": 200,
    "three": 300
```

```
      }
   }
```

The `_id` field is a unique string for each item that is automatically generated by MongoDB. The `options` field contains an array of string options; these are the hash tags we will look for on Twitter. The `results` field is a map where the key represents the option, and the value represents the total number of votes for each item.

Installing the environment

The code we write in this chapter has real external dependencies that we need to set up before we can start to build our system.

 Be sure to check out the chapter notes at `https://github.com/matryer/goblueprints` if you get stuck on installing any of the dependencies.

In most cases, services such as `mongod` and `nsqd` will have to be started before we can run our programs. Since we are writing components of a distributed system, we will have to run each program at the same time, which is as simple as opening many terminal windows.

Introducing NSQ

NSQ is a messaging queue that allows one program to send messages or events to another or to many other programs running either locally on the same machine or on different nodes connected by a network. NSQ guarantees the delivery of each message at least once, which means that it keeps undelivered messages cached until all interested parties have received them. This means that even if we stop our `counter` program, we won't miss any votes. You can contrast this capability with fire-and-forget message queues, where information is deemed out of date, and is, therefore, forgotten if it isn't delivered in time and when the sender of the messages doesn't care whether the consumer received them or not.

A message queue abstraction allows you to have different components of a system running in different places, provided that they have network connectivity to the queue. Your programs are decoupled from others; instead, your designs start to care about the ins and outs of specialized micro services rather than flow of data through a monolithic program.

NSQ transfers raw bytes, which means that it is up to us how we encode data into these bytes. For example, we could encode the data as JSON or in a binary format depending on our needs. In our case, we are going to send the vote option as a string without any additional encoding, since we are only sharing a single data field.

We first need to get NSQ installed and running:

1. Open `http://nsq.io/deployment/installing.html` in a browser (or search `install nsq`) and follow the instructions for your environment. You can either download precompiled binaries or build your own from the source. If you have homebrew installed, installing NSQ is as simple as typing the following:

   ```
   brew install nsq
   ```

2. Once you have installed NSQ, you will need to add the `bin` folder to your `PATH` environment variable so that the tools are available in a terminal.

3. To validate that NSQ is properly installed, open a terminal and run `nsqlookupd`; if the program successfully starts, you should see output similar to the following:

   ```
   nsqlookupd v0.2.27 (built w/go1.3)
   TCP: listening on [::]:4160
   HTTP: listening on [::]:4161
   ```

   We are going to use the default ports to interact with NSQ, so take note of the TCP and HTTP ports listed in the output, as we will be referring to them in our code.

4. Press *Ctrl + C* to stop the process for now; we'll start them properly later.

The key tools from the NSQ installation that we are going to use are `nsqlookupd` and `nsqd`. The `nsqlookupd` program is a daemon that manages topology information about the distributed NSQ environment; it keeps track of all the `nsqd` producers for specific topics and provides interfaces for clients to query such information. The `nsqd` program is a daemon that does the heavy lifting for NSQ, such as receiving, queuing, and delivering messages from and to interested parties.

For more information and background on NSQ, visit `http://nsq.io/`.

NSQ driver for Go

The NSQ tools themselves are written in Go, so it is logical that the Bit.ly team already has a Go package that makes interacting with NSQ very easy. We will need to use it, so in a terminal, you can get it using `go get`:

```
go get github.com/bitly/go-nsq
```

Introducing MongoDB

MongoDB is a document database, which allows you to store and query JSON documents and the data within them. Each document goes into a collection that can be used to group the documents together without enforcing any schema on the data inside them. Unlike rows in a traditional RDBMS, such as Oracle, Microsoft SQL Server, or MySQL, it is perfectly acceptable for documents to have a different shape. For example, a `people` collection can contain the following three JSON documents at the same time:

```
{"name":"Mat","lang":"en","points":57}
{"name":"Laurie","position":"Scrum Master"}
{"position":"Traditional Manager","exists":false}
```

This flexibility allows data with varying structures to coexist without impacting performance or wasting space. It is also extremely useful if you expect your software to evolve over time, as we really always should.

MongoDB was designed to scale while also remaining very easy to work with on single-box installations, such as our development machine. When we host our application for production, we would most likely install a more complex multi-sharded, replicated system, which is distributed across many nodes and locations, but for now, just running `mongod` will do.

Head over to `http://www.mongodb.org/downloads` in order to grab the latest version of MongoDB and install it, making sure to register the `bin` folder with your `PATH` environment variable, as usual.

To validate that MongoDB is successfully installed, run the `mongod` command, and then hit *Ctrl + C* to stop it for now.

MongoDB driver for Go

Gustavo Niemeyer has done a great job in simplifying interactions with MongoDB with his mgo (pronounced *mango*) package hosted at http://labix.org/mgo, which is *go gettable* with the following command:

```
go get gopkg.in/mgo.v2
```

Starting the environment

Now that we have all the pieces we need installed, we need to start our environment. In this section, we are going to:

- Start nsqlookupd so that our nsqd instances are discoverable
- Start nsqd and tell it which nsqlookupd to use
- Start mongod for data services

Each of these daemons should run in their own terminal window, which will make it easy for us to stop them by just hitting *Ctrl + C*.

> Remember the page number for this section as you are likely to revisit it a few times as you work through this chapter.

In a terminal window, run the following:

```
nsqlookupd
```

Take note of the TCP port, which is 4160 by default, and in another terminal window, run the following:

```
nsqd --lookupd-tcp-address=localhost:4160
```

Make sure the port number in the --lookupd-tcp-address flag matches the TCP port of the nsqlookupd instance. Once you start nsqd, you will notice some output printed to the terminal from both nsqlookupd and nsqd; this indicates that the two processes are talking to each other.

In yet another window or tab, start MongoDB by running the following command:

```
mongod --dbpath ./db
```

The dbpath flag tells MongoDB where to store the data files for our database. You can pick any location you like, but you'll have to make sure the folder exists before mongod will run.

 By deleting the dbpath folder at any time, you can effectively erase all data and start afresh. This is especially useful during development.

Now that our environment is running, we are ready to start building our components.

Reading votes from Twitter

In your $GOPATH/src folder, alongside other projects, create a new folder called socialpoll for this chapter. This folder won't be a Go package or a program by itself, but it will contain our three component programs. Inside socialpoll, create a new folder called twittervotes and add the obligatory main.go template (this is important as main packages without a main function won't compile):

```
package main
func main(){}
```

Our twittervotes program is going to:

- Load all polls from the MongoDB database using mgo and collect all options from the options array in each document
- Open and maintain a connection to Twitter's streaming APIs looking for any mention of the options
- Figure out which option is mentioned and push that option through to NSQ for each tweet that matches the filter
- If the connection to Twitter is dropped (which is common in long-running connections that are actually part of Twitter's streaming API specification) after a short delay (so that we do not bombard Twitter with connection requests), reconnect and continue
- Periodically re-query MongoDB for the latest polls and refresh the connection to Twitter to make sure we are always looking out for the right options
- Gracefully stop itself when the user terminates the program by hitting *Ctrl* + *C*

Authorization with Twitter

In order to use the streaming API, we will need authentication credentials from Twitter's Application Management console, much in the same way we did for our Gomniauth service providers in Chapter 3, *Three Ways to Implement Profile Pictures*. Head over to https://apps .twitter.com and create a new app called something like SocialPoll (the names have to be unique, so you can have some fun here; the choice of name doesn't affect the code either way). When your app has been created, visit the **API Keys** tab and locate the **Your access token** section, where you need to create a new access token. After a short delay, refresh the page and note that you, in fact, have two sets of keys and secrets: an API key and a secret and an access token and the corresponding secret. Following good coding practices, we are going to set these values as environment variables so that our program can have access to them without us having to hardcode them in our source files. The keys we will use in this chapter are as follows:

- SP_TWITTER_KEY
- SP_TWITTER_SECRET
- SP_TWITTER_ACCESSTOKEN
- SP_TWITTER_ACCESSSECRET

You may set the environment variables however you like, but since the app relies on them in order to work, creating a new file called setup.sh (for bash shells) or setup.bat (on Windows) is a good idea since you can check such files into your source code repository. Insert the following code in setup.sh by copying the appropriate values from the Twitter app page:

```bash
#!/bin/bash
export SP_TWITTER_KEY=yC2EDnaNrEhN5fd33g...
export SP_TWITTER_SECRET=6n0rToIpskCo1ob...
export SP_TWITTER_ACCESSTOKEN=2427-13677...
export SP_TWITTER_ACCESSSECRET=SpnZf336u...
```

On Windows, the code will look something like this:

```
SET SP_TWITTER_KEY=yC2EDnaNrEhN5fd33g...
SET SP_TWITTER_SECRET=6n0rToIpskCo1ob...
SET SP_TWITTER_ACCESSTOKEN=2427-13677...
SET SP_TWITTER_ACCESSSECRET=SpnZf336u...
```

Run the file with the source or call commands to have the values set appropriately, or add them to your `.bashrc` or `C:\cmdauto.cmd` files to save you from running them every time you open a new terminal window.

If you're not sure how to do this, just search for `Setting environment variables on Linux` or something similar, and the Internet will help you.

Extracting the connection

The Twitter streaming API supports HTTP connections that stay open for a long time, and given the design of our solution, we are going to need to access the `net.Conn` object in order to close it from outside of the goroutine in which requests occur. We can achieve this by providing our own `dial` method to an `http.Transport` object that we will create.

Create a new file called `twitter.go` inside `twittervotes` (which is where all things Twitter-related will live), and insert the following code:

```
var conn net.Conn
func dial(netw, addr string) (net.Conn, error) {
  if conn != nil {
    conn.Close()
    conn = nil
  }
  netc, err := net.DialTimeout(netw, addr, 5*time.Second)
  if err != nil {
    return nil, err
  }
  conn = netc
  return netc, nil
}
```

Our bespoke `dial` function first ensures that `conn` is closed and then opens a new connection, keeping the `conn` variable updated with the current connection. If a connection dies (Twitter's API will do this from time to time) or is closed by us, we can redial without worrying about zombie connections.

We will periodically close the connection ourselves and initiate a new one because we want to reload the options from the database at regular intervals. To do this, we need a function that closes the connection and also closes `io.ReadCloser`, which we will use to read the body of the responses. Add the following code to `twitter.go`:

```
var reader io.ReadCloser
func closeConn() {
  if conn != nil {
```

```
    conn.Close()
  }
  if reader != nil {
    reader.Close()
  }
}
```

Now, we can call `closeConn` at any time in order to break the ongoing connection with Twitter and tidy things up. In most cases, our code will load the options from the database again and open a new connection right away, but if we're shutting the program down (in response to a *Ctrl + C* hit), then we can call `closeConn` just before we exit.

Reading environment variables

Next, we are going to write a function that will read the environment variables and set up the `OAuth` objects we'll need in order to authenticate the requests. Add the following code to the `twitter.go` file:

```
var (
  authClient *oauth.Client
  creds *oauth.Credentials
)
func setupTwitterAuth() {
  var ts struct {
    ConsumerKey    string `env:"SP_TWITTER_KEY,required"`
    ConsumerSecret string `env:"SP_TWITTER_SECRET,required"`
    AccessToken    string `env:"SP_TWITTER_ACCESSTOKEN,required"`
    AccessSecret   string `env:"SP_TWITTER_ACCESSSECRET,required"`
  }
  if err := envdecode.Decode(&ts); err != nil {
    log.Fatalln(err)
  }
  creds = &oauth.Credentials{
    Token:  ts.AccessToken,
    Secret: ts.AccessSecret,
  }
  authClient = &oauth.Client{
    Credentials: oauth.Credentials{
      Token:  ts.ConsumerKey,
      Secret: ts.ConsumerSecret,
    },
  }
}
```

Here, we define a `struct` type to store the environment variables that we need to authenticate with Twitter. Since we don't need to use the type elsewhere, we define it inline and create a variable called `ts` of this anonymous type (that's why we have the somewhat unusual `var ts struct...` code). We then use Joe Shaw's `envdecode` package to pull in these environment variables for us. You will need to run `go get github.com/joeshaw/envdecode` and also import the `log` package. Our program will try to load appropriate values for all the fields marked `required` and return an error if it fails to do so, which reminds people that the program won't work without Twitter credentials.

The strings inside the back ticks alongside each field in `struct` are called tags and are available through a reflection interface, which is how `envdecode` knows which variables to look for. We added the `required` argument to this package, which indicates that it is an error for any of the environment variables to be missing (or empty).

Once we have the keys, we use them to create `oauth.Credentials` and an `oauth.Client` object from Gary Burd's `go-oauth` package, which will allow us to authorize requests with Twitter.

Now that we have the ability to control the underlying connection and authorize requests, we are ready to write the code that will actually build the authorized request and return the response. In `twitter.go`, add the following code:

```
var (
  authSetupOnce sync.Once
  httpClient    *http.Client
)
func makeRequest(req *http.Request, params url.Values) (*http.Response,
error) {
  authSetupOnce.Do(func() {
    setupTwitterAuth()
    httpClient = &http.Client{
      Transport: &http.Transport{
        Dial: dial,
      },
    }
  })
  formEnc := params.Encode()
  req.Header.Set("Content-Type", "application/x-www-form- urlencoded")
  req.Header.Set("Content-Length", strconv.Itoa(len(formEnc)))
  req.Header.Set("Authorization", authClient.AuthorizationHeader(creds,
  "POST",
  req.URL, params))
  return httpClient.Do(req)
}
```

We use `sync.Once` to ensure our initialization code gets run only once despite the number of times we call `makeRequest`. After calling the `setupTwitterAuth` method, we create a new `http.Client` function using an `http.Transport` function that uses our custom `dial` method. We then set the appropriate headers required for authorization with Twitter by encoding the specified `params` object that will contain the options we are querying for.

Reading from MongoDB

In order to load the polls, and therefore the options to search Twitter for, we need to connect to and query MongoDB. In `main.go`, add the two functions `dialdb` and `closedb`:

```
var db *mgo.Session
func dialdb() error {
  var err error
  log.Println("dialing mongodb: localhost")
  db, err = mgo.Dial("localhost")
  return err
}
func closedb() {
  db.Close()
  log.Println("closed database connection")
}
```

These two functions will connect to and disconnect from the locally running MongoDB instance using the `mgo` package and store `mgo.Session` (the database connection object) in a global variable called `db`.

> As an additional assignment, see whether you can find an elegant way to make the location of the MongoDB instance configurable so that you don't need to run it locally.

Assuming MongoDB is running and our code is able to connect, we need to load the poll objects and extract all the options from the documents, which we will then use to search Twitter. Add the following `loadOptions` function to `main.go`:

```
type poll struct {
  Options []string
}
func loadOptions() ([]string, error) {
  var options []string
  iter := db.DB("ballots").C("polls").Find(nil).Iter()
  var p poll
  for iter.Next(&p) {
```

```
        options = append(options, p.Options...)
    }
    iter.Close()
    return options, iter.Err()
}
```

Our poll document contains more than just `Options`, but our program doesn't care about anything else, so there's no need for us to bloat our `poll` struct. We use the `db` variable to access the `polls` collection from the `ballots` database and call the `mgo` package's fluent `Find` method, passing `nil` (meaning no filtering).

A fluent interface (first coined by Eric Evans and Martin Fowler) refers to an API design that aims to make the code more readable by allowing you to chain method calls together. This is achieved by each method returning the context object itself so that another method can be called directly afterwards. For example, `mgo` allows you to write queries such as this:
`query := col.Find(q).Sort("field").Limit(10).Skip(10)`

We then get an iterator by calling the `Iter` method, which allows us to access each poll one by one. This is a very memory-efficient way of reading the poll data because it only ever uses a single `poll` object. If we were to use the `All` method instead, the amount of memory we'd use would depend on the number of polls we had in our database, which could be out of our control.

When we have a poll, we use the `append` method to build up the `options` slice. Of course, with millions of polls in the database, this slice too would grow large and unwieldy. For that kind of scale, we would probably run multiple `twittervotes` programs, each dedicated to a portion of the poll data. A simple way to do this would be to break polls into groups based on the letters the titles begin with, such as group A-N and O-Z. A somewhat more sophisticated approach would be to add a field to the `poll` document, grouping it up in a more controlled manner, perhaps based on the stats for the other groups so that we are able to balance the load across many `twittervotes` instances.

The `append` built-in function is actually a `variadic` function, which means you can pass multiple elements for it to append. If you have a slice of the correct type, you can add . . . to the end, which simulates the passing of each item of the slice as a different argument.

Finally, we close the iterator and clean up any used memory before returning the options and any errors that occurred while iterating (by calling the `Err` method in the `mgo.Iter` object).

Reading from Twitter

Now we are able to load the options and make authorized requests to the Twitter API. We are ready to write the code that initiates the connection and continuously reads from the stream until either we call our `closeConn` method or Twitter closes the connection for one reason or another. The structure contained in the stream is a complex one, containing all kinds of information about the tweet who made it and when and even what links or mentions of users occur in the body (refer to Twitter's API documentation for more details). However, we are only interested in the tweet text itself; so, don't worry about all the other noise and add the following structure to `twitter.go`:

```
type tweet struct {
  Text string
}
```

> This may feel incomplete, but think about how clear it makes our intentions to other programmers who might see our code: a tweet has some text, and that is all we care about.

Using this new structure, in `twitter.go`, add the following `readFromTwitter` function that takes a send only channel called `votes`; this is how this function will inform the rest of our program that it has noticed a vote on Twitter:

```
func readFromTwitter(votes chan<- string) {
  options, err := loadOptions()
  if err != nil {
    log.Println("failed to load options:", err)
    return
  }
  u, err := url.Parse("https://stream.twitter.com/1.1/statuses
/filter.json")
  if err != nil {
    log.Println("creating filter request failed:", err)
    return
  }
  query := make(url.Values)
  query.Set("track", strings.Join(options, ","))
  req, err := http.NewRequest("POST",u.String(),strings.NewReader
(query.Encode()))
  if err != nil {
    log.Println("creating filter request failed:", err)
    return
  }
  resp, err := makeRequest(req, query)
  if err != nil {
```

```
      log.Println("making request failed:", err)
      return
    }
    reader := resp.Body
    decoder := json.NewDecoder(reader)
    for {
      var t tweet
      if err := decoder.Decode(&t); err != nil {
        break
      }
      for _, option := range options {
        if strings.Contains(
          strings.ToLower(t.Text),
          strings.ToLower(option),
        ) {
          log.Println("vote:", option)
          votes <- option
        }
      }
    }
  }
}
```

In the preceding code, after loading the options from all the polls data (by calling the loadOptions function), we use url.Parse to create a url.URL object that describes the appropriate endpoint on Twitter. We build a url.Values object called query and set the options as a comma-separated list. As per the API, we make a new POST request using the encoded url.Values object as the body and pass it to makeRequest along with the query object itself. If all is well, we make a new json.Decoder from the body of the request and keep reading inside an infinite for loop by calling the Decode method. If there is an error (probably due to the connection being closed), we simply break the loop and exit the function. If there is a tweet to read, it will be decoded into the t variable, which will give us access to the Text property (the 140 characters of the tweet itself). We then iterate over all the possible options, and if the tweet has mentioned it, we send it on the votes channel. This technique also allows a tweet to contain many votes at the same time, something you may or may not decide to change based on the rules of the election.

The votes channel is send-only (which means we cannot receive on it), since it is of the chan<- string type. Think of the little arrow that tells us which way messages will flow: either into the channel (chan<-) or out of it (<-chan). This is a great way to express intent to other programmers or our future selves-it's clear that we never intend to read votes using our readFromTwitter function; rather, we will only send them on that channel.

Terminating the program whenever `Decode` returns an error doesn't provide a very robust solution. This is because the Twitter API documentation states that the connection will drop from time to time, and clients should consider this when consuming the services. And remember, we are going to terminate the connection periodically too, so we need to think about a way to reconnect once the connection is dropped.

Signal channels

A great use of channels in Go is to signal events between code running in different goroutines. We are going to see a real-world example of this when we write our next function.

The purpose of the function is to start a goroutine that continually calls the `readFromTwitter` function (with the specified `votes` channel to receive the votes on) until we signal that we want it to stop. And once it has stopped, we want to be notified through another signal channel. The return of the function will be a channel of `struct{}`: a signal channel.

Signal channels have some interesting properties that are worth taking a closer look at. Firstly, the type sent down the channels is an empty `struct{}`, instances of which actually take up zero bytes, since it has no fields. So, `struct{}{}` is a great memory-efficient option for signaling events. Some people use `bool` types, which are also fine, although `true` and `false` both take up a byte of memory.

Head over to `http://play.golang.org` and try this out for yourself. The size of `bool` is one:
`fmt.Println(reflect.TypeOf(true).Size())` = 1 On the other hand, the size of `struct{}{}` is zero:
`fmt.Println(reflect.TypeOf(struct{}{}).Size())` = 0

The signal channels also have a buffer size of 1, which means that execution will not get blocked until something reads the signal from the channel.

We are going to employ two signal channels in our code: one that we pass into our function that tells our goroutine that it should stop and another (provided by the function) that signals once the stopping is complete.

In `twitter.go`, add the following function:

```go
func startTwitterStream(stopchan <-chan struct{}, votes chan<- string) <-
chan struct{} {
  stoppedchan := make(chan struct{}, 1)
  go func() {
    defer func() {
      stoppedchan <- struct{}{}
    }()
    for {
      select {
      case <-stopchan:
        log.Println("stopping Twitter...")
        return
      default:
        log.Println("Querying Twitter...")
        readFromTwitter(votes)
        log.Println("  (waiting)")
        time.Sleep(10 * time.Second) // wait before
         reconnecting
      }
    }
  }()
  return stoppedchan
}
```

In the preceding code, the first argument, `stopchan`, is a channel of type `<-chan struct{}`, a receive-only signal channel. It is this channel that, outside the code, will signal on, which will tell our goroutine to stop. Remember that it's receive-only inside this function; the actual channel itself will be capable of sending. The second argument is the `votes` channel on which votes will be sent. The return type of our function is also a signal channel of type `<-chan struct{}`: a receive-only channel that we will use to indicate that we have stopped.

These channels are necessary because our function triggers its own goroutine and immediately returns; so without this, calling code would have no idea whether the spawned code was still running or not.

The first thing we do in the `startTwitterStream` function is make our `stoppedchan` argument, and defer the sending of `struct{}{}` to indicate that we have finished when our function exits. Note that `stoppedchan` is a normal channel, so even though it is returned as receive-only, we will be able to send it from within this function.

We then start an infinite `for` loop in which we select from one of two channels. The first is `stopchan` (the first argument), which would indicate that it was time to stop and return (thus triggering the deferred signaling on `stoppedchan`). If that hasn't happened, we will call `readFromTwitter` (passing in the `votes` channel), which will go and load the options from the database and open the connection to Twitter.

When the Twitter connection dies, our code will return, where we sleep for 10 seconds using the `time.Sleep` function. This is to give the Twitter API rest in case it closed the connection due to overuse. Once we've rested, we re-enter the loop and check on `stopchan` again to see whether calling code wants us to stop or not.

To make this flow clear, we are logging out key statements that will not only help us debug our code, but also let us peek into the inner workings of this somewhat complicated mechanism.

 Signal channels are a great solution for simple cases where all code lives inside a single package. If you need to cross API boundaries, the context package is the recommended way to deal with deadlines, cancelation and, stopping since it was promoted to the standard library in Go 1.7.

Publishing to NSQ

Once our code successfully notices votes on Twitter and sends them down the `votes` channel, we need a way to publish them into an NSQ topic; after all, this is the point of the `twittervotes` program.

We will write a function called `publishVotes`, which will take the `votes` channel, this time of type `<-chan string` (a receive only channel), and publish each string that is received from it.

 In our previous functions, the `votes` channel was of type `chan<-string`, but this time, it's of the type `<-chan string`. You might think this is a mistake or even that it means that we cannot use the same channel for both, but you would be wrong. The channel we create later will be made with `make(chan string)`, neither receive nor only send, and can act in both cases. The reason for using the `<-` operator on a channel in arguments is to make the intent of what the channel will be used for clear, or in the case where it is the return type, to prevent users from accidentally sending on channels intended for receiving or vice versa. The compiler will actually produce an error if they use such a channel incorrectly.

Once the `votes` channel is closed (this is how the external code will tell our function to stop working), we will stop publishing and send a signal down the returned stop signal channel.

Add the `publishVotes` function to `main.go`:

```
func publishVotes(votes <-chan string) <-chan struct{} {
  stopchan := make(chan struct{}, 1)
  pub, _ := nsq.NewProducer("localhost:4150",
   nsq.NewConfig())
  go func() {
    for vote := range votes {
      pub.Publish("votes", []byte(vote)) // publish vote
    }
    log.Println("Publisher: Stopping")
    pub.Stop()
    log.Println("Publisher: Stopped")
    stopchan <- struct{}{}
  }()
  return stopchan
}
```

Again, the first thing we do is create `stopchan`, which we later return, this time not deferring the signaling but doing it inline by sending `struct{}{}` down `stopchan`.

 The difference in how we handle `stopchan` is to show alternative options. Within one code base, you should pick a style you like and stick with it until a standard emerges within the community; in which case, we should all go with that. It is also possible to close `stopchan` rather than send anything down it, which will also unblock the code waiting on that channel. But once a channel is closed, it cannot be reopened.

We then create an NSQ producer by calling `NewProducer` and connecting to the default NSQ port on `localhost` using a default configuration. We start a goroutine, which uses another great built-in feature of the Go language that lets us continually pull values from a channel (in our case, the `votes` channel) just by doing a normal `for...range` operation on it. Whenever the channel has no values, execution will be blocked until one comes down the line. If the `votes` channel is closed, the `for` loop will exit.

To learn more about the power of channels in Go, it is highly recommended that you seek out blog posts and videos by John Graham-Cumming, in particular, one entitled *A Channel Compendium* that he presented at Gophercon 2014 and which contains a brief history of channels, including their origin (interestingly, John was also the guy who successfully petitioned the British government to officially apologize for its treatment of the late, great Alan Turing).

When the loop exits (after the `votes` channel is closed), the publisher is stopped, following which the `stopchan` signal is sent. Did anything stand-out as unusual in the `publishVotes` function? We are breaking a cardinal rule of Go by ignoring an error (assigning it to an underscore variables; therefore dismissing it). As an additional exercise, catch the error and deal with it in a way that seems suitable.

Gracefully starting and stopping programs

When our program is terminated, we want to do a few things before actually exiting, namely closing our connection to Twitter and stopping the NSQ publisher (which actually deregisters its interest in the queue). To achieve this, we have to override the default *Ctrl + C* behavior.

The upcoming code blocks all go inside the `main` function; they are broken up so that we can discuss each section before continuing.

Add the following code inside the `main` function:

```
var stoplock sync.Mutex // protects stop
stop := false
stopChan := make(chan struct{}, 1)
signalChan := make(chan os.Signal, 1)
go func() {
  <-signalChan
  stoplock.Lock()
  stop = true
  stoplock.Unlock()
  log.Println("Stopping...")
  stopChan <- struct{}{}
  closeConn()
}()
signal.Notify(signalChan, syscall.SIGINT, syscall.SIGTERM)
```

Here, we create a stop `bool` with an associated `sync.Mutex` function so that we can access it from many goroutines at the same time. We then create two more signal channels, `stopChan` and `signalChan`, and use `signal.Notify` to ask Go to send the signal down `signalChan` when someone tries to halt the program (either with the `SIGINT` interrupt or the `SIGTERM` termination POSIX signals). The `stopChan` function is how we indicate that we want our processes to terminate, and we pass it as an argument to `startTwitterStream` later.

We then run a goroutine that blocks waiting for the signal by trying to read from `signalChan`; this is what the `<-` operator does in this case (it's trying to read from the channel). Since we don't care about the type of signal, we don't bother capturing the object returned on the channel. Once a signal is received, we set `stop` to `true` and close the connection. Only when one of the specified signals is sent will the rest of the goroutine code run, which is how we are able to perform teardown code before exiting the program.

Add the following piece of code (inside the main function) to open and defer the closing of the database connection:

```
if err := dialdb(); err != nil {
  log.Fatalln("failed to dial MongoDB:", err)
}
defer closedb()
```

Since the `readFromTwitter` method reloads the options from the database each time and because we want to keep our program updated without having to restart it, we are going to introduce one final goroutine. This goroutine will simply call `closeConn` every minute, causing the connection to die and cause `readFromTwitter` to be called all over again. Insert the following code at the bottom of the `main` function to start all of these processes and then wait for them to gracefully stop:

```
// start things
votes := make(chan string) // chan for votes
publisherStoppedChan := publishVotes(votes)
twitterStoppedChan := startTwitterStream(stopChan, votes)
go func() {
  for {
    time.Sleep(1 * time.Minute)
    closeConn()
    stoplock.Lock()
    if stop {
      stoplock.Unlock()
      return
    }
    stoplock.Unlock()
  }
}
```

```
}()
<-twitterStoppedChan
close(votes)
<-publisherStoppedChan
```

First, we make the `votes` channel that we have been talking about throughout this section, which is a simple channel of strings. Note that it is neither a send (`chan<-`) nor a receive (`<-chan`) channel; in fact, making such channels makes little sense. We then call `publishVotes`, passing in the `votes` channel for it to receive from and capturing the returned stop signal channel as `publisherStoppedChan`. Similarly, we call `startTwitterStream`, passing in our `stopChan` function from the beginning of the `main` function and the `votes` channel for it to send to while capturing the resulting stop signal channel as `twitterStoppedChan`.

We then start our refresher goroutine, which immediately enters an infinite `for` loop before sleeping for a minute and closing the connection via the call to `closeConn`. If the stop `bool` has been set to true (in that previous goroutine), we will break the loop and exit; otherwise, we will loop around and wait another minute before closing the connection again. The use of `stoplock` is important because we have two goroutines that might try to access the stop variable at the same time, but we want to avoid collisions.

Once the goroutine has started, we block `twitterStoppedChan` by attempting to read from it. When successful (which means the signal was sent on `stopChan`), we close the `votes` channel, which will cause the publisher's `for...range` loop to exit and the publisher itself to stop, after which the signal will be sent on `publisherStoppedChan`, which we wait for before exiting.

Testing

To make sure our program works, we need to do two things: first, we need to create a poll in the database, and second, we need to peer inside the messaging queue to see whether the messages are indeed being generated by `twittervotes`.

In a terminal, run the `mongo` command to open a database shell that allows us to interact with MongoDB. Then, enter the following commands to add a test poll:

```
> use ballots
  switched to db ballots
> db.polls.insert({"title":"Test poll","options":
  ["happy","sad","fail","win"]})
```

The preceding commands add a new item to the `polls` collection in the `ballots` database. We are using some common words for options that are likely to be mentioned by people on Twitter so that we can observe real tweets being translated into messages. You might notice that our poll object is missing the `results` field; this is fine since we are dealing with unstructured data where documents do not have to adhere to a strict schema. The `counter` program we are going to write in the next section will add and maintain the `results` data for us later.

Press *Ctrl + Ci»¿* to exit the MongoDB shell and type the following command:

```
nsq_tail --topic="votes" --lookupd-http-
    address=localhost:4161
```

The `nsq_tail` tool connects to the specified messaging queue topic and outputs any messages that it notices. This is where we will validate that our `twittervotes` program is sending messages.

In a separate terminal window, let's build and run the `twittervotes` program:

```
go build -o twittervotes
./twittervotes
```

Now switch back to the window running `nsq_tail` and note that messages are indeed being generated in response to live Twitter activity.

If you don't see much activity, try to look up trending hash tags on Twitter and add another poll containing these options.

Counting votes

The second program we are going to implement is the `counter` tool, which will be responsible for watching out for votes in NSQ, counting them, and keeping MongoDB up to date with the latest numbers.

Create a new folder called `counter` alongside `twittervotes`, and add the following code to a new `main.go` file:

```
package main
import (
  "flag"
  "fmt"
```

```
   "os"
)
var fatalErr error
func fatal(e error) {
   fmt.Println(e)
   flag.PrintDefaults()
   fatalErr = e
}
func main() {
   defer func() {
     if fatalErr != nil {
       os.Exit(1)
     }
   }()
}
```

Normally when we encounter an error in our code, we use a call such as `log.Fatal` or `os.Exit`, which immediately terminates the program. Exiting the program with a nonzero exit code is important because it is our way of telling the operating system that something went wrong, and we didn't complete our task successfully. The problem with the normal approach is that any deferred functions we have scheduled (and therefore any teardown code we need to run) won't get a chance to execute.

The pattern employed in the preceding code snippet lets us call the `fatal` function to record that an error has occurred. Note that only when our main function exits will the deferred function run, which in turn calls `os.Exit(1)` to exit the program with an exit code of `1`. Because the deferred statements are run in LIFO (last in, first out) order, the first function we defer will be the last function to be executed, which is why the first thing we do in the `main` function is defer the exiting code. This allows us to be sure that other functions we defer will be called *before* the program exits. We'll use this feature to ensure that our database connection gets closed regardless of any errors.

Connecting to the database

The best time to think about cleaning up resources, such as database connections, is immediately after you have successfully obtained the resource; Go's `defer` keyword makes this easy. At the bottom of the main function, add the following code:

```
log.Println("Connecting to database...")
db, err := mgo.Dial("localhost")
if err != nil {
   fatal(err)
   return
}
```

```
defer func() {
  log.Println("Closing database connection...")
  db.Close()
}()
pollData := db.DB("ballots").C("polls")
```

This code uses the familiar `mgo.Dial` method to open a session to the locally running MongoDB instance and immediately defers a function that closes the session. We can be sure that this code will run before our previously deferred statement containing the exit code (because deferred functions are run in the reverse order in which they were called). Therefore, whatever happens in our program, we know that the database session will definitely and properly close.

 The log statements are optional, but they will help us see what's going on when we run and exit our program.

At the end of the snippet, we use the `mgo` fluent API to keep a reference of the `ballots.polls` data collection in the `pollData` variable, which we will use later to make queries.

Consuming messages in NSQ

In order to count the votes, we need to consume the messages in the `votes` topic in NSQ, and we'll need a place to store them. Add the following variables to the `main` function:

```
var counts map[string]int
var countsLock sync.Mutex
```

A map and a lock (`sync.Mutex`) is a common combination in Go because we will have multiple goroutines trying to access the same map, and we need to avoid corrupting it by trying to modify or read it at the same time.

Add the following code to the `main` function:

```
log.Println("Connecting to nsq...")
q, err := nsq.NewConsumer("votes", "counter", nsq.NewConfig())
if err != nil {
  fatal(err)
  return
}
```

The NewConsumer function allows us to set up an object that will listen on the votes NSQ topic, so when twittervotes publishes a vote on that topic, we can handle it in this program. If NewConsumer returns an error, we'll use our fatal function to record it and return.

Next, we are going to add the code that handles messages (votes) from NSQ:

```
q.AddHandler(nsq.HandlerFunc(func(m *nsq.Message) error {
  countsLock.Lock()
  defer countsLock.Unlock()
  if counts == nil {
    counts = make(map[string]int)
  }
  vote := string(m.Body)
  counts[vote]++
  return nil
}))
```

We call the AddHandler method on nsq.Consumer and pass it a function that will be called for every message received on the votes topic.

When a vote comes in, the first thing we do is lock the countsLock mutex. Next, we defer the unlocking of the mutex for when the function exits. This allows us to be sure that while NewConsumer is running, we are the only ones allowed to modify the map; others will have to wait until our function exits before they can use it. Calls to the Lock method block execution while the lock is in place, and it only continues when the lock is released by a call to Unlock. This is why it's vital that every Lock call has an Unlock counterpart; otherwise, we will deadlock our program.

Every time we receive a vote, we check whether counts is nil and make a new map if it is because once the database has been updated with the latest results, we want to reset everything and start at zero. Finally, we increase the int value by one for the given key and return nil, indicating no errors.

Although we have created our NSQ consumer and added our handler function, we still need to connect to the NSQ service, which we will do by adding the following code:

```
if err := q.ConnectToNSQLookupd("localhost:4161");
 err !=nil {
  fatal(err)
  return
}
```

It is important to note that we are actually connecting to the HTTP port of the `nsqlookupd` instance rather than NSQ instances; this abstraction means that our program doesn't need to know *where* the messages are coming from in order to consume them. If we fail to connect to the server (for instance, if we forget to start it), we'll get an error, which we report to our fatal function before immediately returning.

Keeping the database updated

Our code will listen out for votes and keep a map of the results in the memory, but that information is trapped inside our program so far. Next, we need to add the code that will periodically push the results to the database. Add the following `doCount` function:

```go
func doCount(countsLock *sync.Mutex, counts *map[string]int, pollData
*mgo.Collection) {
  countsLock.Lock()
  defer countsLock.Unlock()
  if len(*counts) == 0 {
    log.Println("No new votes, skipping database update")
    return
  }
  log.Println("Updating database...")
  log.Println(*counts)
  ok := true
  for option, count := range *counts {
    sel := bson.M{"options": bson.M{"$in":
     []string{option}}}
    up := bson.M{"$inc": bson.M{"results." +
     option:count}}
    if _, err := pollData.UpdateAll(sel, up); err != nil {
      log.Println("failed to update:", err)
      ok = false
    }
  }
  if ok {
    log.Println("Finished updating database...")
    *counts = nil // reset counts
  }
}
```

When our `doCount` function runs, the first thing we do is lock `countsLock` and defer its unlocking. We then check to see whether there are any values in the `counts` map. If there aren't, we just log that we're skipping the update and wait for next time.

We are taking all arguments in as pointers (note the * character before the type name) because we want to be sure that we are interacting with the underlying data itself and not a copy of it. For example, the *counts = nil line will actually reset the underlying map to nil rather than just invalidate our local copy of it. If there are some votes, we iterate over the counts map, pulling out the option and the number of votes (since the last update), and use some MongoDB magic to update the results.

MongoDB stores **BSON** (short for **Binary JSON**) documents internally, which are easier to traverse than normal JSON documents, and that is why the mgo package comes with the mgo/bson encoding package. When using mgo, we will often use bson types, such as the bson.M map, to describe concepts for MongoDB.

We first create the selector for our update operation using the bson.M shortcut type, which is similar to creating map[string]interface{} types. The selector we create here will look something like this:

```
{
  "options": {
    "$in": ["happy"]
  }
}
```

In MongoDB, the preceding BSON specifies that we want to select polls where "happy" is one of the items in the options array.

Next, we use the same technique to generate the update operation, which looks something like this:

```
{
  "$inc": {
    "results.happy": 3
  }
}
```

In MongoDB, the preceding BSON specifies that we want to increase the results.happy field by three. If there is no results map in the poll, one will be created, and if there is no happy key inside results, zero will be assumed.

We then call the UpdateAll method in our pollsData query to issue the command to the database, which will in turn update every poll that matches the selector (contrast this to the Update method, which will update only one). If something goes wrong, we report it and set the ok Boolean to false. If all goes well, we set the counts map to nil, since we want to reset the counter.

We are going to specify `updateDuration` as a constant at the top of the file, which will make it easy for us to change when we are testing our program. Add the following code above the `main` function:

```
const updateDuration = 1 * time.Second
```

Next, we will add `time.Ticker` and make sure our `doCount` function gets called in the same `select` block that we use when responding to *Ctrl + C*.

Responding to Ctrl + C

The last thing to do before our program is ready is set up a select block that periodically calls `doCount` and be sure that our `main` function waits for operations to complete before exiting, like we did in our `twittervotes` program. Add the following code at the end of the `main` function:

```
ticker := time.NewTicker(updateDuration)
 termChan := make(chan os.Signal, 1)
signal.Notify(termChan, syscall.SIGINT, syscall.SIGTERM, syscall.SIGHUP)
for {
   select {
   case <-ticker.C:
    doCount(&countsLock, &counts, pollData)   case <- termChan:ticker.Stop()
      q.Stop()
   case <-q.StopChan:
     // finished
     return
   }
 }
```

The `time.Ticker` function is a type that gives us a channel (via the C field) on which the current time is sent at the specified interval (in our case, `updateDuration`). We use this in a `select` block to call our `doCount` function while `termChan` and `q.StopChan` are quiet.

To handle termination, we have employed a slightly different tactic than before. We trap the termination event, which will cause a signal to go down `termChan` when we hit *Ctrl + C*. Next, we start an infinite loop, inside which we use the `select` structure to allow us to run the code if we receive something on either `termChan` or `StopChan` of the consumer.

In fact, we will only ever get a `termChan` signal first in response to a *Ctrl + C* press, at which point we stop `time.Ticker` and ask the consumer to stop listening for votes. Execution then re-enters the loop and blocks until the consumer reports that it has indeed stopped by signaling on its `StopChan` function. When that happens, we're done and we exit, at which point our deferred statement runs, which, if you remember, tidies up the database session.

Running our solution

It's time to see our code in action. Ensure that you have `nsqlookupd`, `nsqd`, and `mongod` running in separate terminal windows with the following:

```
nsqlookupd
nsqd --lookupd-tcp-address=127.0.0.1:4160
mongod --dbpath ./db
```

If you haven't already done so, make sure the `twittervotes` program is running too. Then, in the `counter` folder, build and run our counting program:

```
go build -o counter
./counter
```

You should see a periodic output describing what work `counter` is doing, such as the following:

```
No new votes, skipping database update
Updating database...
map[win:2 happy:2 fail:1]
Finished updating database...
No new votes, skipping database update
Updating database...
map[win:3]
Finished updating database...
```

The output will, of course, vary since we are actually responding to real, live activity on Twitter.

We can see that our program is receiving vote data from NSQ and reports to update the database with the results. We can confirm this by opening the MongoDB shell and querying the poll data to see whether the `results` map is being updated. In another terminal window, open the MongoDB shell:

```
mongo
```

Ask it to use the ballots database:

```
> use ballots
switched to db ballots
```

Use the `find` method with no arguments to get all polls (add the `pretty` method to the end to get nicely formatted JSON):

```
> db.polls.find().pretty()
{
  "_id" : ObjectId("53e2a3afffbff195c2e09a02"),
  "options" : [
  "happy","sad","fail","win"
  ],
  "results" : {
    "fail" : 159, "win" : 711,
    "happy" : 233, "sad" : 166,
  },
  title" : "Test poll"
}
```

The `results` map is indeed updated, and at any point in time, it contains the total number of votes for each option.

Summary

In this chapter, we covered a lot of ground. We learned different techniques to gracefully shut down programs using signaling channels, which is especially important when our code has some work to do before it can exit. We saw that deferring the reporting of fatal errors at the start of our program can give our other deferred functions a chance to execute before the process ends.

We also discovered how easy it is to interact with MongoDB using the `mgo` package and how to use BSON types when describing concepts for the database. The `bson.M` alternative to `map[string]interface{}` helps us keep our code more concise while still providing all the flexibility we need when working with unstructured or schemaless data.

We learned about message queues and how they allow us to break apart the components of a system into isolated and specialized micro-services. We started an instance of NSQ by first running the `nsqlookupd` lookup daemon before running a single `nsqd` instance and connecting them via a TCP interface. We were then able to publish votes to the queue in `twittervotes` and connect to the lookup daemon to run a handler function for every vote sent in our `counter` program.

While our solution is actually performing a pretty simple task, the architecture we have put together in this chapter is capable of doing some pretty great things.

We eliminated the need for our `twittervotes` and counter programs to run on the same machine-as long as they can both connect to the appropriate NSQ, they will function as expected regardless of where they are running.

We can distribute our MongoDB and NSQ nodes across many physical machines, which would mean our system is capable of gigantic scale-whenever resources start running low, we can add new boxes to cope with the demand.

When we add other applications that need to query and read the results from polls, we can be sure that our database services are highly available and capable of delivering.

We can spread our database across geographical expanses, replicating data for backup so we don't lose anything when disaster strikes.

We can build a multinode, fault-tolerant NSQ environment, which means that when our `twittervotes` program learns of interesting tweets, there will always be some place to send the data.

We can write many more programs that generate votes from different sources; the only requirement is that they know how to put messages into NSQ.

In the next chapter, we will build a RESTful data service of our own, through which we will expose the functionality of our social polling application. We will also build a web interface that lets users create their own polls and have the results visualized.

6
Exposing Data and Functionality through a RESTful Data Web Service API

In the previous chapter, we built a service that reads tweets from Twitter, counts the hash tag votes, and stores the results in a MongoDB database. We also used the MongoDB shell to add polls and see the poll results. This approach is fine if we are the only ones using our solution, but it would be madness if we released our project and expected users to connect directly to our MongoDB instance in order to use the service we built.

Therefore, in this chapter, we are going to build a RESTful data service through which the data and functionality will be exposed. We will also put together a simple website that consumes the new API. Users may then either use our website to create and monitor polls or build their own application on top of the web services we release.

 Code in this chapter depends on the code in `Chapter 5`, *Building Distributed Systems and Working with Flexible Data*, so it is recommended that you complete that chapter first, especially since it covers setting up the environment that the code in this chapter runs on.

Specifically, you will learn:

- How wrapping `http.HandlerFunc` types can give us a simple but powerful pipeline of execution for our HTTP requests
- How to safely share data between HTTP handlers using the `context` package
- Best practices for the writing of handlers responsible for exposing data

- Where small abstractions can allow us to write the simplest possible implementations now but leave room to improve them later without changing the interface
- How adding simple helper functions and types to our project will prevent us from (or at least defer) adding dependencies on external packages

RESTful API design

For an API to be considered RESTful, it must adhere to a few principles that stay true to the original concepts behind the Web and are already known to most developers. Such an approach allows us to make sure we aren't building anything strange or unusual into our API while also giving our users a head start toward consuming it, since they are already familiar with its concepts.

Some of the important RESTful design concepts are:

- HTTP methods describe the kind of action to take; for example, GET methods will only ever read data, while POST requests will create something
- Data is expressed as a collection of resources
- Actions are expressed as changes to data
- URLs are used to refer to specific data
- HTTP headers are used to describe the kind of representation coming into and going out of the server

The following table shows the HTTP methods and URLs that represent the actions that we will support in our API, along with a brief description and an example use case of how we intend the call to be used.

Request	Description	Use case
GET /polls	Read all polls	Show a list of polls to the users
GET /polls/{id}	Read the poll	Show details or results of a specific poll
POST /polls	Create a poll	Create a new poll
DELETE /polls/{id}	Delete a poll	Delete a specific poll

The {id} placeholder represents where in the path the unique ID for a poll will go.

Sharing data between handlers

Occasionally, we need to share a state between our middleware and handlers. Go 1.7 brought the `context` package into the standard library, which gives us, among other things, a way to share basic request-scoped data.

Every `http.Request` method comes with a `context.Context` object accessible via the `request.Context()` method, from which we can create new context objects. We can then call `request.WithContext()` to get a (cheap) shallow copied `http.Request` method that uses our new `Context` object.

To add a value, we can create a new context (based on the existing one from the request) via the `context.WithValue` method:

```
ctx := context.WithValue(r.Context(), "key", "value")
```

While you can technically store any type of data using this approach, it is only recommended that you store simple primitive types such as Strings and Integers and do not use it to inject dependencies or pointers to other objects that your handlers might need. Later in this chapter, we will explore patterns to access dependencies, such as a database connection.

In middleware code, we can then use our new `ctx` object when we pass execution to the wrapped handler:

```
Handler.ServeHTTP(w, r.WithContext(ctx))
```

It is worth exploring the documentation for the context package at `https://golang.org/pkg/context/` in order to find out what other features it provides.

We are going to use this technique to allow our handlers to have access to an API key that is extracted and validated elsewhere.

Context keys

Setting a value in a context object requires us to use a key, and while it might seem obvious that the value argument is of type `interface{}`, which means we can (but not necessarily should) store anything we like, it might surprise you to learn the type of the key:

```
func WithValue(parent Context, key, val interface{}) Context
```

The key is also an `interface{}`. This means we are not restricted to using only strings as the key, which is good news when you consider how disparate code might well attempt to set values with the same name in the same context, which would create problems.

Instead, a pattern of a more stable way of keying values is emerging from the Go community (and is already used in some places inside the standard library). We are going to create a simple (private) `struct` for our keys and a helper method in order to get the value out of the context.

Add the essential minimal `main.go` file inside a new `api` folder:

```
package main
func main(){}
```

Add a new type called `contextKey`:

```
type contextKey struct {
  name string
}
```

This structure contains only the name of the key, but pointers to it will remain unique even if the `name` field is the same in two keys. Next, we are going to add a key to store our API key value in:

```
var contextKeyAPIKey = &contextKey{"api-key"}
```

It is good practice to group related variables together with a common prefix; in our case, we can start the name all of our context key types with the `contextKey` prefix. Here, we have created a key called `contextKeyAPIKey`, which is a pointer to a `contextKey` type, setting the name as `api-key`.

Next, we are going to write a helper that will, given a context, extract the key:

```
func APIKey(ctx context.Context) (string, bool) {
  key, ok := ctx.Value(contextKeyAPIKey).(string)
  return key, ok
}
```

The function takes `context.Context` and returns the API key string along with an `ok` bool indicating whether the key was successfully obtained and cast to a string or not. If the key is missing, or if it's the wrong type, the second return argument will be false, but our code will not panic.

Note that `contextKey` and `contextKeyAPIKey` are internal (they start with a lowercase letter) but `APIKey` will be exported. In `main` packages, this doesn't really matter, but if you were writing a package, it's nice to know that the complexity of how you are storing and extracting data from a context is hidden from users.

Wrapping handler functions

We are going to utilize one of the most valuable patterns to learn when building services and websites in Go, something we already explored a little in `Chapter 2`, *Adding User Accounts*: wrapping handlers. We have seen how we can wrap `http.Handler` types to run code before and after our main handlers execute, and we are going to apply the same technique to `http.HandlerFunc` function alternatives.

API keys

Most web APIs require clients to register an API key for their application, which they are asked to send along with every request. Such keys have many purposes, ranging from simply identifying which app the requests are coming from to addressing authorization concerns in situations where some apps are only able to do limited things based on what a user has allowed. While we don't actually need to implement API keys for our application, we are going to ask clients to provide one, which will allow us to add an implementation later, while keeping the interface constant.

We are going to add our first `HandlerFunc` wrapper function called `withAPIKey` to the bottom of `main.go`:

```
func withAPIKey(fn http.HandlerFunc) http.HandlerFunc {
  return func(w http.ResponseWriter, r *http.Request) {
    key := r.URL.Query().Get("key")
    if !isValidAPIKey(key) {
      respondErr(w, r, http.StatusUnauthorized, "invalid
       API key")
      return
    }
    ctx := context.WithValue(r.Context(),
     contextKeyAPIKey, key)
    fn(w, r.WithContext(ctx))
  }
}
```

As you can see, our `withAPIKey` function both takes an `http.HandlerFunc` type as an argument and returns one; this is what we mean by wrapping in this context.
The `withAPIKey` function relies on a number of other functions that we are yet to write, but you can clearly see what's going on. Our function immediately returns a new `http.HandlerFunc` type that performs a check for the `key` query parameter by calling `isValidAPIKey`. If the key is deemed invalid (by the return of `false`), we respond with an `invalid API key` error; otherwise, we put the key into the context and call the next handler. To use this wrapper, we simply pass an `http.HandlerFunc` type into this function in order to enable the `key` parameter check. Since it returns an `http.HandlerFunc` type too, the result can then be passed on to other wrappers or given directly to the `http.HandleFunc` function to actually register it as the handler for a particular path pattern.

Let's add our `isValidAPIKey` function next:

```
func isValidAPIKey(key string) bool {
   return key == "abc123"
}
```

For now, we are simply going to hardcode the API key as `abc123`; anything else will return `false` and therefore be considered invalid. Later, we can modify this function to consult a configuration file or database to check the authenticity of a key without affecting how we use the `isValidAPIKey` method or the `withAPIKey` wrapper.

Cross-origin resource sharing

The same-origin security policy mandates that AJAX requests in web browsers be allowed only for services hosted on the same domain, which would make our API fairly limited since we won't necessarily be hosting all of the websites that use our web service. The **CORS (Cross-origin resource sharing)** technique circumnavigates the same-origin policy, allowing us to build a service capable of serving websites hosted on other domains. To do this, we simply have to set the `Access-Control-Allow-Origin` header in response to `*`. While we're at it, since we're going to use the `Location` header in our create poll call âⓔⓔwe'll allow this header to be accessible by the client too, which can be done by listing it in the `Access-Control-Expose-Headers` header. Add the following code to `main.go`:

```
func withCORS(fn http.HandlerFunc) http.HandlerFunc {
   return func(w http.ResponseWriter, r *http.Request) {
     w.Header().Set("Access-Control-Allow-Origin", "*")
     w.Header().Set("Access-Control-Expose-Headers",
       "Location")
```

```
        fn(w, r)
    }
}
```

This is the simplest wrapper function yet; it just sets the appropriate header on the
ResponseWriter type and calls the specified http.HandlerFunc type.

> In this chapter, we are handling CORS explicitly so we can understand
> exactly what is going on; for real production code, you should consider
> employing an open source solution, such as https://github.com/faster
> ness/cors.

Injecting dependencies

Now that we can be sure that a request has a valid API key and is CORS-compliant, we
must consider how handlers will connect to the database. One option is to have each
handler dial its own connection, but this isn't very **DRY (Don't Repeat Yourself)** and leaves
room for potentially erroneous code, such as code that forgets to close a database session
once it is finished with it. It also means that if we wanted to change how we connected to
the database (perhaps we want to use a domain name instead of a hardcoded IP address),
we might have to modify our code in many places, rather than one.

Instead, we will create a new type that encapsulates all the dependencies for our handlers
and construct it with a database connection in main.go.

Create a new type called Server:

```
// Server is the API server.
type Server struct {
  db *mgo.Session
}
```

Our handler functions will be methods of this server, which is how they will be able to
access the database session.

Responding

A big part of any API is responding to requests with a combination of status codes, data,
errors, and sometimes headers â@@the net/http package makes all of this very easy to do.
One option we have, which remains the best option for tiny projects or even the early stages
of big projects, is to just build the response code directly inside the handler.

As the number of handlers grows, however, we will end up duplicating a lot of code and sprinkling representation decisions all over our project. A more scalable approach is to abstract the response code into helper functions.

For the first version of our API, we are going to speak only JSON, but we want the flexibility to add other representations later if we need to.

Create a new file called `respond.go` and add the following code:

```
func decodeBody(r *http.Request, v interface{}) error {
  defer r.Body.Close()
  return json.NewDecoder(r.Body).Decode(v)
}
func encodeBody(w http.ResponseWriter, r *http.Request, v  interface{})
error {
  return json.NewEncoder(w).Encode(v)
}
```

These two functions abstract the decoding and encoding of data from and to the `Request` and `ResponseWriter` objects, respectively. The decoder also closes the request body, which is recommended. Although we haven't added much functionality here, it means that we do not need to mention JSON anywhere else in our code, and if we decide to add support for other representations or switch to a binary protocol instead, we only need to touch these two functions.

Next, we are going to add a few more helpers that will make responding even easier. In `respond.go`, add the following code:

```
func respond(w http.ResponseWriter, r *http.Request,
  status int, data interface{}) {
  w.WriteHeader(status)
  if data != nil {
    encodeBody(w, r, data)
  }
}
```

This function makes it easy to write the status code and some data to the `ResponseWriter` object using our `encodeBody` helper.

Handling errors is another important aspect that is worth abstracting. Add the following `respondErr` helper:

```
func respondErr(w http.ResponseWriter, r *http.Request,
  status int, args ...interface{}) {
  respond(w, r, status, map[string]interface{}{
    "error": map[string]interface{}{
```

```
      "message": fmt.Sprint(args...),
    },
  })
}
```

This method gives us an interface similar to the `respond` function, but the data written will be enveloped in an `error` object in order to make it clear that something went wrong. Finally, we can add an HTTP-error-specific helper that will generate the correct message for us using the `http.StatusText` function from the Go standard library:

```
func respondHTTPErr(w http.ResponseWriter, r *http.Request, status int) {
  respondErr(w, r, status, http.StatusText(status))
}
```

Note that these functions are all dog food, which means that they use each other (as in, eating your own dog food), which is important since we want actual responding to happen in only one place for if (or more likely, when) we need to make changes.

Understanding the request

The `http.Request` object gives us access to every piece of information we might need about the underlying HTTP request; therefore, it is worth glancing through the `net/http` documentation to really get a feel for its power. Examples include, but are not limited to, the following:

- The URL, path, and query string
- The HTTP method
- Cookies
- Files
- Form values
- The referrer and user agent of requester
- Basic authentication details
- The request body
- The header information

There are a few things it doesn't address, which we need to either solve ourselves or look to an external package to help us with. URL path parsing is one such example —while we can access a path (such as `/people/1/books/2`) as a string via the `http.Request` type's `URL.Path` field, there is no easy way to pull out the data encoded in the path, such as the people ID of 1 or the book ID of 2.

A few projects do a good job of addressing this problem, such as Goweb or Gorillz's `mux` package. They let you map path patterns that contain placeholders for values that they then pull out of the original string and make available to your code. For example, you can map a pattern of `/users/{userID}/comments/{commentID}`, which will map paths such as `/users/1/comments/2`. In your handler code, you can then get the values by the names placed inside the curly braces rather than having to parse the path yourself.

Since our needs are simple, we are going to knock together a simple path-parsing utility; we can always use a different package later if we have to, but that would mean adding a dependency to our project.

Create a new file called `path.go` and insert the following code:

```go
package main
import (
  "strings"
)
const PathSeparator = "/"
type Path struct {
  Path string
  ID   string
}
func NewPath(p string) *Path {
  var id string
  p = strings.Trim(p, PathSeparator)
  s := strings.Split(p, PathSeparator)
  if len(s) > 1 {
    id = s[len(s)-1]
    p = strings.Join(s[:len(s)-1], PathSeparator)
  }
  return &Path{Path: p, ID: id}
}
func (p *Path) HasID() bool {
  return len(p.ID) > 0
}
```

This simple parser provides a `NewPath` function that parses the specified path string and returns a new instance of the `Path` type. Leading and trailing slashes are trimmed (using `strings.Trim`) and the remaining path is split (using `strings.Split`) by the `PathSeparator` constant, which is just a forward slash. If there is more than one segment (`len(s) > 1`), the last one is considered to be the ID. We re-slice the slice of strings to select the last item for the ID using `s[len(s)-1]` and the rest of the items for the remainder of the path using `s[:len(s)-1]`. On the same lines, we also rejoin the path segments with the `PathSeparator` constant to form a single string containing the path without the ID.

This supports any `collection/id` pair, which is all we need for our API. The following table shows the state of the `Path` type for the given original path string:

Original path string	Path	ID	HasID
/	/	nil	false
/people/	people	nil	false
/people/1/	people	1	true

Serving our API with one function

A web service is nothing more than a simple Go program that binds to a specific HTTP address and port and serves requests, so we get to use all our command-line tool writing knowledge and techniques.

> We also want to ensure that our `main` function is as simple and modest as possible, which is always a goal of coding, especially in Go.

Before writing our `main` function, let's look at a few design goals of our API program:

- We should be able to specify the HTTP address and port to which our API listens and the address of the MongoDB instances without having to recompile the program (through command-line flags)

  We want the program to gracefully shut down when we terminate it, allowing the in-flight requests (requests that are still being processed when the termination signal is sent to our program) to complete

- We want the program to log out status updates and report errors properly

Atop the `main.go` file, replace the `main` function placeholder with the following code:

```
func main() {
  var (
    addr  = flag.String("addr", ":8080", "endpoint
      address")
    mongo = flag.String("mongo", "localhost", "mongodb
      address")
  )
  log.Println("Dialing mongo", *mongo)
  db, err := mgo.Dial(*mongo)
  if err != nil {
    log.Fatalln("failed to connect to mongo:", err)
  }
  defer db.Close()
  s := &Server{
    db: db,
  }
  mux := http.NewServeMux()
  mux.HandleFunc("/polls/",
   withCORS(withAPIKey(s.handlePolls)))
  log.Println("Starting web server on", *addr)
  http.ListenAndServe(":8080", mux)
  log.Println("Stopping...")
}
```

This function is the entirety of our API `main` function. The first thing we do is specify two command-line flags, `addr` and `mongo`, with some sensible defaults and ask the `flag` package to parse them. We then attempt to dial the MongoDB database at the specified address. If we are unsuccessful, we abort with a call to `log.Fatalln`. Assuming the database is running and we are able to connect, we store the reference in the `db` variable before deferring the closing of the connection. This ensures that our program properly disconnects and tidies up after itself when it ends.

We create our server and specify the database dependency. We are calling our server `s`, which some people think is a bad practice because it's difficult to read code referring to a single letter variable and know what it is. However, since the scope of this variable is so small, we can be sure that its use will be very near to its definition, removing the potential for confusion.

We then create a new `http.ServeMux` object, which is a request multiplexer provided by the Go standard library, and register a single handler for all requests that begin with the `/polls/` path. Note that the `handlePolls` handler is a method on our server, and this is how it will be able to access the database.

Using handler function wrappers

It is when we call `HandleFunc` on the `ServeMux` handler that we are making use of our handler function wrappers with this line:

```
withCORS(withAPIKey(handlePolls))
```

Since each function takes an `http.HandlerFunc` type as an argument and also returns one, we are able to chain the execution just by nesting the function calls, as we have done previously. So when a request comes in with a path prefix of `/polls/`, the program will take the following execution path:

1. The `withCORS` function is called, which sets the appropriate header.
2. The `withAPIKey` function is called next, which checks the request for an API key and aborts if it's invalid or else calls the next handler function.
3. The `handlePolls` function is then called, which may use the helper functions in `respond.go` to write a response to the client.
4. Execution goes back to `withAPIKey`, which exits.
5. Execution finally goes back to `withCORS`, which exits.

Handling endpoints

The final piece of the puzzle is the `handlePolls` function, which will use the helpers to understand the incoming request and access the database and generate a meaningful response that will be sent back to the client. We also need to model the poll data that we were working with in the previous chapter.

Create a new file called `polls.go` and add the following code:

```
package main
import "gopkg.in/mgo.v2/bson"
type poll struct {
    ID      bson.ObjectId `bson:"_id" json:"id"`
    Title   string        `json:"title"`
    Options []string      `json:"options"`
```

```
    Results map[string]int `json:"results,omitempty"`
    APIKey  string          `json:"apikey"`
}
```

Here, we define a structure called `poll`, which has five fields that in turn describe the polls being created and maintained by the code we wrote in the previous chapter. We have also added the `APIKey` field, which you probably wouldn't do in the real world but which will allow us to demonstrate how we extract the API key from the context. Each field also has a tag (two in the `ID` case), which allows us to provide some extra metadata.

Using tags to add metadata to structs

Tags are just a string that follows a field definition within a `struct` type on the same line. We use the black tick character to denote literal strings, which means we are free to use double quotes within the tag string itself. The `reflect` package allows us to pull out the value associated with any key; in our case, both `bson` and `json` are examples of keys, and they are each key/value pair separated by a space character. Both the `encoding/json` and `gopkg.in/mgo.v2/bson` packages allow you to use tags to specify the field name that will be used with encoding and decoding (along with some other properties) rather than having it infer the values from the name of the fields themselves. We are using BSON to talk with the MongoDB database and JSON to talk to the client, so we can actually specify different views of the same `struct` type. For example, consider the ID field:

```
    ID bson.ObjectId `bson:"_id" json:"id"`
```

The name of the field in Go is `ID`, the JSON field is `id`, and the BSON field is `_id`, which is the special identifier field used in MongoDB.

Many operations with a single handler

Because our simple path-parsing solution cares only about the path, we have to do some extra work when looking at the kind of RESTful operation the client is making. Specifically, we need to consider the HTTP method so that we know how to handle the request. For example, a `GET` call to our `/polls/` path should read polls, where a `POST` call would create a new one. Some frameworks solve this problem for you by allowing you to map handlers based on more than the path, such as the HTTP method or the presence of specific headers in the request. Since our case is ultra simple, we are going to use a simple `switch` case. In `polls.go`, add the `handlePolls` function:

```
    func (s *Server) handlePolls(w http.ResponseWriter,
      r *http.Request) {
```

```
switch r.Method {
  case "GET":
  s.handlePollsGet(w, r)
  return
  case "POST":
  s.handlePollsPost(w, r)
  return
  case "DELETE":
  s.handlePollsDelete(w, r)
  return
}
// not found
respondHTTPErr(w, r, http.StatusNotFound)
}
```

We switch on the HTTP method and branch our code depending on whether it
is GET, POST, or DELETE. If the HTTP method is something else, we just respond with a 404
http.StatusNotFound error. To make this code compile, you can add the following
function stubs underneath the handlePolls handler:

```
func (s *Server) handlePollsGet(w http.ResponseWriter,
 r *http.Request) {
  respondErr(w, r, http.StatusInternalServerError,
   errors.New("not
  implemented"))
}
func (s *Server) handlePollsPost(w http.ResponseWriter,
 r *http.Request) {
  respondErr(w, r, http.StatusInternalServerError,
   errors.New("not
  implemented"))
}
func (s *Server) handlePollsDelete(w http.ResponseWriter,
  r *http.Request) {
  respondErr(w, r, http.StatusInternalServerError,
   errors.New("not
  implemented"))
}
```

In this section, we learned how to manually parse elements of the requests
(the HTTP method) and make decisions in code. This is great for simple
cases, but it's worth looking at packages such as Gorilla's mux package for
some more powerful ways of solving these problems. Nevertheless,
keeping external dependencies to a minimum is a core philosophy of
writing good and contained Go code.

Reading polls

Now it's time to implement the functionality of our web service. Add the following code:

```
func (s *Server) handlePollsGet(w http.ResponseWriter,
  r *http.Request) {
  session := s.db.Copy()
  defer session.Close()
  c := session.DB("ballots").C("polls")
  var q *mgo.Query
  p := NewPath(r.URL.Path)
  if p.HasID() {
    // get specific poll
    q = c.FindId(bson.ObjectIdHex(p.ID))
  } else {
    // get all polls
    q = c.Find(nil)
  }
  var result []*poll
  if err := q.All(&result); err != nil {
    respondErr(w, r, http.StatusInternalServerError, err)
    return
  }
  respond(w, r, http.StatusOK, &result)
}
```

The very first thing we do in each of our sub handler functions is create a copy of the database session that will allow us to interact with MongoDB. We then use mgo to create an object referring to the polls collection in the database —if you remember, this is where our polls live.

We then build up an mgo.Query object by parsing the path. If an ID is present, we use the FindId method on the polls collection; otherwise, we pass nil to the Find method, which indicates that we want to select all the polls. We are converting the ID from a string to a bson.ObjectId type with the ObjectIdHex method so that we can refer to the polls with their numerical (hex) identifiers.

Since the All method expects to generate a collection of poll objects, we define the result as []*poll or a slice of pointers to poll types. Calling the All method on the query will cause mgo to use its connection to MongoDB to read all the polls and populate the result object.

For small scale, such as a small number of polls, this approach is fine, but as the polls grow, we will need to consider a more sophisticated approach. We can page the results by iterating over them using the `Iter` method on the query and using the `Limit` and `Skip` methods, so we do not try to load too much data into the memory or present too much information to users in one go.

Now that we have added some functionality, let's try out our API for the first time. If you are using the same MongoDB instance that we set up in the previous chapter, you should already have some data in the `polls` collection; to see our API working properly, you should ensure there are at least two polls in the database.

If you need to add other polls to the database, in a terminal, run the `mongo` command to open a database shell that will allow you to interact with MongoDB. Then, enter the following commands to add some test polls:

```
> use ballots
switched to db ballots
> db.polls.insert({"title":"Test  poll","options":
  ["one","two","three"]})
> db.polls.insert({"title":"Test poll  two","options":
  ["four","five","six"]})
```

In a terminal, navigate to your `api` folder and build and run the project:

```
go build -o api
./api
```

Now make a GET request to the `/polls/` endpoint by navigating to `http://localhost:8080/polls/?key=abc123` in your browser; remember to include the trailing slash. The result will be an array of polls in the JSON format.

Copy and paste one of the IDs from the polls list and insert it before the ? character in the browser to access the data for a specific poll, for example, `http://localhost:8080/polls/5415b060a02cd4adb487c3ae?key=abc123`. Note that instead of returning all the polls, it only returns one.

Test the API key functionality by removing or changing the key parameter to see what the error looks like.

You might have also noticed that although we are only returning a single poll, this poll value is still nested inside an array. This is a deliberate design decision made for two reasons: the first and most important reason is that nesting makes it easier for users of the API to write code to consume the data. If users are always expecting a JSON array, they can write strong types that describe that expectation rather than having one type for single polls and another for collections of polls. As an API designer, this is your decision to make. The second reason we left the object nested in an array is that it makes the API code simpler, allowing us to just change the mgo.Query object and leave the rest of the code the same.

Creating a poll

Clients should be able to make a POST request to /polls/ in order to create a poll. Let's add the following code inside the POST case:

```go
func (s *Server) handlePollsPost(w http.ResponseWriter,
  r *http.Request) {
  session := s.db.Copy()
  defer session.Close()
  c := session.DB("ballots").C("polls")
  var p poll
  if err := decodeBody(r, &p); err != nil {
    respondErr(w, r, http.StatusBadRequest, "failed to
     read poll from request", err)
    return
  }
  apikey, ok := APIKey(r.Context())
  if ok {
    p.APIKey = apikey
  }
  p.ID = bson.NewObjectId()
  if err := c.Insert(p); err != nil {
    respondErr(w, r, http.StatusInternalServerError,
     "failed to insert
    poll", err)
    return
  }
  w.Header().Set("Location", "polls/"+p.ID.Hex())
  respond(w, r, http.StatusCreated, nil)
}
```

After we get a copy of the database session like earlier, we attempt to decode the body of the request that, according to RESTful principles, should contain a representation of the poll object the client wants to create. If an error occurs, we use the `respondErr` helper to write the error to the user and immediately exit from the function. We then generate a new unique ID for the poll and use the `mgo` package's `Insert` method to send it into the database. We then set the `Location` header of the response and respond with a `201` `http.StatusCreated` message, pointing to the URL from which the newly created poll may be accessed. Some APIs return the object instead of providing a link to it; there is no concrete standard so it's up to you as the designer.

Deleting a poll

The final piece of functionality we are going to include in our API is the ability to delete polls. By making a request with the `DELETE` HTTP method to the URL of a poll (such as `/polls/5415b060a02cd4adb487c3ae`), we want to be able to remove the poll from the database and return a `200 Success` response:

```
func (s *Server) handlePollsDelete(w http.ResponseWriter,
  r *http.Request) {
  session := s.db.Copy()
  defer session.Close()
  c := session.DB("ballots").C("polls")
  p := NewPath(r.URL.Path)
  if !p.HasID() {
    respondErr(w, r, http.StatusMethodNotAllowed,
      "Cannot delete all polls.")
    return
  }
  if err := c.RemoveId(bson.ObjectIdHex(p.ID)); err != nil {
    respondErr(w, r, http.StatusInternalServerError,
      "failed to delete poll", err)
    return
  }
  respond(w, r, http.StatusOK, nil) // ok
}
```

Similar to the GET case, we parse the path, but this time, we respond with an error if the path does not contain an ID. For now, we don't want people to be able to delete all polls with one request, and so we use the suitable StatusMethodNotAllowed code. Then, using the same collection we used in the previous cases, we call RemoveId, passing the ID in the path after converting it into a bson.ObjectId type. Assuming things go well, we respond with an http.StatusOK message with no body.

CORS support

In order for our DELETE capability to work over CORS, we must do a little extra work to support the way CORS browsers handle some HTTP methods such as DELETE. A CORS browser will actually send a preflight request (with an HTTP method of OPTIONS), asking for permission to make a DELETE request (listed in the Access-Control-Request-Method request header), and the API must respond appropriately in order for the request to work. Add another case in the switch statement for OPTIONS:

```
case "OPTIONS":
  w.Header().Add("Access-Control-Allow-Methods", "DELETE")
  respond(w, r, http.StatusOK, nil)
  return
```

If the browser asks for permission to send a DELETE request, the API will respond by setting the Access-Control-Allow-Methods header to DELETE, thus overriding the default * value that we set in our withCORS wrapper handler. In the real world, the value for the Access-Control-Allow-Methods header will change in response to the request made, but since DELETE is the only case we are supporting, we can hardcode it for now.

 The details of CORS are out of the scope of this book, but it is recommended that you research the particulars online if you intend to build truly accessible web services and APIs. Head over to http://enable -cors.org/ to get started.

Testing our API using curl

Curl is a command-line tool that allows us to make HTTP requests to our service so that we can access it as though we were a real app or client consuming the service.

Windows users do not have access to curl by default and will need to seek an alternative. Check out `http://curl.haxx.se/dlwiz/?type=bin` or search the Web for Windows curl alternative.

In a terminal, let's read all the polls in the database through our API. Navigate to your `api` folder and build and run the project and also ensure MongoDB is running:

```
go build -o api
./api
```

We then perform the following steps:

1. Enter the following `curl` command that uses the `-x` flag to denote we want to make a `GET` request to the specified URL:

```
curl -X GET http://localhost:8080/polls/?
key=abc123
```

2. The output is printed after you hit *Enter*:

```
[{"id":"541727b08ea48e5e5d5bb189","title":"Best
  Beatle?",
  "options": ["john","paul","george","ringo"]},
{"id":"541728728ea48e5e5d5bb18a","title":"Favorite
  language?",
  "options": ["go","java","javascript","ruby"]}]
```

3. While it isn't pretty, you can see that the API returns the polls from your database. Issue the following command to create a new poll:

```
curl --data '{"title":"test","options":
["one","two","three"]}'
-X POST http://localhost:8080/polls/?key=abc123
```

4. Get the list again to see the new poll included:

```
curl -X GET http://localhost:8080/polls/?
key=abc123
```

5. Copy and paste one of the IDs and adjust the URL to refer specifically to that poll:

```
curl -X GET
  http://localhost:8080/polls/541727b08ea48e5e5d5bb189?
  key=abc123
[{"id":"541727b08ea48e5e5d5bb189",","title":"Best  Beatle?",
  "options": ["john","paul","george","ringo"]}]
```

6. Now we see only the selected poll. Let's make a `DELETE` request to remove the poll:

```
curl -X DELETE
  http://localhost:8080/polls/541727b08ea48e5e5d5bb189?
  key=abc123
```

7. Now when we get all the polls again, we'll see that the Beatles poll has gone:

```
curl -X GET http://localhost:8080/polls/?key=abc123
[{"id":"541728728ea48e5e5d5bb18a","title":"Favorite
  language?","options":["go","java","javascript","ruby"]}]
```

So now that we know that our API is working as expected, it's time to build something that consumes the API properly.

A web client that consumes the API

We are going to put together an ultra simple web client that consumes the capabilities and data exposed through our API, allowing users to interact with the polling system we built in the previous chapter and earlier in this chapter. Our client will be made up of three web pages:

- An `index.html` page that shows all the polls
- A `view.html` page that shows the results of a specific poll
- A `new.html` page that allows users to create new polls

Create a new folder called `web` alongside the `api` folder and add the following content to the `main.go` file:

```go
package main
import (
  "flag"
  "log"
  "net/http"
)
func main() {
  var addr = flag.String("addr", ":8081", "website address")
  flag.Parse()
  mux := http.NewServeMux()
  mux.Handle("/", http.StripPrefix("/",
    http.FileServer(http.Dir("public"))))
  log.Println("Serving website at:", *addr)
```

```
    http.ListenAndServe(*addr, mux)
}
```

These few lines of Go code really highlight the beauty of the language and the Go standard library. They represent a complete, highly scalable, static website hosting program. The program takes an `addr` flag and uses the familiar `http.ServeMux` type to serve static files from a folder called `public`.

> Building the next few pages âⓞⓞwhile we're building the UI âⓞⓞconsists of writing a lot of HTML and JavaScript code. Since this is not Go code, if you'd rather not type it all out, feel free to head over to the GitHub repository for this book and copy and paste it from `https://github.com/matryer/goblueprints`. You are also free to include the latest versions of the Bootstrap and jQuery libraries as you see fit, but there may be implementation differences with subsequent versions.

Index page showing a list of polls

Create the `public` folder insideweb and add the `index.html` file after writing the following HTML code in it:

```html
<!DOCTYPE html>
<html>
<head>
  <title>Polls</title>
  <link rel="stylesheet"
    href="//maxcdn.bootstrapcdn.com/bootstrap/3.2.0/css/
    bootstrap.min.css">
</head>
<body>
</body>
</html>
```

We will use Bootstrap again to make our simple UI look nice, but we need to add two additional sections to the `body` tag of the HTML page. First, add the DOM elements that will display the list of polls:

```html
<div class="container">
  <div class="col-md-4"></div>
  <div class="col-md-4">
    <h1>Polls</h1>
    <ul id="polls"></ul>
    <a href="new.html" class="btn btn-primary">Create new poll</a>
  </div>
```

```
      <div class="col-md-4"></div>
    </div>
```

Here, we are using Bootstrap's grid system to center-align our content that is made up of a list of polls and a link to `new.html`, where users can create new polls.

Next, add the following `script` tags and JavaScript underneath that:

```
<script
src="//ajax.googleapis.com/ajax/libs/jquery/2.1.1/jquery.min.js"></script>
 <script>
  $(function(){
    var update = function(){
      $.get("http://localhost:8080/polls/?key=abc123", null, null,  "json")
        .done(function(polls){
          $("#polls").empty();
          for (var p in polls) {
            var poll = polls[p];
            $("#polls").append(
              $("<li>").append(
                $("<a>")
                  .attr("href", "view.html?poll=polls/" + poll.id)
                  .text(poll.title)
              )
            )
          }
        }
      );
      window.setTimeout(update, 10000);
    }
    update();
  });
</script>
```

We are using jQuery's `$.get` function to make an AJAX request to our web service. We are hardcoding the API URL âⓞⓞwhich, in practice, you might decide against âⓞⓞor at least use a domain name to abstract it. Once the polls have loaded, we use jQuery to build up a list containing hyperlinks to the `view.html` page, passing the ID of the poll as a query parameter.

Creating a new poll

To allow users to create a new poll, create a file called `new.html` inside the `public` folder, and add the following HTML code to the file:

```
<!DOCTYPE html>
<html>
<head>
  <title>Create Poll</title>
  <link rel="stylesheet"
    href="//maxcdn.bootstrapcdn.com/bootstrap/3.2.0/css/
    bootstrap.min.css">
</head>
<body>
  <script src="//ajax.googleapis.com/ajax/libs/jquery/2.1.1/jquery.min.js">
</script>
</body>
</html>
```

We are going to add the elements for an HTML form that will capture the information we need when creating a new poll, namely the title of the poll and the options. Add the following code inside the `body` tags:

```
<div class="container">
  <div class="col-md-4"></div>
  <form id="poll" role="form" class="col-md-4">
    <h2>Create Poll</h2>
    <div class="form-group">
      <label for="title">Title</label>
      <input type="text" class="form-control" id="title"
        placeholder="Title">
    </div>
    <div class="form-group">
      <label for="options">Options</label>
      <input type="text" class="form-control" id="options"
        placeholder="Options">
      <p class="help-block">Comma separated</p>
    </div>
    <button type="submit" class="btn btn-primary">
      Create Poll</button> or <a href="/">cancel</a>
  </form>
  <div class="col-md-4"></div>
</div>
```

Since our API speaks JSON, we need to do a bit of work to turn the HTML form into a JSON-encoded string and also break the comma-separated options string into an array of options. Add the following `script` tag:

```
<script>
  $(function(){
    var form = $("form#poll");
    form.submit(function(e){
      e.preventDefault();
      var title = form.find("input[id='title']").val();
      var options = form.find("input[id='options']").val();
      options = options.split(",");
      for (var opt in options) {
        options[opt] = options[opt].trim();
      }
      $.post("http://localhost:8080/polls/?key=abc123",
        JSON.stringify({
          title: title, options: options
        })
      ).done(function(d, s, r){
        location.href = "view.html?poll=" +
        r.getResponseHeader("Location");
      });
    });
  });
</script>
```

Here, we add a listener to the `submit` event of our form and use jQuery's `val` method to collect the input values. We split the options with a comma and trim the spaces away before using the `$.post` method to make the `POST` request to the appropriate API endpoint. `JSON.stringify` allows us to turn the data object into a JSON string, and we use that string as the body of the request, as expected by the API. On success, we pull out the `Location` header and redirect the user to the `view.html` page, passing a reference to the newly created poll as the parameter.

Showing the details of a poll

The final page of our app we need to complete is the `view.html` page, where users can see the details and live results of the poll. Create a new file called `view.html` inside the `public` folder and add the following HTML code to it:

```
<!DOCTYPE html>
<html>
<head>
```

```
<title>View Poll</title>
<link rel="stylesheet"
 href="//maxcdn.bootstrapcdn.com/bootstrap/3.2.0/css/bootstrap.min.css">
</head>
<body>
  <div class="container">
    <div class="col-md-4"></div>
    <div class="col-md-4">
      <h1 data-field="title">...</h1>
      <ul id="options"></ul>
      <div id="chart"></div>
      <div>
        <button class="btn btn-sm" id="delete">Delete this poll</button>
      </div>
    </div>
    <div class="col-md-4"></div>
  </div>
</body>
</html>
```

This page is mostly similar to the other pages; it contains elements to present the title of the poll, the options, and a pie chart. We will be mashing up Google's Visualization API with our API to present the results. Underneath the final div tag in view.html (and above the closing body tag), add the following script tags:

```
<script src="//www.google.com/jsapi"></script>
<script  src="//ajax.googleapis.com/ajax/libs/jquery/2.1.1/jquery.min.js">
</script>
<script>
google.load('visualization', '1.0', {'packages':['corechart']});
google.setOnLoadCallback(function(){
  $(function(){
    var chart;
    var poll = location.href.split("poll=")[1];
    var update = function(){
      $.get("http://localhost:8080/"+poll+"?key=abc123", null, null,
        "json")
        .done(function(polls){
          var poll = polls[0];
          $('[data-field="title"]').text(poll.title);
          $("#options").empty();
          for (var o in poll.results) {
            $("#options").append(
              $("<li>").append(
                $("<small>").addClass("label label
                default").text(poll.results[o]),
                " ", o
              )
```

```
          )
        }
        if (poll.results) {
          var data = new google.visualization.DataTable();
          data.addColumn("string","Option");
          data.addColumn("number","Votes");
          for (var o in poll.results) {
            data.addRow([o, poll.results[o]])
          }
          if (!chart) {
            chart = new                 google.visualization.PieChart
              (document.getElementById('chart'));
          }
          chart.draw(data, {is3D: true});
        }
      }
    );
    window.setTimeout(update, 1000);
  };
  update();
  $("#delete").click(function(){
    if (confirm("Sure?")) {
      $.ajax({
        url:"http://localhost:8080/"+poll+"?key=abc123",
        type:"DELETE"
      })
      .done(function(){
        location.href = "/";
      })
    }
  });
});
});
</script>
```

We include the dependencies we will need in order to power our page, jQuery and Bootstrap, and also the Google JavaScript API. The code loads the appropriate visualization libraries from Google and waits for the DOM elements to load before extracting the poll ID from the URL by splitting it on poll=. We then create a variable called update that represents a function responsible for generating the view of the page. This approach is taken to make it easy for us to use window.setTimeout in order to issue regular calls to update the view. Inside the update function, we use $.get to make a GET request to our /polls/{id} endpoint, replacing {id} with the actual ID we extracted from the URL earlier. Once the poll has loaded, we update the title on the page and iterate over the options to add them to the list. If there are results (remember, in the previous chapter, the results map was only added to the data as votes started being counted), we create a new

`google.visualization.PieChart` object and build a
`google.visualization.DataTable` object containing the results. Calling `draw` on the
chart causes it to render the data and thus update the chart with the latest numbers. We
then use `setTimeout` to tell our code to call `update` again in another second.

Finally, we bind to the `click` event of the `delete` button we added to our page, and after
asking the user whether they are sure, make a `DELETE` request to the polls URL and then
redirect them back to the home page. It is this request that will actually cause the `OPTIONS`
request to be made first, asking for permission, which is why we added explicit support for
it in our `handlePolls` function earlier.

Running the solution

We built many components over the previous two chapters, and it is now time to see them
all working together. This section contains everything you need in order to get all the items
running, assuming you have the environment set up properly, as described at the beginning
of the previous chapter. This section assumes you have a single folder that contains the four
subfolders: `api`, `counter`, `twittervotes`, and `web`.

Assuming nothing is running, take the following steps (each step in its own terminal
window):

1. In the top-level folder, start the `nsqlookupd` daemon:

   ```
   nsqlookupd
   ```

2. In the same directory, start the `nsqd` daemon:

   ```
   nsqd --lookupd-tcp-address=localhost:4160
   ```

3. Start the MongoDB daemon:

   ```
   mongod
   ```

4. Navigate to the `counter` folder and build and run it:

   ```
   cd counter
   go build -o counter
   ./counter
   ```

5. Navigate to the `twittervotes` folder and build and run it. Ensure that you have the appropriate environment variables set; otherwise, you will see errors when you run the program:

```
cd ../twittervotes
go build -o twittervotes
./twittervotes
```

6. Navigate to the `api` folder and build and run it:

```
cd ../api
go build -o api
./api
```

7. Navigate to the `web` folder and build and run it:

```
cd ../web
go build -o web
./web
```

Now that everything is running, open a browser and head to `http://localhost:8081/`. Using the user interface, create a poll called `Moods` and input the options as `happy`, `sad`, `fail`, `success`. These are common enough words that we are likely to see some relevant activity on Twitter.

Once you have created your poll, you will be taken to the view page where you will start to see the results coming in. Wait for a few seconds and enjoy the fruits of your hard work as the UI updates in real time, showing live, real-time results:

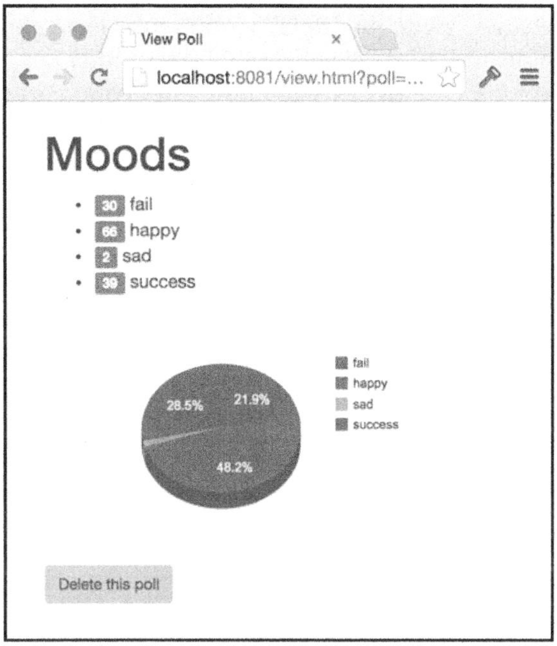

Summary

In this chapter, we exposed the data for our social polling solution through a highly scalable RESTful API and built a simple website that consumes the API to provide an intuitive way for users to interact with it. The website consists of static content only, with no server-side processing (since the API does the heavy lifting for us). This allows us to host the website very cheaply on static hosting sites, such as `bitballoon.com`, or distribute the files to content delivery networks.

Within our API service, we learned how to share data between handlers without breaking or obfuscating the handler pattern from the standard library. We also saw how writing wrapped handler functions allows us to build a pipeline of functionality in a very simple and intuitive way.

We wrote some basic encoding and decoding functions that â◎◎while only simply wrapping their counterparts from the `encoding/json` package for now â◎◎could be improved later to support a range of different data representations without changing the internal interface to our code. We wrote a few simple helper functions that make responding to data requests easy while providing the same kind of abstraction that would allow us to evolve our API later.

We saw how, for simple cases, switching to HTTP methods is an elegant way to support many functions for a single endpoint. We also saw how, with a few extra lines of code, we are able to build support for CORS in order to allow applications running on different domains to interact with our services âⓞⓞwithout the need for hacks such as JSONP.

In the next chapter, we will evolve our API and web skills to build a brand new startup app called Meander. We'll also explore an interesting way of representing enumerators in a language that doesn't officially support them.

7
Random Recommendations Web Service

The concept behind the project that we will build in this chapter is a simple one: we want users to be able to generate random recommendations for things to do in specific geographical locations based on a predefined set of journey types that we will expose through the API. We will give our project the codename Meander.

Often on projects in the real world, you are not responsible for the full stack; somebody else builds the website, a different person might write the iOS app, and maybe an outsourced company builds the desktop version. On more successful API projects, you might not even know who the consumers of your API are, especially if it's a public API.

In this chapter, we will simulate this reality by designing and agreeing a minimal API design with a fictional partner up front before going on to implement the API. Once we have finished our side of the project, we will download a user interface built by our teammates to see the two work together to produce the final application.

In this chapter, you will:

- Learn to express the general goals of a project using short and simple Agile user stories
- Discover that you can agree on a meeting point in a project by agreeing on the design of an API, which allows many people to work in parallel
- See how early versions can have data fixtures written in code and compiled into the program, allowing us to change the implementation later without touching the interface
- Learn a strategy that allows structs (and other types) to represent a public version of themselves for cases where we want to hide or transform internal representations

- Learn to use embedded structs to represent nested data while keeping the interface of our types simple
- Learn to use `http.Get` to make external API requests, specifically to the Google Places API, with no code bloat
- Learn to effectively implement enumerators in Go even though they aren't really a language feature
- Experience a real-world example of TDD
- Look at how the `math/rand` package makes it easy to select an item from a slice at random
- Learn an easy way to grab data from the URL parameters of the `http.Request` type

The project overview

Following Agile methodologies, let's write two user stories that describe the functionality of our project. User stories shouldn't be comprehensive documents describing the entire set of features of an application; rather, small cards are perfect for not only describing what the user is trying to do, but also why. Also, we should do this without trying to design the whole system up front or delving too deep into implementation details.

First, we need a story about seeing the different journey types from which our users can select:

As a	traveler
I want	to see the different types of journeys I can get recommendations for
So that	I can decide what kind of evening to take my partner on

Secondly, we need a story about providing random recommendations for a selected journey type:

As a	traveler
I want	to see a random recommendation for my selected journey type
So that	I know where to go and what the evening will entail

These two stories represent the two core capabilities that our API needs to provide and actually ends up representing two endpoints.

In order to discover places around specified locations, we are going to make use of the Google Places API, which allows us to search for listings of businesses with given types, such as `bar`, `café`, or `movie_theater`. We will then use Go's `math/rand` package to pick from these places at random, building up a complete journey for our users.

 The Google Places API supports many business types; refer to `https://developers.google.com/places/documentation/supported_types` for the complete list.

Project design specifics

In order to turn our stories into an interactive application, we are going to provide two JSON endpoints: one to deliver the kinds of journeys users will be able to select in the application and another to actually generate the random recommendations for the selected journey type.

```
GET /journeys
```

The preceding call should return a list similar to the following:

```
[
  {
    name: "Romantic",
    journey: "park|bar|movie_theater|restaurant|florist"
  },
  {
    name: "Shopping",
    journey: "department_store|clothing_store|jewelry_store"
  }
]
```

The `name` field is a human-readable label for the type of recommendations the app generates, and the `journey` field is a pipe-separated list of the supported journey types. It is the journey value that we will pass, as a URL parameter, into our other endpoint, which generates the actual recommendations:

```
GET /recommendations?
  lat=1&lng=2&journey=bar|cafe&radius=10&cost=$...$$$$$
```

This endpoint is responsible for querying the Google Places API and generating the recommendations before returning an array of place objects. We will use the parameters in the URL to control the kind of query to make. The `lat` and `lng` parameters representing latitude and longitude, respectively tell our API where in the world we want recommendations from, and the `radius` parameter represents the distance in meters around the point in which we are interested.

The `cost` value is a human-readable way of representing the price range for places that the API returns. It is made up of two values: a lower and upper range separated by three dots. The number of dollar characters represents the price level, with $ being the most affordable and $$$$$ being the most expensive. Using this pattern, a value of $...$$ would represent very low-cost recommendations, where $$$$...$$$$$ would represent a pretty expensive experience.

Some programmers might insist that the cost range is represented by numerical values, but since our API is going to be consumed by people, why not make things a little more interesting? It is up to you as the API designer.

An example payload for this call might look something like this:

```
[
  {
    icon: "http://maps.gstatic.com/mapfiles/place_api/icons/cafe-
    71.png",
    lat: 51.519583, lng: -0.146251,
    vicinity: "63 New Cavendish St, London",
    name: "Asia House",
    photos: [{
      url: "https://maps.googleapis.com/maps/api/place/photo?
      maxwidth=400&photoreference=CnRnAAAAyLRN"
    }]
  }, ...
]
```

The array returned contains a place object representing a random recommendation for each segment in the journey in the appropriate order. The preceding example is a cafÃ© in London. The data fields are fairly self-explanatory; the `lat` and `lng` fields represent the location of the place, the `name` and `vicinity` fields tell us what and where the business is, and the `photos` array gives us a list of relevant photographs from Google's servers. The `vicinity` and `icon` fields will help us deliver a richer experience to our users.

Representing data in code

We are first going to expose the journeys that users can select from; so, create a new folder called `meander` in GOPATH and add the following `journeys.go` code:

```go
package meander
type j struct {
  Name       string
  PlaceTypes []string
}
var Journeys = []interface{}{
  j{Name: "Romantic", PlaceTypes: []string{"park", "bar",
   "movie_theater", "restaurant", "florist", "taxi_stand"}},
  j{Name: "Shopping", PlaceTypes: []string{"department_store",  "cafe",
   "clothing_store", "jewelry_store", "shoe_store"}},
  j{Name: "Night Out", PlaceTypes: []string{"bar", "casino", "food",
   "bar", "night_club", "bar", "bar", "hospital"}},
  j{Name: "Culture", PlaceTypes: []string{"museum", "cafe", "cemetery",
   "library", "art_gallery"}},
  j{Name: "Pamper", PlaceTypes: []string{"hair_care",  "beauty_salon",
   "cafe", "spa"}},
}
```

Here, we define an internal type called `j` inside the `meander` package, which we then use to describe the journeys by creating instances of them inside the `Journeys` slice. This approach is an ultra-simple way of representing data in the code without building a dependency on an external data store.

> As an additional assignment, why not see if you can keep `golint` happy throughout this process? Every time you add some code, run `golint` for the packages and satisfy any suggestions that emerge. It cares a lot about exported items that have no documentation; so adding simple comments in the correct format will keep it happy. To learn more about `golint`, refer to https://github.com/golang/lint.

Of course, this is likely to evolve into just that later, maybe even with the ability for users to create and share their own journeys. Since we are exposing our data via an API, we are free to change the internal implementation without affecting the interface, so this approach is great for a version 1.

> We are using a slice of type `[]interface{}` because we will later implement a general way of exposing public data regardless of the actual types.

A romantic journey consists of a visit first to a park, then a bar, a movie theater, then a restaurant before a visit to a florist, and finally, a taxi ride home; you get the general idea. Feel free to get creative and add others by consulting the supported types in the Google Places API.

You might have noticed that since we are containing our code inside a package called `meander` (rather than `main`), our code can never be run as a tool like the other APIs we have written so far. Create two new folders inside meander so that you have a path that looks like `meander/cmd/meander`; this will house the actual command-line tool that exposes the `meander` package's capabilities via an HTTP endpoint.

Since we are primarily building a package for our meandering project (something that other tools can import and make use of), the code in the root folder is the `meander` package, and we nest our command (the `main` package) inside the `cmd` folder. We include the additional final `meander` folder to follow good practices where the command name is the same as the folder if we omitted it, our command would be called `cmd` instead of `meander`, which would get confusing.

Inside the `cmd/meander` folder, add the following code to the `main.go` file:

```
package main
func main() {
  //meander.APIKey = "TODO"
  http.HandleFunc("/journeys", func(w http.ResponseWriter,
  r *http.Request) {
    respond(w, r, meander.Journeys)
  })
  http.ListenAndServe(":8080", http.DefaultServeMux)
}
func respond(w http.ResponseWriter, r *http.Request, data  []interface{})
error {
  return json.NewEncoder(w).Encode(data)
}
```

You will recognize this as a simple API endpoint program, mapping to the `/journeys` endpoint.

You'll have to import the `encoding/json`, `net/http`, and `runtime` packages, along with your own `meander` package you created earlier.

We set the value of APIKey in the meander package (which is commented out for now, since we are yet to implement it) before calling the familiar HandleFunc function on the net/http package to bind our endpoint, which then just responds with the meander.Journeys variable. We borrow the abstract responding concept from the previous chapter by providing a respond function that encodes the specified data to the http.ResponseWriter type.

Let's run our API program by navigating to the cmd/meander folder in a terminal and using go run. We don't need to build this into an executable file at this stage since it's just a single file:

```
go run main.go
```

Hit the http://localhost:8080/journeys endpoint, and note that our Journeys data payload is served, which looks like this:

```
[{
  Name: "Romantic",
  PlaceTypes: [
    "park",
    "bar",
    "movie_theater",
    "restaurant",
    "florist",
    "taxi_stand"
  ]
}, ...]
```

This is perfectly acceptable, but there is one major flaw: it exposes internals about our implementation. If we changed the PlaceTypes field name to Types, promises made in our API would break, and it's important that we avoid this.

Projects evolve and change over time, especially successful ones, and as developers, we should do what we can to protect our customers from the impact of the evolution. Abstracting interfaces is a great way to do this, as is taking ownership of the public-facing view of our data objects.

Public views of Go structs

In order to control the public view of structs in Go, we need to invent a way to allow individual journey types to tell us how they want to be exposed. In the root meander folder, create a new file called public.go and add the following code:

```
package meander
type Facade interface {
  Public() interface{}
}
func Public(o interface{}) interface{} {
  if p, ok := o.(Facade); ok {
    return p.Public()
  }
  return o
}
```

The Facade interface exposes a single Public method, which will return the public view of a struct. The exported Public function takes any object and checks whether it implements the Facade interface (does it have a Public() interface{} method?); if it is implemented, it calls the method and returns the result otherwise, it just returns the original object untouched. This allows us to pass anything through the Public function before writing the result to the ResponseWriter object, allowing individual structs to control their public appearance.

> Normally, single method interfaces such as our Facade are named after the method they describe, such as Reader and Writer. However, Publicer is just confusing, so I deliberately broke the rule.

Let's implement a Public method for our j type by adding the following code to journeys.go:

```
func (j j) Public() interface{} {
  return map[string]interface{}{
    "name":    j.Name,
    "journey": strings.Join(j.PlaceTypes, "|"),
  }
}
```

The public view of our j type joins the PlaceTypes field into a single string separated by the pipe character as per our API design.

Head back to `cmd/meander/main.go` and replace the `respond` method with one that makes use of our new `Public` function:

```
func respond(w http.ResponseWriter, r *http.Request, data []interface{})
error {
  publicData := make([]interface{}, len(data))
  for i, d := range data {
    publicData[i] = meander.Public(d)
  }
  return json.NewEncoder(w).Encode(publicData)
}
```

Here, we iterate over the data slice calling the `meander.Public` function for each item, building the results into a new slice of the same size. In the case of our `j` type, its `Public` method will be called to serve the public view of the data rather than the default view. In a terminal, navigate to the `cmd/meander` folder again and run `go run main.go` before hitting `http://localhost:8080/journeys`. Note that the same data has now changed to a new structure:

```
[{
  journey: "park|bar|movie_theater|restaurant|florist|taxi_stand",
  name: "Romantic"
}, ...]
```

 An alternative way of achieving the same result would be to use tags to control the field names, as we have done in previous chapters, and implement your own `[]string` type that provides a `MarshalJSON` method which tells the encoder how to marshal your type. Both are perfectly acceptable, but the `Facade` interface and `Public` method are probably more expressive (if someone reads the code, isn't it obvious what's going on?) and give us more control.

Generating random recommendations

In order to obtain the places from which our code will randomly build up recommendations, we need to query the Google Places API. In the root `meander` folder, add the following `query.go` file:

```
package meander
type Place struct {
  *googleGeometry `json:"geometry"`
  Name            string          `json:"name"`
  Icon            string          `json:"icon"`
```

```
    Photos          []*googlePhoto `json:"photos"`
    Vicinity        string          `json:"vicinity"`
  }
  type googleResponse struct {
    Results []*Place `json:"results"`
  }
  type googleGeometry struct {
    *googleLocation `json:"location"`
  }
  type googleLocation struct {
    Lat float64 `json:"lat"`
    Lng float64 `json:"lng"`
  }
  type googlePhoto struct {
    PhotoRef string `json:"photo_reference"`
    URL      string `json:"url"`
  }
```

This code defines the structures we will need in order to parse the JSON response from the Google Places API into usable objects.

> Head over to the Google Places API documentation for an example of the response we are expecting. Refer to http://developers.google.com/pla ces/documentation/search.

Most of the preceding code will be obvious, but it's worth noting that the Place type embeds the googleGeometry type, which allows us to represent the nested data as per the API while essentially flattening it in our code. We do this with googleLocation inside googleGeometry, which means that we will be able to access the Lat and Lng values directly on a Place object even though they're technically nested in other structures.

Because we want to control how a Place object appears publically, let's give this type the following Public method:

```
  func (p *Place) Public() interface{} {
    return map[string]interface{}{
      "name":     p.Name,
      "icon":     p.Icon,
      "photos":   p.Photos,
      "vicinity": p.Vicinity,
      "lat":      p.Lat,
      "lng":      p.Lng,
    }
  }
```

Remember to run `golint` on this code to see which comments need to be added to the exported items.

The Google Places API key

Like with most APIs, we will need an API key in order to access the remote services. Head over to the Google APIs Console, sign in with a Google account, and create a key for the Google Places API. For more detailed instructions, refer to the documentation on the Google's developer website.

Once you have your key, let's create a variable inside the `meander` package that can hold it. At the top of `query.go`, add the following definition:

```
var APIKey string
```

Now nip back into `main.go`, remove the double slash `//` from the `APIKey` line, and replace the `TODO` value with the actual key provided by the Google APIs Console. Remember that it is bad practice to hardcode keys like this directly in your code; instead, it's worth breaking them out into environment variables, which keeps them out of your source code repository.

Enumerators in Go

To handle the various cost ranges for our API, it makes sense to use an enumerator (or **enum**) to denote the various values and handle conversions to and from string representations. Go doesn't explicitly provide enumerators as a language feature, but there is a neat way of implementing them, which we will explore in this section.

A simple flexible checklist to write enumerators in Go is as follows:

- Define a new type based on a primitive integer type
- Use that type whenever you need users to specify one of the appropriate values
- Use the `iota` keyword to set the values in a `const` block, disregarding the first zero value
- Implement a map of sensible string representations to the values of your enumerator

- Implement a `String` method on the type that returns the appropriate string representation from the map
- Implement a `ParseType` function that converts from a string to your type using the map

Now, we will write an enumerator to represent the cost levels in our API. Create a new file called `cost_level.go` inside the root `meander` folder and add the following code:

```
package meander
type Cost int8
const (
  _ Cost = iota
  Cost1
  Cost2
  Cost3
  Cost4
  Cost5
)
```

Here, we define the type of our enumerator, which we have called `Cost`, and since we need to represent a only few values, we have based it on an `int8` range. For enumerators where we need larger values, you are free to use any of the integer types that work with `iota`. The `Cost` type is now a real type in its own right, and we can use it wherever we need to represent one of the supported values for example, we can specify a `Cost` type as an argument in functions, or we can use it as the type for a field in a struct.

We then define a list of constants of that type and use the `iota` keyword to indicate that we want incrementing values for the constants. By disregarding the first `iota` value (which is always zero), we indicate that one of the specified constants must be explicitly used rather than the zero value.

To provide a string representation of our enumerator, we only need to add a `String` method to the `Cost` type. This is a useful exercise even if you don't need to use the strings in your code, because whenever you use the print calls from the Go standard library (such as `fmt.Println`), the numerical values will be used by default. Often, these values are meaningless and will require you to look them up and even count the lines to determine the numerical value for each item.

For more information on the `String()` method in Go, refer to the `Stringer` and `GoStringer` interfaces in the `fmt` package at `http://gola ng.org/pkg/fmt/#Stringer`.

Test-driven enumerator

To ensure that our enumerator code is working correctly, we are going to write unit tests that make some assertions about expected behavior.

Alongside `cost_level.go`, add a new file called `cost_level_test.go` and add the following unit test:

```
package meander_test
import (
  "testing"
  "github.com/cheekybits/is"
  "path/to/meander"
)
func TestCostValues(t *testing.T) {
  is := is.New(t)
  is.Equal(int(meander.Cost1), 1)
  is.Equal(int(meander.Cost2), 2)
  is.Equal(int(meander.Cost3), 3)
  is.Equal(int(meander.Cost4), 4)
  is.Equal(int(meander.Cost5), 5)
}
```

You will need to run `go get` in order to get the CheekyBits `is` package (from `https://github.com/cheekybits/is`).

The `is` package is an alternative testing helper package, but this one is ultra-simple and deliberately bare-bones. You get to pick your favorite when you write your own projects or use none at all.

Normally, we wouldn't worry about the actual integer value of constants in our enumerator, but since the Google Places API uses numerical values to represent the same thing, we need to care about the values.

You might have noticed something strange about this test file that breaks from convention. Although it is inside the root `meander` folder, it is not a part of the `meander` package; rather, it's in `meander_test`.
In Go, this is an error in every case except for tests. Because we are putting our test code into its own package, it means that we no longer have access to the internals of the `meander` package. Note how we have to use the package prefix. This may seem like a disadvantage, but in fact, it allows us to be sure that we are testing the package as though we were a real user of it. We may only call exported methods and only have visibility into exported types; just like our users. And we cannot mess around with

internals to do things that our users cannot; it's a true user test. In testing, sometimes you do need to fiddle with an internal state, in which case your tests would need to be in the same package as the code instead.

Run the tests by running `go test` in a terminal and note that it passes.

Let's add another test to make assertions about the string representations for each `Cost` constant. In `cost_level_test.go`, add the following unit test:

```
func TestCostString(t *testing.T) {
    is := is.New(t)
    is.Equal(meander.Cost1.String(), "$")
    is.Equal(meander.Cost2.String(), "$$")
    is.Equal(meander.Cost3.String(), "$$$")
    is.Equal(meander.Cost4.String(), "$$$$")
    is.Equal(meander.Cost5.String(), "$$$$$")
}
```

This test asserts that calling the `String` method for each constant yields the expected value. Running these tests will, of course, fail because we haven't implemented the `String` method yet.

Underneath the `Cost` constants, add the following map and the `String` method:

```
var costStrings = map[string]Cost{
    "$":     Cost1,
    "$$":    Cost2,
    "$$$":   Cost3,
    "$$$$":  Cost4,
    "$$$$$": Cost5,
}
func (l Cost) String() string {
    for s, v := range costStrings {
        if l == v {
            return s
        }
    }
    return "invalid"
}
```

The `map[string]Cost` variable maps the cost values to the string representation, and the `String` method iterates over the map to return the appropriate value.

In our case, a simple `strings.Repeat("$", int(1))` return would work just as well (and wins because it's simpler code); but it often won't; therefore, this section explores the general approach.

Now if we were to print out the `Cost3` value, we would actually see $$$, which is much more useful than numerical values. As we want to use these strings in our API, we are also going to add a `ParseCost` method.

In `cost_value_test.go`, add the following unit test:

```
func TestParseCost(t *testing.T) {
  is := is.New(t)
  is.Equal(meander.Cost1, meander.ParseCost("$"))
  is.Equal(meander.Cost2, meander.ParseCost("$$"))
  is.Equal(meander.Cost3, meander.ParseCost("$$$"))
  is.Equal(meander.Cost4, meander.ParseCost("$$$$"))
  is.Equal(meander.Cost5, meander.ParseCost("$$$$$"))
}
```

Here, we assert that calling `ParseCost` will, in fact, yield the appropriate value depending on the input string.

In `cost_value.go`, add the following implementation code:

```
func ParseCost(s string) Cost {
  return costStrings[s]
}
```

Parsing a `Cost` string is very simple since this is how our map is laid out.

As we need to represent a range of cost values, let's imagine a `CostRange` type and write the tests out for how we intend to use it. Add the following tests to `cost_value_test.go`:

```
func TestParseCostRange(t *testing.T) {
  is := is.New(t)
  var l meander.CostRange
  var err error
  l, err = meander.ParseCostRange("$$...$$$")
  is.NoErr(err)
  is.Equal(l.From, meander.Cost2)
  is.Equal(l.To, meander.Cost3)
  l, err = meander.ParseCostRange("$...$$$$$")
  is.NoErr(err)
  is.Equal(l.From, meander.Cost1)
  is.Equal(l.To, meander.Cost5)
}
```

```
func TestCostRangeString(t *testing.T) {
  is := is.New(t)
  r := meander.CostRange{
    From: meander.Cost2,
    To:   meander.Cost4,
  }
  is.Equal("$$...$$$$", r.String())
}
```

We specify that passing in a string with two dollar characters first, followed by three dots and then three dollar characters should create a new `meander.CostRange` type that has `From` set to `meander.Cost2` and `To` set to `meander.Cost3`. We also use `is.NoErr` in order to assert that no error is returned when we parse our strings. The second test does the reverse by testing that the `CostRange.String` method, which returns the appropriate value.

To make our tests pass, add the following `CostRange` type and the associated `String` and `ParseString` functions:

```
type CostRange struct {
  From Cost
  To   Cost
}
func (r CostRange) String() string {
  return r.From.String() + "..." + r.To.String()
}
func ParseCostRange(s string) (CostRange, error) {
  var r CostRange
  segs := strings.Split(s, "...")
  if len(segs) != 2 {
    return r, errors.New("invalid cost range")
  }
  r.From = ParseCost(segs[0])
  r.To = ParseCost(segs[1])
  return r, nil
}
```

This allows us to convert a string such as `$...$$$$$` to a structure that contains two `Cost` values: a `From` and `To` set and vice versa. If somebody passes in an invalid cost range (we just perform a simple check on the number of segments after splitting on the dots), then we return an error. You can do additional checking here if you want to, such as ensuring only dots and dollar signs are mentioned in the strings.

Querying the Google Places API

Now that we are capable of representing the results of the API, we need a way to represent and initiate the actual query. Add the following structure to query.go:

```
type Query struct {
  Lat          float64
  Lng          float64
  Journey      []string
  Radius       int
  CostRangeStr string
}
```

This structure contains all the information we will need in order to build up the query, all of which will actually come from the URL parameters in the requests from the client. Next, add the following find method, which will be responsible for making the actual request to Google's servers:

```
func (q *Query) find(types string) (*googleResponse, error) {
  u := "https://maps.googleapis.com/maps/api/place/nearbysearch/json"
  vals := make(url.Values)
  vals.Set("location", fmt.Sprintf("%g,%g", q.Lat, q.Lng))
  vals.Set("radius", fmt.Sprintf("%d", q.Radius))
  vals.Set("types", types)
  vals.Set("key", APIKey)
  if len(q.CostRangeStr) > 0 {
    r, err := ParseCostRange(q.CostRangeStr)
    if err != nil {
      return nil, err
    }
    vals.Set("minprice", fmt.Sprintf("%d", int(r.From)-1))
    vals.Set("maxprice", fmt.Sprintf("%d", int(r.To)-1))
  }
  res, err := http.Get(u + "?" + vals.Encode())
  if err != nil {
    return nil, err
  }
  defer res.Body.Close()
  var response googleResponse
  if err := json.NewDecoder(res.Body).Decode(&response); err != nil {
    return nil, err
  }
  return &response, nil
}
```

First, we build the request URL as per the Google Places API specification by appending the `url.Values` encoded string of the data for `lat`, `lng`, `radius`, and, of course, the `APIKey` values.

The `url.Values` type is actually a `map[string][]string` type, which is why we use `make` rather than `new`.

The `types` value we specify as an argument represents the kind of business to look for. If there is `CostRangeStr`, we parse it and set the `minprice` and `maxprice` values before finally calling `http.Get` to actually make the request. If the request is successful, we defer the closing of the response body and use a `json.Decoder` method to decode the JSON that comes back from the API into our `googleResponse` type.

Building recommendations

Next, we need to write a method that will allow us to make many calls to find for the different steps in a journey. Underneath the `find` method, add the following `Run` method to the `Query` struct:

```go
// Run runs the query concurrently, and returns the results.
func (q *Query) Run() []interface{} {
  rand.Seed(time.Now().UnixNano())
  var w sync.WaitGroup
  var l sync.Mutex
  places := make([]interface{}, len(q.Journey))
  for i, r := range q.Journey {
    w.Add(1)
    go func(types string, i int) {
      defer w.Done()
      response, err := q.find(types)
      if err != nil {
        log.Println("Failed to find places:", err)
        return
      }
      if len(response.Results) == 0 {
        log.Println("No places found for", types)
        return
      }
      for _, result := range response.Results {
        for _, photo := range result.Photos {
          photo.URL =
            "https://maps.googleapis.com/maps/api/place/photo?" +
```

```
                "maxwidth=1000&photoreference=" + photo.PhotoRef + "&key="
                + APIKey
        }
    }
    randI := rand.Intn(len(response.Results))
    l.Lock()
    places[i] = response.Results[randI]
    l.Unlock()
  }(r, i)
}
w.Wait() // wait for everything to finish
return places
}
```

The first thing we do is set the random seed to the current time in nanoseconds since January 1, 1970 UTC. This ensures that every time we call the Run method and use the rand package, the results will be different. If we don't do this, our code would suggest the same recommendations every time, which defeats the object.

Since we need to make many requests to Google and since we want to make sure this is as quick as possible we are going to run all the queries at the same time by making concurrent calls to our Query.find method. So next, we create sync.WaitGroup and a map to hold the selected places along with a sync.Mutex method to allow many goroutines to safely access the map concurrently.

We then iterate over each item in the Journey slice, which might be bar, cafe, or movie_theater. For each item, we add 1 to the WaitGroup object and start a goroutine. Inside the routine, we first defer the w.Done call, informing the WaitGroup object that this request has completed before calling our find method to make the actual request. Assuming no errors occurred and it was indeed able to find some places, we iterate over the results and build up a usable URL for any photos that might be present. According to the Google Places API, we are given a photoreference key, which we can use in another API call to get the actual image. To save our clients from having to have knowledge of the Google Places API at all, we build the complete URL for them.

We then lock the map locker and with a call to rand.Intn, pick one of the options at random and insert it into the right position in the places slice before unlocking sync.Mutex.

Finally, we wait for all goroutines to complete with a call to w.Wait before returning the places.

Handlers that use query parameters

Now we need to wire up our /recommendations call, so head back to main.go in the cmd/meander folder and add the following code inside the main function:

```
http.HandleFunc("/recommendations", cors(func(w
http.ResponseWriter, r *http.Request) {
    q := &meander.Query{
        Journey: strings.Split(r.URL.Query().Get("journey"), "|"),
    }
    var err error
    q.Lat, err = strconv.ParseFloat(r.URL.Query().Get("lat"), 64)
    if err != nil {
        http.Error(w, err.Error(), http.StatusBadRequest)
        return
    }
    q.Lng, err = strconv.ParseFloat(r.URL.Query().Get("lng"), 64)
    if err != nil {
        http.Error(w, err.Error(), http.StatusBadRequest)
        return
    }
    q.Radius, err = strconv.Atoi(r.URL.Query().Get("radius"))
    if err != nil {
        http.Error(w, err.Error(), http.StatusBadRequest)
        return
    }
    q.CostRangeStr = r.URL.Query().Get("cost")
    places := q.Run()
    respond(w, r, places)
}))
```

This handler is responsible for preparing the meander.Query object and calling its Run method before responding with the results. The http.Request type's URL value exposes the Query data that provides a Get method which, in turn, looks up a value for a given key.

The journey string is translated from the bar|cafe|movie_theater format to a slice of strings by splitting on the pipe character. Then, a few calls to functions in the strconv package turn the string latitude, longitude, and radius values into numerical types. If the values are in an incorrect format, we will get an error, which we will then write out to the client using the http.Error helper with an http.StatusBadRequest status.

CORS

The final piece of the first version of our API will be to implement CORS, as we did in the previous chapter. See if you can solve this problem yourself before reading on about the solution in the next section.

If you are going to tackle this yourself, remember that your aim is to set the `Access-Control-Allow-Origin` response header to `*`. Also, consider the `http.HandlerFunc` wrapping we did in the previous chapter. The best place for this code is probably in the `cmd/meander` program, since that is what exposes the functionality through an HTTP endpoint.

In `main.go`, add the following `cors` function:

```
func cors(f http.HandlerFunc) http.HandlerFunc {
  return func(w http.ResponseWriter, r *http.Request) {
    w.Header().Set("Access-Control-Allow-Origin", "*")
    f(w, r)
  }
}
```

This familiar pattern takes in an `http.HandlerFunc` type and returns a new one that sets the appropriate header before calling the passed-in function. Now, we can modify our code to make sure that the `cors` function gets called for both of our endpoints. Update the appropriate lines in the `main` function:

```
func main() {
  meander.APIKey = "YOUR_API_KEY"
  http.HandleFunc("/journeys", cors(func(w http.ResponseWriter,
  r *http.Request)
  {
    respond(w, r, meander.Journeys)
  }))
  http.HandleFunc("/recommendations", cors(func(w http.ResponseWriter,
  r *http.Request) {
    q := &meander.Query{
      Journey: strings.Split(r.URL.Query().Get("journey"), "|"),
    }
    var err error
    q.Lat, err = strconv.ParseFloat(r.URL.Query().Get("lat"), 64)
    if err != nil {
      http.Error(w, err.Error(), http.StatusBadRequest)
      return
    }
    q.Lng, err = strconv.ParseFloat(r.URL.Query().Get("lng"), 64)
```

```
      if err != nil {
        http.Error(w, err.Error(), http.StatusBadRequest)
        return
      }
      q.Radius, err = strconv.Atoi(r.URL.Query().Get("radius"))
      if err != nil {
        http.Error(w, err.Error(), http.StatusBadRequest)
        return
      }
      q.CostRangeStr = r.URL.Query().Get("cost")
      places := q.Run()
      respond(w, r, places)
    }))
    log.Println("serving meander API on :8080")
    http.ListenAndServe(":8080", http.DefaultServeMux)
  }
```

Now, calls to our API will be allowed from any domain without a cross-origin error occurring.

> Can you see a way to smarten up the code by removing the multiple calls to r.URL.Query()? Perhaps do this once and cache the result in a local variable. Then, you can avoid parsing the query many times.

Testing our API

Now that we are ready to test our API, head to a console and navigate to the cmd/meander folder. Because our program imports the meander package, building the program will automatically build our meander package too.

Build and run the program:

```
go build -o meanderapi
./meanderapi
```

To see meaningful results from our API, let's take a minute to find your actual latitude and longitude. Head over to http://mygeoposition.com/ and use the web tools to get the x, y values for a location you are familiar with.

Or, pick from these popular cities:

- London, England: 51.520707 x 0.153809
- New York, USA: 40.7127840 x -74.0059410

- Tokyo, Japan: `35.6894870 x 139.6917060`
- San Francisco, USA: `37.7749290 x -122.4194160`

Now, open a web browser and access the `/recommendations` endpoint with some appropriate values for the fields:

```
http://localhost:8080/recommendations?
  lat=51.520707&lng=-0.153809&radius=5000&
  journey=cafe|bar|casino|restaurant&
  cost=$...$$$
```

The following screenshot shows what a sample recommendation around London might look like:

Feel free to play around with the values in the URL to see how powerful the simple API is by trying various journey strings, tweaking the locations, and trying different cost range value strings.

Web application

We are going to download a complete web application built to the same API specifications and point it at our implementation to see it come to life before our eyes. Head over to `https://github.com/matryer/goblueprints/tree/master/chapter7/meanderweb` and download the `meanderweb` project into your `GOPATH` folder (alongside your root meander folder will do).

In a terminal, navigate to the `meanderweb` folder and build and run it:

```
go build -o meanderweb
./meanderweb
```

This will start a website running on `localhost:8081`, which is hardcoded to look for the API running at `localhost:8080`. Because we added the CORS support, this won't be a problem despite them running on different domains.

Open a browser to `http://localhost:8081/` and interact with the application; while somebody else built the UI, it would be pretty useless without the API that we built in order to power it.

Summary

In this chapter, we built an API that consumes and abstracts the Google Places API to provide a fun and interesting way of letting users plan their days and evenings.

We started by writing some simple and short user stories that described what we wanted to achieve at a really high level without trying to design the implementation up front. In order to parallelize the project, we agreed upon the meeting point of the project as the API design, and we built toward it (as would our partners).

We embedded data directly in the code, avoiding the need to investigate, design, and implement a data store in the early stages of a project. By caring about how that data is accessed (via the API endpoint) instead, we allowed our future selves to completely change how and where the data is stored without breaking any apps that have been written with our API.

We implemented the `Facade` interface, which allows our structs and other types to provide public representations of them without revealing messy or sensitive details about our implementation.

Our foray into enumerators gave us a useful starting point to build enumerated types, even though there is no official support for them in the language. The `iota` keyword that we used lets us specify constants of our own numerical type, with incrementing values. The common `String` method that we implemented showed us how to make sure that our enumerated types don't become obscure numbers in our logs. At the same time, we also saw a real-world example of TDD and red/green programming, where we wrote unit tests that first fail but which we then go on to make pass by writing the implementation code.

In the next chapter, we are going to take a break from web services in order to build a backup tool for our code, where we'll explore how easy Go makes it for us to interact with the local filesystem.

8
Filesystem Backup

There are many solutions that provide filesystem backup capabilities. These include everything from apps such as Dropbox, Box, and Carbonite to hardware solutions such as Apple's Time Machine, Seagate, or network-attached storage products, to name a few. Most consumer tools provide some key automatic functionality, along with an app or website for you to manage your policies and content. Often, especially for developers, these tools don't quite do the things we need them to. However, thanks to Go's standard library (which includes packages such as ioutil and os), we have everything we need to build a backup solution that behaves exactly the way we need it to.

For our next project, we will build a simple filesystem backup for our source code projects that archive specified folders and save a snapshot of them every time we make a change. The change could be when we tweak a file and save it, when we add new files and folders, or even when we delete a file. We want to be able to go back to any point in time to retrieve old files.

Specifically, in this chapter, you will learn about the following topics:

- How to structure projects that consist of packages and command-line tools
- A pragmatic approach to persisting simple data across tool executions
- How the os package allows you to interact with a filesystem
- How to run code in an infinite timed loop while respecting *Ctrl + C*
- How to use filepath.Walk to iterate over files and folders
- How to quickly determine whether the contents of a directory have changed
- How to use the archive/zip package to zip files
- How to build tools that care about a combination of command-line flags and normal arguments

Solution design

We will start by listing some high-level acceptance criteria for our solution and the approach we want to take:

- The solution should create a snapshot of our files at regular intervals as we make changes to our source code projects
- We want to control the interval at which the directories are checked for changes
- Code projects are primarily text-based, so zipping the directories to generate archives will save a lot of space
- We will build this project quickly, while keeping a close watch over where we might want to make improvements later
- Any implementation decisions we make should be easily modified if we decide to change our implementation in the future
- We will build two command-line tools: the backend daemon that does the work and a user interaction utility that will let us list, add, and remove paths from the backup service

The project structure

It is common in Go solutions to have, in a single project, both a package that allows other Go programmers to use your capabilities and a command-line tool that allows end users to use your programs.

As we saw in the last chapter, a convention to structure such projects is emerging whereby we have the package in the main project project folder and the command-line tool inside a subfolder called `cmd` or `cmds` if you have multiple commands. Because all packages are equal in Go (regardless of the directory tree), you can import the package from the command subpackages, knowing you'll never need to import the commands from the project package (which is illegal as you can't have cyclical dependencies). This may seem like an unnecessary abstraction, but it is actually quite a common pattern and can be seen in the standard Go tool chain with examples such as `gofmt` and `goimports`.

For example, for our project, we are going to write a package called `backup` and two command-line tools: the daemon and the user interaction tool. We will structure our project in the following way:

```
/backup - package
/backup/cmds/backup - user interaction tool
/backup/cmds/backupd - worker daemon
```

The reason we don't just put code directly inside the cmd folder (even if we only had one command) is that when go install builds projects, it uses the name of the folder as the command name, and it wouldn't be very useful if all of our tools were called cmd.

The backup package

We are first going to write the backup package, of which we will become the first customer when we write the associated tools. The package will be responsible for deciding whether directories have changed and need backing up or not as well as actually performing the backup procedure.

Considering obvious interfaces first

One of the early things to think about when embarking on a new Go program is whether any interfaces stand out to you. We don't want to over-abstract or waste too much time upfront designing something that we know will change as we start to code, but that doesn't mean we shouldn't look for obvious concepts that are worth pulling out. If you're not sure, that is perfectly acceptable; you should write your code using concrete types and revisit potential abstractions after you have actually solved the problems.

However, since our code will archive files, the Archiver interface pops out as a candidate.

Create a new folder inside your GOPATH/src folder called backup, and add the following archiver.go code:

```
package backup
type Archiver interface {
  Archive(src, dest string) error
}
```

An Archiver interface will specify a method called Archive, which takes source and destination paths and returns an error. Implementations of this interface will be responsible for archiving the source folder and storing it in the destination path.

Defining an interface up front is a nice way to get some concepts out of our heads and into the code; it doesn't mean that this interface can't change as we evolve our solution as long as we remember the power of simple interfaces. Also, remember that most of the I/O interfaces in the io package expose only a single method.

From the very beginning, we have made the case that while we are going to implement ZIP files as our archive format, we could easily swap this out later with another kind of `Archiver` format.

Testing interfaces by implementing them

Now that we have the interface for our `Archiver` types, we are going to implement one that uses the ZIP file format.

Add the following `struct` definition to `archiver.go`:

```
type zipper struct{}
```

We are not going to export this type, which might make you jump to the conclusion that users outside of the package won't be able to make use of it. In fact, we are going to provide them with an instance of the type for them to use in order to save them from having to worry about creating and managing their own types.

Add the following exported implementation:

```
// Zip is an Archiver that zips and unzips files.
var ZIP Archiver = (*zipper)(nil)
```

This curious snippet of Go voodoo is actually a very interesting way of exposing the intent to the compiler without using any memory (literally 0 bytes). We are defining a variable called `ZIP` of type `Archiver`, so from outside the package, it's pretty clear that we can use that variable wherever `Archiver` is needed if you want to zip things. Then, we assign it with `nil` cast to the type `*zipper`. We know that `nil` takes no memory, but since it's cast to a `zipper` pointer, and given that our `zipper` struct has no state, it's an appropriate way of solving a problem, which hides the complexity of code (and indeed the actual implementation) from outside users. There is no reason anybody outside of the package needs to know about our `zipper` type at all, which frees us up to change the internals without touching the externals at any time: the true power of interfaces.

Another handy side benefit to this trick is that the compiler will now be checking whether our zipper type properly implements the `Archiver` interface or not, so if you try to build this code, you'll get a compiler error:

```
./archiver.go:10: cannot use (*zipper)(nil) (type *zipper) as type
Archiver in assignment:
  *zipper does not implement Archiver (missing Archive method)
```

We see that our `zipper` type does not implement the `Archive` method as mandated in the interface.

> You can also use the `Archive` method in test code to ensure that your types implement the interfaces they should. If you don't need to use the variable, you can always throw it away using an underscore and you'll still get the compiler help:
>
> ```
> var _ Interface = (*Implementation)(nil)
> ```

To make the compiler happy, we are going to add the implementation of the `Archive` method for our `zipper` type.

Add the following code to `archiver.go`:

```go
func (z *zipper) Archive(src, dest string) error {
  if err := os.MkdirAll(filepath.Dir(dest), 0777); err != nil {
    return err
  }
  out, err := os.Create(dest)
  if err != nil {
    return err
  }
  defer out.Close()
  w := zip.NewWriter(out)
  defer w.Close()
  return filepath.Walk(src, func(path string, info os.FileInfo, err error)
  error {
    if info.IsDir() {
      return nil // skip
    }
    if err != nil {
      return err
    }
    in, err := os.Open(path)
    if err != nil {
      return err
    }
    defer in.Close()
    f, err := w.Create(path)
    if err != nil {
      return err
    }
    _, err = io.Copy(f, in)
    if err != nil {
      return err
```

```
        }
        return nil
    })
}
```

You will also have to import the `archive/zip` package from the Go standard library. In our `Archive` method, we take the following steps to prepare writing to a ZIP file:

- Use `os.MkdirAll` to ensure that the destination directory exists. The `0777` code represents the file permissions with which you may need to create any missing directories
- Use `os.Create` to create a new file as specified by the `dest` path
- If the file is created without an error, defer the closing of the file with `defer out.Close()`
- Use `zip.NewWriter` to create a new `zip.Writer` type that will write to the file we just created and defer the closing of the writer

Once we have a `zip.Writer` type ready to go, we use the `filepath.Walk` function to iterate over the source directory, `src`.

The `filepath.Walk` function takes two arguments: the root path and a callback function to be called for every item (files and folders) it encounters while iterating over the filesystem.

Functions are first class types in Go, which means you can use them as argument types as well as global functions and methods. The `filepath.Walk` function specifies the second argument type as `filepath.WalkFunc`, which is a function with a specific signature. As long as we adhere to the signature (correct input and return arguments) we can write inline functions rather than worrying about the `filepath.WalkFunc` type at all.
Taking a quick look at the Go source code tell us that the signature for `filepath.WalkFunc` matches the function we are passing in `func(path string, info os.FileInfo, err error) error`

The `filepath.Walk` function is recursive, so it will travel deep into subfolders too. The callback function itself takes three arguments: the full path of the file, the `os.FileInfo` object that describes the file or folder itself, and an error (it also returns an error in case something goes wrong). If any calls to the callback function result in an error (other than the special `SkipDir` error value) being returned, the operation will be aborted and `filepath.Walk` returns that error. We simply pass this up to the caller of `Archive` and let them worry about it, since there's nothing more we can do.

For each item in the tree, our code takes the following steps:

- If the `info.IsDir` method tells us that the item is a folder, we just return `nil`, effectively skipping it. There is no reason to add folders to ZIP archives because the path of the files will encode that information for us.
- If an error is passed in (via the third argument), it means something went wrong when trying to access information about the file. This is uncommon, so we just return the error, which will eventually be passed out to the caller of `Archive`. As the implementor of `filepath.Walk`, you aren't forced to abort the operation here; you are free to do whatever makes sense in your individual case.
- Use `os.Open` to open the source file for reading, and if successful, defer its closing.
- Call `Create` on the `ZipWriter` object to indicate that we want to create a new compressed file and give it the full path of the file, which includes the directories it is nested inside.
- Use `io.Copy` to read all of the bytes from the source file and write them through the `ZipWriter` object to the ZIP file we opened earlier.
- Return `nil` to indicate no errors.

This chapter will not cover unit testing or **Test-driven Development** (TDD) practices, but feel free to write a test to ensure that our implementation does what it is meant to do.

 Since we are writing a package, spend some time commenting on the exported pieces so far. You can use `golint` to help you find anything you may have missed.

Has the filesystem changed?

One of the biggest problems our backup system has is deciding whether a folder has changed or not in a cross-platform, predictable, and reliable way. After all, there's no point in creating a backup if nothing is different from the previous backup. A few things spring to mind when we think about this problem: should we just check the last modified date on the top-level folder? Should we use system notifications to be informed whenever a file we care about changes? There are problems with both of these approaches, and it turns out it's not a simple problem to solve.

Check out the `fsnotify` project at `https://fsnotify.org` (project source: `https://github.com/fsnotify`). The authors are attempting to build a cross-platform package for subscription to filesystem events. At the time of writing this, the project is still in its infancy and it not a viable option for this chapter, but in the future, it could well become the standard solution for filesystem events.

We are, instead, going to generate an MD5 hash made up of all of the information that we care about when considering whether something has changed or not.

Looking at the `os.FileInfo` type, we can see that we can find out a lot of information about a file or folder:

```
type FileInfo interface {
  Name()  string      // base name of the file
  Size()  int64       // length in bytes for regular files;
                      // system-dependent for others
  Mode()  FileMode    // file mode bits
  ModTime() time.Time // modification time
  IsDir() bool        // abbreviation for Mode().IsDir()
  Sys()  interface{}  // underlying data source (can return nil)
}
```

To ensure we are aware of a variety of changes to any file in a folder, the hash will be made up of the filename and path (so if they rename a file, the hash will be different), size (if a file changes size, it's obviously different), the last modified date, whether the item is a file or folder, and the file mode bits. Even though we won't be archiving the folders, we still care about their names and the tree structure of the folder.

Create a new file called `dirhash.go` and add the following function:

```
package backup
import (
  "crypto/md5"
  "fmt"
  "io"
  "os"
  "path/filepath"
)
func DirHash(path string) (string, error) {
  hash := md5.New()
  err := filepath.Walk(path, func(path string, info os.FileInfo, err error)
  error {
    if err != nil {
      return err
    }
```

```
    io.WriteString(hash, path)
    fmt.Fprintf(hash, "%v", info.IsDir())
    fmt.Fprintf(hash, "%v", info.ModTime())
    fmt.Fprintf(hash, "%v", info.Mode())
    fmt.Fprintf(hash, "%v", info.Name())
    fmt.Fprintf(hash, "%v", info.Size())
    return nil
  })
  if err != nil {
    return "", err
  }
  return fmt.Sprintf("%x", hash.Sum(nil)), nil
}
```

We first create a new hash.Hash function that knows how to calculate MD5s before using filepath.Walk again to iterate over all of the files and folders inside the specified path directory. For each item, assuming there are no errors, we write the differential information to the hash generator using io.WriteString, which lets us write a string to io.Writer and fmt.Fprintf, which does the same but exposes formatting capabilities at the same time, allowing us to generate the default value format for each item using the %v format verb.

Once each file has been processed, and assuming no errors occurred, we then use fmt.Sprintf to generate the result string. The Sum method in hash.Hash calculates the final hash value with the specified values appended. In our case, we do not want to append anything since we've already added all of the information we care about, so we just pass nil. The %x format verb indicates that we want the value to be represented in hex (base 16) with lowercase letters. This is the usual way of representing an MD5 hash.

Checking for changes and initiating a backup

Now that we have the ability to hash a folder and perform a backup, we are going to put the two together in a new type called Monitor. The Monitor type will have a map of paths with their associated hashes, a reference to any Archiver type (of course, we'll use backup.ZIP for now), and a destination string representing where to put the archives.

Create a new file called monitor.go and add the following definition:

```
type Monitor struct {
  Paths        map[string]string
  Archiver     Archiver
  Destination  string
}
```

In order to trigger a check for changes, we are going to add the following `Now` method:

```go
func (m *Monitor) Now() (int, error) {
  var counter int
  for path, lastHash := range m.Paths {
    newHash, err := DirHash(path)
    if err != nil {
      return counter, err
    }
    if newHash != lastHash {
      err := m.act(path)
      if err != nil {
        return counter, err
      }
      m.Paths[path] = newHash // update the hash
      counter++
    }
  }
  return counter, nil
}
```

The `Now` method iterates over every path in the map and generates the latest hash of that folder. If the hash does not match the hash from the map (generated the last time it checked), then it is considered to have changed and needs backing up again. We do this with a call to the as-yet-unwritten `act` method before then updating the hash in the map with this new hash.

To give our users a high-level indication of what happened when they called `Now`, we are also maintaining a counter, which we increment every time we back up a folder. We will use this later to keep our end users up to date on what the system is doing without bombarding them with information:

```
m.act undefined (type *Monitor has no field or method act)
```

The compiler is helping us again and reminding us that we have yet to add the `act` method:

```go
func (m *Monitor) act(path string) error {
  dirname := filepath.Base(path)
  filename := fmt.Sprintf("%d.zip", time.Now().UnixNano())
  return m.Archiver.Archive(path, filepath.Join(m.Destination,  dirname,
filename))
}
```

Because we have done the heavy lifting in our ZIP `Archiver` type, all we have to do here is generate a filename, decide where the archive will go, and call the `Archive` method.

If the `Archive` method returns an error, the `act` method and then the `Now` method will each return it. This mechanism of passing errors up the chain is very common in Go and allows you to either handle cases where you can do something useful to recover or else defer the problem to somebody else.

The `act` method in the preceding code uses `time.Now().UnixNano()` to generate a timestamp filename and hardcodes the `.zip` extension.

Hardcoding is OK for a short while

Hardcoding the file extension like we have is OK in the beginning, but if you think about it, we have blended concerns a little here. If we change the `Archiver` implementation to use RAR or a compression format of our making, the `.zip` extension would no longer be appropriate.

Before reading on, think about what steps you might take to avoid this hardcoding. Where does the filename extension decision live? What changes would you need to make in order to avoid hardcoding?

The right place for the filename extensions decision is probably in the `Archiver` interface, since it knows the kind of archiving it will be doing. So we could add an `Ext()` string method and access that from our `act` method. But we can add a little extra power with not much extra work by allowing `Archiver` authors to specify the entire filename format rather than just the extension instead.

Back in `archiver.go`, update the `Archiver` interface definition:

```
type Archiver interface {
  DestFmt() string
  Archive(src, dest string) error
}
```

Our `zipper` type needs to now implement this:

```
func (z *zipper) DestFmt() string {
  return "%d.zip"
}
```

Now that we can ask our `act` method to get the whole format string from the `Archiver` interface, update the `act` method:

```
func (m *Monitor) act(path string) error {
```

```
    dirname := filepath.Base(path)
    filename := fmt.Sprintf(m.Archiver.DestFmt(), time.Now().UnixNano())
    return m.Archiver.Archive(path, filepath.Join(m.Destination, dirname,
    filename))
}
```

The user command-line tool

The first of two tools we will build allows the user to add, list, and remove paths for the backup daemon tool (which we will write later). You can expose a web interface or even use the binding packages for the desktop user interface integration, but we are going to keep things simple and build ourselves a command-line tool.

Create a new folder called cmds inside the backup folder and create another backup folder inside that so you have backup/cmds/backup.

Inside our new backup folder, add the following code to main.go:

```
func main() {
  var fatalErr error
  defer func() {
    if fatalErr != nil {
      flag.PrintDefaults()
      log.Fatalln(fatalErr)
    }
  }()
  var (
    dbpath = flag.String("db", "./backupdata", "path to database
directory")
  )
  flag.Parse()
  args := flag.Args()
  if len(args) < 1 {
    fatalErr = errors.New("invalid usage; must specify command")
    return
  }
}
```

We first define our fatalErr variable and defer the function that checks to ensure that value is nil. If it is not, it will print the error along with flag defaults and exit with a nonzero status code. We then define a flag called db that expects the path to the filedb database directory before parsing the flags and getting the remaining arguments and ensuring that there is at least one.

Persisting small data

In order to keep track of the paths and the hashes that we generate, we will need some kind of data storage mechanism that ideally works even when we stop and start our programs. We have lots of choices here: everything from a text file to a full horizontally scalable database solution. The Go ethos of simplicity tells us that building-in a database dependency to our little backup program would not be a great idea; rather, we should ask what the simplest way in which we can solve this problem is.

The `github.com/matryer/filedb` package is an experimental solution for just this kind of problem. It lets you interact with the filesystem as though it were a very simple, schemaless database. It takes its design lead from packages such as `mgo` and can be used in cases where data querying needs are very simple. In `filedb`, a database is a folder, and a collection is a file where each line represents a different record. Of course, this could all change as the `filedb` project evolves, but the interface, hopefully, won't.

 Adding dependencies such as this to a Go project should be done very carefully because over time, dependencies go stale, change beyond their initial scope, or disappear altogether in some cases. While it sounds counterintuitive, you should consider whether copying and pasting a few files into your project is a better solution than relying on an external dependency. Alternatively, consider vendoring the dependency by copying the entire package into the `vendor` folder of your command. This is akin to storing a snapshot of the dependency that you know works for your tool.

Add the following code to the end of the `main` function:

```
db, err := filedb.Dial(*dbpath)
if err != nil {
  fatalErr = err
  return
}
defer db.Close()
col, err := db.C("paths")
if err != nil {
  fatalErr = err
  return
}
```

Here, we use the `filedb.Dial` function to connect with the `filedb` database. In actuality, nothing much happens here except specifying where the database is, since there are no real database servers to connect to (although this might change in the future, which is why such provisions exist in the interface). If that was successful, we defer the closing of the database.

Closing the database does actually do something, since files may be open that need to be cleaned up.

Following the `mgo` pattern, next we specify a collection using the `C` method and keep a reference to it in the `col` variable. If an error occurs at any point, we assign it to the `fatalErr` variable and return.

To store data, we are going to define a type called `path`, which will store the full path and the last hash value and use JSON encoding to store this in our `filedb` database. Add the following `struct` definition above the `main` function:

```
type path struct {
  Path string
  Hash string
}
```

Parsing arguments

When we call `flag.Args` (as opposed to `os.Args`), we receive a slice of arguments excluding the flags. This allows us to mix flag arguments and non-flag arguments in the same tool.

We want our tool to be able to be used in the following ways:

- To add a path:

  ```
  backup -db=/path/to/db add {path} [paths...]
  ```

- To remove a path:

  ```
  backup -db=/path/to/db remove {path} [paths...]
  ```

- To list all paths:

  ```
  backup -db=/path/to/db list
  ```

To achieve this, since we have already dealt with flags, we must check the first (non-flag) argument.

Add the following code to the `main` function:

```
switch strings.ToLower(args[0]) {
case "list":
case "add":
case "remove":
}
```

Here, we simply switch on the first argument after setting it to lowercase (if the user types `backup LIST`, we still want it to work).

Listing the paths

To list the paths in the database, we are going to use a `ForEach` method on the path's `col` variable. Add the following code to the list case:

```
var path path
col.ForEach(func(i int, data []byte) bool {
  err := json.Unmarshal(data, &path)
  if err != nil {
    fatalErr = err
    return true
  }
  fmt.Printf("= %s\n", path)
  return false
})
```

We pass in a callback function to `ForEach`, which will be called for every item in that collection. We then unmarshal it from JSON into our `path` type, and just print it out using `fmt.Printf`. We return `false` as per the `filedb` interface, which tells us that returning `true` would stop iterating and that we want to make sure we list them all.

String representations for your own types

If you print structs in Go in this way, using the `%s` format verbs, you can get some messy results that are difficult for users to read. If, however, the type implements a `String()` string method, it will be used instead, and we can use this to control what gets printed. Below the path struct, add the following method:

```
func (p path) String() string {
  return fmt.Sprintf("%s [%s]", p.Path, p.Hash)
}
```

This tells the `path` type how it should represent itself as a string.

Adding paths

To add a path, or many paths, we are going to iterate over the remaining arguments and call the `InsertJSON` method for each one. Add the following code to the `add` case:

```
if len(args[1:]) == 0 {
  fatalErr = errors.New("must specify path to add")
  return
}
for _, p := range args[1:] {
  path := &path{Path: p, Hash: "Not yet archived"}
  if err := col.InsertJSON(path); err != nil {
    fatalErr = err
    return
  }
  fmt.Printf("+ %s\n", path)
}
```

If the user hasn't specified any additional arguments, for example if they just called `backup add` without typing any paths, we will return a fatal error. Otherwise, we do the work and print out the path string (prefixed with a + symbol) to indicate that it was successfully added. By default, we'll set the hash to the `Not yet archived` string literal this is an invalid hash but serves the dual purposes of letting the user know that it hasn't yet been archived as well as indicating as such to our code (given that a hash of the folder will never equal that string).

Removing paths

To remove a path, or many paths, we use the `RemoveEach` method for the path's collection. Add the following code to the `remove` case:

```
var path path
col.RemoveEach(func(i int, data []byte) (bool, bool) {
  err := json.Unmarshal(data, &path)
  if err != nil {
    fatalErr = err
    return false, true
  }
  for _, p := range args[1:] {
    if path.Path == p {
      fmt.Printf("- %s\n", path)
      return true, false
    }
  }
  return false, false
```

```
})
```

The callback function we provide to `RemoveEach` expects us to return two bool types: the first one indicates whether the item should be removed or not, and the second one indicates whether we should stop iterating or not.

Using our new tool

We have completed our simple `backup` command-line tool. Let's look at it in action. Create a folder called `backupdata` inside `backup/cmds/backup`; this will become the `filedb` database.

Build the tool in a terminal by navigating to the `main.go` file and running this:

```
go build -o backup
```

If all is well, we can now add a path:

```
./backup -db=./backupdata add ./test ./test2
```

You should see the expected output:

```
+ ./test [Not yet archived]
+ ./test2 [Not yet archived]
```

Now let's add another path:

```
./backup -db=./backupdata add ./test3
```

You should now see the complete list:

```
./backup -db=./backupdata list
```

Our program should yield the following:

```
= ./test [Not yet archived]
= ./test2 [Not yet archived]
= ./test3 [Not yet archived]
```

Let's remove `test3` in order to make sure the `remove` functionality is working:

```
./backup -db=./backupdata remove ./test3
./backup -db=./backupdata list
```

This will take us back to this:

```
+ ./test [Not yet archived]
+ ./test2 [Not yet archived]
```

We are now able to interact with the `filedb` database in a way that makes sense for our use case. Next, we build the daemon program that will actually use our `backup` package to do the work.

The daemon backup tool

The `backup` tool, which we will call `backupd`, will be responsible for periodically checking the paths listed in the `filedb` database, hashing the folders to see whether anything has changed, and using the `backup` package to actually perform the archiving of the folders that need it.

Create a new folder called `backupd` alongside the `backup/cmds/backup` folder, and let's jump right into handling the fatal errors and flags:

```
func main() {
  var fatalErr error
  defer func() {
    if fatalErr != nil {
      log.Fatalln(fatalErr)
    }
  }()
  var (
    interval = flag.Duration("interval", 10 * time.Second, "interval
between
    checks")
    archive  = flag.String("archive", "archive", "path to archive
location")
    dbpath   = flag.String("db", "./db", "path to filedb database")
  )
  flag.Parse()
}
```

You must be quite used to seeing this kind of code by now. We defer the handling of fatal errors before specifying three flags: `interval`, `archive`, and `db`. The `interval` flag represents the number of seconds between checks to see whether folders have changed, the `archive` flag is the path to the archive location where ZIP files will go, and the `db` flag is the path to the same `filedb` database that the `backup` command is interacting with. The usual call to `flag.Parse` sets the variables up and validates whether we're ready to move on.

In order to check the hashes of the folders, we are going to need an instance of `Monitor` that we wrote earlier. Append the following code to the `main` function:

```
m := &backup.Monitor{
  Destination: *archive,
  Archiver:    backup.ZIP,
  Paths:       make(map[string]string),
}
```

Here, we create `backup.Monitor` using the `archive` value as the `Destination` type. We'll use the `backup.ZIP` archiver and create a map ready for it to store the paths and hashes internally. At the start of the daemon, we want to load the paths from the database so that it doesn't archive unnecessarily as we stop and start things.

Add the following code to the `main` function:

```
db, err := filedb.Dial(*dbpath)
if err != nil {
  fatalErr = err
  return
}
defer db.Close()
col, err := db.C("paths")
if err != nil {
  fatalErr = err
  return
}
```

You have seen this code earlier too; it dials the database and creates an object that allows us to interact with the `paths` collection. If anything fails, we set `fatalErr` and return.

Duplicated structures

Since we're going to use the same path structure as we used in our user command-line tool program, we need to include a definition of it for this program too. Insert the following structure above the `main` function:

```
type path struct {
  Path string
  Hash string
}
```

The object-oriented programmers out there are no doubt screaming at the pages by now, demanding for this shared snippet to exist in one place only and not be duplicated in both programs. I urge you to resist this compulsion. These four lines of code hardly justify a new package, and therefore dependency for our code, when they can just as easily exist in both programs with very little overhead. Also, consider that we might want to add a `LastChecked` field to our `backupd` program so that we can add rules where each folder only gets archived once an hour at most. Our `backup` program doesn't care about this and will chug along perfectly happy with its view into what fields constitute a `path` structure.

Caching data

We can now query all existing paths and update the `Paths` map, which is a useful technique to increase the speed of a program, especially given slow or disconnected data stores. By loading the data into a cache (in our case, the `Paths` map), we can access it at lightning speed without having to consult the files each time we need information.

Add the following code to the body of the `main` function:

```
var path path
col.ForEach(func(_ int, data []byte) bool {
  if err := json.Unmarshal(data, &path); err != nil {
    fatalErr = err
    return true
  }
  m.Paths[path.Path] = path.Hash
  return false // carry on
})
if fatalErr != nil {
  return
}
if len(m.Paths) < 1 {
  fatalErr = errors.New("no paths - use backup tool to add at least one")
  return
```

```
}
```

Using the `ForEach` method again allows us to iterate over all the paths in the database. We unmarshal the JSON bytes into the same `path` structure as we used in our other program and set the values in the `Paths` map. Assuming that nothing goes wrong, we do a final check to make sure there is at least one path, and if not, we return with an error.

 One limitation to our program is that it will not dynamically add paths once it has started. The daemon would need to be restarted. If this bothers you, you can always build in a mechanism that updates the `Paths` map periodically or uses some other kind of configuration management.

Infinite loops

The next thing we need to do is perform a check on the hashes right away to see whether anything needs archiving before entering into an infinite timed loop where we perform the check again at regular, specified intervals.

An infinite loop sounds like a bad idea; in fact, to some, it sounds like a bug. However, since we're talking about an infinite loop within this program, and since infinite loops can be easily broken with a simple `break` command, they're not as dramatic as they might sound. When we mix an infinite loop with a select statement that has no default case, we are able to run the code in a manageable way without gobbling up CPU cycles as we wait for something to happen. The execution will be blocked until one of the two channels receive data.

In Go, to write an infinite loop is as simple as running this:

```
for {}
```

The instructions inside the braces get executed over and over again, as quickly as the machine running the code can execute them. Again, this sounds like a bad plan unless you're careful about what you're asking it to do. In our case, we are immediately initiating a `select` case on the two channels that will block safely until one of the channels has something interesting to say.

Add the following code:

```
check(m, col)
signalChan := make(chan os.Signal, 1)
signal.Notify(signalChan, syscall.SIGINT, syscall.SIGTERM)
for {
  select {
```

```
    case <-time.After(*interval):
      check(m, col)
    case <-signalChan:
      // stop
      fmt.Println()
      log.Printf("Stopping...")
      return
    }
  }
```

Of course, as responsible programmers, we care about what happens when the user terminates our programs. So after a call to the check method (which doesn't yet exist), we make a signal channel and use signal.Notify to ask for the termination signal to be given to the channel rather than it being handled automatically. In our infinite for loop, we select two possibilities: either the timer channel sends a message or the termination signal channel sends a message. If it's the timer channel message, we call check again; if it's signalChan, we go about terminating the program; otherwise, we'll loop back and wait.

The time.After function returns a channel that will send a signal (actually, the current time) after the specified time has elapsed. Since we are using flag.Duration, we can pass this (deferenced via *) as the time.Duration argument directly into the function. Using flag.Duration also means that users can specify time durations in a human readable way, such as 10s for 10 seconds or 1m for a minute.

Finally, we return from the main function, causing the deferred statements to execute, such as closing the database connection.

Updating filedb records

All that is left is for us is implement the check function that should call the Now method on the Monitor type and update the database with new hashes if there are any.

Underneath the main function, add the following code:

```
func check(m *backup.Monitor, col *filedb.C) {
  log.Println("Checking...")
  counter, err := m.Now()
  if err != nil {
    log.Fatalln("failed to backup:", err)
  }
  if counter > 0 {
    log.Printf("  Archived %d directories\n", counter)
    // update hashes
    var path path
```

```
    col.SelectEach(func(_ int, data []byte) (bool, []byte, bool) {
      if err := json.Unmarshal(data, &path); err != nil {
        log.Println("failed to unmarshal data (skipping):", err)
        return true, data, false
      }
      path.Hash, _ = m.Paths[path.Path]
      newdata, err := json.Marshal(&path)
      if err != nil {
        log.Println("failed to marshal data (skipping):", err)
        return true, data, false
      }
      return true, newdata, false
    })
  } else {
    log.Println("  No changes")
  }
}
```

The check function first tells the user that a check is happening before immediately calling Now. If the Monitor type did any work for us, which is to ask whether it archived any files, we output them to the user and go on to update the database with the new values. The SelectEach method allows us to change each record in the collection if we so wish by returning the replacement bytes. So we unmarshal the bytes to get the path structure, update the hash value, and return the marshaled bytes. This ensures that the next time we start a backupd process, it will do so with the correct hash values.

Testing our solution

Let's see whether our two programs play nicely together. You may want to open two terminal windows for this, since we'll be running two programs.

We have already added some paths to the database, so let's use backup to see them:

```
./backup -db="./backupdata" list
```

You should see the two test folders; if you don't, refer to the *Adding paths* section:

```
= ./test [Not yet archived]
= ./test2 [Not yet archived]
```

In another window, navigate to the backupd folder and create our two test folders, called test and test2.

Build `backupd` using the usual method:

```
go build -o backupd
```

Assuming all is well, we can now start the backup process, being sure to point the `db` path to the same path as we used for the `backup` program and specifying that we want to use a new folder called `archive` to store the ZIP files. For testing purposes, let's specify an interval of 5 seconds in order to save time:

```
./backupd -db="../backup/backupdata/" -archive="./archive" -
interval=5s
```

Immediately, `backupd` should check the folders, calculate the hashes, note that they are different (to `Not yet archived`), and initiate the archive process for both folders. It will print the output that tells us this:

```
Checking...
Archived 2 directories
```

Open the newly created `archive` folder inside `backup/cmds/backupd` and note that it has created two subfolders: `test` and `test2`. Inside these are compressed archive versions of the empty folders. Feel free to unzip one and see; nothing very exciting so far.

Meanwhile, back in the terminal window, `backupd` has been checking the folders for changes again:

```
Checking...
  No changes
Checking...
  No changes
```

In your favorite text editor, create a new text file inside the `test2` folder, containing the word `test`, and save it as `one.txt`. After a few seconds, you will see that `backupd` has noticed the new file and created another snapshot inside the `archive/test2` folder.

Of course, it has a different filename because the time is different, but if you unzip it, you will notice that it has indeed created a compressed archive version of the folder.

Play around with the solution by taking the following actions:

- Change the contents of the `one.txt` file
- Add a file to the `test` folder too
- Delete a file

Summary

In this chapter, we successfully built a very simple backup system for your code projects. You can see how simple it would be to extend or modify the behavior of these programs. The scope for potential problems that you could go on to solve is limitless.

Rather than having a local archive destination folder like we did in the previous section, imagine mounting a network storage device and using that instead. Suddenly, you have off-site (or at least off-machine) backups of these vital files. You can easily set a Dropbox folder as the archive destination, which would mean that not only do you get access to the snapshots yourself, but a copy is also stored in the cloud and can even be shared with other users.

Extending the `Archiver` interface to support `Restore` operations (which would just use the `encoding/zip` package to unzip the files) allows you to build tools that can peer inside the archives and access the changes of individual files, much like Time Machine on a Mac allows you to do. Indexing the files gives you the complete search across the entire history of your code, much like GitHub does.

Since the filenames are timestamps, you could have backupd retiring old archives to less active storage mediums or summarized the changes into a daily dump.

Obviously, backup software exists, is well tested, and is used throughout the world, and it may be a smart move to focus on solving problems that haven't been solved yet. But when it requires such little effort to write small programs to get things done, it is often worth doing because of the control it gives you. When you write the code, you can get exactly what you want without compromise, and it's down to each individual to make that call.

Specifically, in this chapter, we explored how easy Go's standard library makes it to interact with the filesystem: opening files for reading, creating new files, and making directories. The `os` package mixed in with the powerful types from the `io` package, blended further with capabilities such as `encoding/zip` and others, gives a clear example of how extremely simple Go interfaces can be composed to deliver very powerful results.

9
Building a Q&A Application for Google App Engine

Google App Engine gives developers a **NoOps** (short for **No Operations**, indicating that developers and engineers have no work to do in order to have their code running and available) way of deploying their applications, and Go has been officially supported as a language option for some years now. Google's architecture runs some of the biggest applications in the world, such as Google Search, Google Maps, and Gmail, among others, so is a pretty safe bet when it comes to deploying our own code.

Google App Engine allows you to write a Go application, add a few special configuration files, and deploy it to Google's servers, where it will be hosted and made available in a highly available, scalable, and elastic environment. Instances will automatically spin up to meet demand and tear down gracefully when they are no longer needed with a healthy free quota and preapproved budgets.

Along with running application instances, Google App Engine makes available a myriad of useful services, such as fast and high-scale data stores, search, memcache, and task queues. Transparent load balancing means you don't need to build and maintain additional software or hardware to ensure servers don't get overloaded and that requests are fulfilled quickly.

In this chapter, we will build the API backend for a question and answer service similar to Stack Overflow or Quora and deploy it to Google App Engine. In the process, we'll explore techniques, patterns, and practices that can be applied to all such applications, as well as dive deep into some of the more useful services available to our application.

Specifically, in this chapter, you will learn:

- How to use the Google App Engine SDK for Go to build and test applications locally before deploying to the cloud
- How to use `app.yaml` to configure your application
- How Modules in Google App Engine let you independently manage the different components that make up your application
- How the Google Cloud Datastore lets you persist and query data at scale
- A sensible pattern for the modeling of data and working with keys in Google Cloud Datastore
- How to use the Google App Engine Users API to authenticate people with Google accounts
- A pattern to embed denormalized data into entities
- How to ensure data integrity and build counters using transactions
- Why maintaining a good line of sight in code helps improve maintainability
- How to achieve simple HTTP routing without adding a dependency to a third-party package

The Google App Engine SDK for Go

In order to run and deploy Google App Engine applications, we must download and configure the Go SDK. Head over to `https://cloud.google.com/appengine/downloads` and download the latest *Google App Engine SDK for Go* for your computer. The ZIP file contains a folder called `go_appengine`, which you should place in an appropriate folder outside of your `GOPATH`, for example, in `/Users/yourname/work/go_appengine`.

 It is possible that the names of these SDKs will change in the future; if that happens, ensure that you consult the project home page for notes pointing you in the right direction at `https://github.com/matryer/goblueprints`.

Next, you will need to add the `go_appengine` folder to your `$PATH` environment variable, much like what you did with the `go` folder when you first configured Go.

To test your installation, open a terminal and type this:

```
goapp version
```

You should see something like the following:

```
go version go1.6.1 (appengine-1.9.37) darwin/amd64
```

 The actual version of Go is likely to differ and is often a few months behind actual Go releases. This is because the Cloud Platform team at Google needs to do work on its end to support new releases of Go.

The `goapp` command is a drop-in replacement for the `go` command with a few additional subcommands; so you can do things like `goapp test` and `goapp vet`, for example.

Creating your application

In order to deploy an application to Google's servers, we must use the Google Cloud Platform Console to set it up. In a browser, go to `https://console.cloud.google.com` and sign in with your Google account. Look for the **Create Project** menu item, which often gets moved around as the console changes from time to time. If you already have some projects, click on a project name to open a submenu, and you'll find it in there.

 If you can't find what you're looking for, just search **Creating App Engine project** and you'll find it.

When the **New Project** dialog box opens, you will be asked for a name for your application. You are free to call it whatever you like (for example, Answers), but note the Project ID that is generated for you; you will need to refer to this when you configure your app later. You can also click on **Edit** and specify your own ID, but know that the value must be globally unique, so you'll have to get creative when thinking one up. In this book, we will use `answersapp` as the application ID, but you won't be able to use that one since it has already been taken.

You may need to wait a minute or two for your project to get created; there's no need to watch the page you can continue and check back later.

App Engine applications are Go packages

Now that the Google App Engine SDK for Go is configured and our application has been created, we can start building it.

In Google App Engine, an application is just a normal Go package with an `init` function that registers handlers via the `http.Handle` or `http.HandleFunc` functions. It does not need to be the `main` package like normal tools.

Create a new folder (somewhere inside your `GOPATH` folder) called `answersapp/api` and add the following `main.go` file:

```
package api
import (
  "io"
  "net/http"
)
func init() {
  http.HandleFunc("/", handleHello)
}
func handleHello(w http.ResponseWriter, r *http.Request) {
  io.WriteString(w, "Hello from App Engine")
}
```

You will be familiar with most of this by now, but note that there is no `ListenAndServe` call, and the handlers are set inside the `init` function rather than `main`. We are going to handle every request with our simple `handleHello` function, which will just write a welcoming string.

The app.yaml file

In order to turn our simple Go package into a Google App Engine application, we must add a special configuration file called `app.yaml`. The file will go at the root of the application or module, so create it inside the `answersapp/api` folder with the following contents:

```
application: YOUR_APPLICATION_ID_HERE
version: 1
runtime: go
api_version: go1
handlers:
- url: /.*
  script: _go_app
```

The file is a simple human-(and machine) readable configuration file in **YAML (Yet Another Markup Language** format refer to yaml.org for more details). The following table describes each property:

Property	Description
application	The application ID (copied and pasted from when you created your project).
version	Your application version number you can deploy multiple versions and even split traffic between them to test new features, among other things. We'll just stick with version 1 for now.
runtime	The name of the runtime that will execute your application. Since this is a Go book and since we're building a Go application, we'll use go.
api_version	The go1 api version is the runtime version supported by Google; you can imagine that this could be go2 in the future.
handlers	A selection of configured URL mappings. In our case, everything will be mapped to the special _go_app script, but you can also specify static files and folders here.

Running simple applications locally

Before we deploy our application, it makes sense to test it locally. We can do this using the App Engine SDK we downloaded earlier.

Navigate to your answersapp/api folder and run the following command in a terminal:

```
goapp serve
```

You should see the following output:

This indicates that an API server is running locally on port :56443, an admin server is running on :8000, and our application (the module `default`) is now serving at `localhost:8080`, so let's hit that one in a browser.

As you can see by the `Hello from App Engine` response, our application is running locally. Navigate to the admin server by changing the port from `:8080` to `:8000`.

The preceding screenshot shows the web portal that we can use to interrogate the internals of our application, including viewing running instances, inspecting the data store, managing task queues, and more.

Deploying simple applications to Google App Engine

To truly understand the power of Google App Engine's NoOps promise, we are going to deploy this simple application to the cloud. Back in the terminal, stop the server by hitting *Ctrl+C* and run the following command:

```
goapp deploy
```

Your application will be packaged and uploaded to Google's servers. Once it's finished, you should see something like the following:

```
Completed update of app: theanswersapp, version: 1
```

It really is as simple as that.

You can prove this by navigating to the endpoint you get for free with every Google App Engine application, remembering to replace the application ID with your own: `https://YOUR_APPLICATION_ID_HERE.appspot.com/`.

You will see the same output as earlier (the font may render differently since Google's servers will make assumptions about the content type that the local dev server doesn't).

 The application is being served over HTTP/2 and is already capable of pretty massive scale, and all we did was write a `config` file and a few lines of code.

Modules in Google App Engine

A module is a Go package that can be versioned, updated, and managed independently. An app might have a single module, or it can be made up of many modules, each distinct but part of the same application with access to the same data and services. An application must have a default module even if it doesn't do much.

Our application will be made up of the following modules:

Description	The module name
The obligatory default module	default
An API package delivering RESTful JSON	api
A static website serving HTML, CSS, and JavaScript that makes AJAX calls to the API module	web

Each module will be a Go package and will, therefore, live inside its own folder.

Let's reorganize our project into modules by creating a new folder alongside the `api` folder called `default`.

We are not going to make our default module do anything other than use it for configuration, as we want our other modules to do all the meaningful work. But if we leave this folder empty, the Google App Engine SDK will complain that it has nothing to build.

Inside the `default` folder, add the following placeholder `main.go` file:

```
package defaultmodule
func init() {}
```

This file does nothing except allow our `default` module to exist

 It would have been nice for our package names to match the folders, but `default` is a reserved keyword in Go, so we have a good reason to break that rule.

The other module in our application will be called `web`, so create another folder alongside the `api` and `default` folders called `web`. In this chapter, we are only going to build the API for our application and cheat by downloading the web module.

Head over to the project home page at `https://github.com/matryer/goblueprints`, access the content for **Second Edition**, and look for the download link for the *web components for* `Chapter` 9, *Building a Q&A Application for Google App Engine* in the Downloads section of the `README` file. The ZIP file contains the source files for the web component, which should be unzipped and placed inside the `web` folder.

Now, our application structure should look like this:

```
/answersapp/api
/answersapp/default
/answersapp/web
```

Specifying modules

To specify which module our `api` package will become, we must add a property to the `app.yaml` inside our **api** folder. Update it to include the `module` property:

```
application: YOUR_APPLICATION_ID_HERE
version: 1
runtime: go
module: api
api_version: go1
handlers:
- url: /.*
  script: _go_app
```

Since our default module will need to be deployed as well, we also need to add an
`app.yaml` configuration file to it. Duplicate the `api/app.yaml` file inside
`default/app.yaml`, changing the module to `default`:

```
application: YOUR_APPLICATION_ID_HERE
version: 1
runtime: go
module: default
api_version: go1
handlers:
- url: /.*
  script: _go_app
```

Routing to modules with dispatch.yaml

In order to route traffic appropriately to our modules, we will create another configuration
file called `dispatch.yaml`, which will let us map URL patterns to the modules.

We want all traffic beginning with the `/api/` path to be routed to the `api` module and
everything else to the `web` module. As mentioned earlier, we won't expect our `default`
module to handle any traffic, but it will have more utility later.

In the `answersapp` folder (alongside our module folders not inside any of the module
folders), create a new file called `dispatch.yaml` with the following contents:

```
application: YOUR_APPLICATION_ID_HERE
dispatch:
  - url: "*/api/*"
    module: api
  - url: "*/*"
    module: web
```

The same `application` property tells the Google App Engine SDK for Go which
application we are referring to, and the `dispatch` section routes URLs to modules.

Google Cloud Datastore

One of the services available to App Engine developers is Google Cloud Datastore, a
NoSQL document database built for automatic scaling and high performance. Its limited
featureset guarantees very high scale, but understanding the caveats and best practices is
vital to a successful project.

Denormalizing data

Developers with experience of relational databases (RDBMS) will often aim to reduce data redundancy (trying to have each piece of data appear only once in their database) by **normalizing** data, spreading it across many tables, and adding references (foreign keys) before joining it back via a query to build a complete picture. In schemaless and NoSQL databases, we tend to do the opposite. We **denormalize** data so that each document contains the complete picture it needs, making read times extremely fast since it only needs to go and get a single thing.

For example, consider how we might model tweets in a relational database such as MySQL or Postgres:

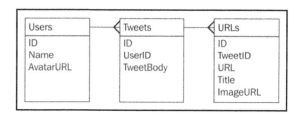

A tweet itself contains only its unique ID, a foreign key reference to the Users table representing the author of the tweet, and perhaps many URLs that were mentioned in `TweetBody`.

One nice feature of this design is that a user can change their Name or AvatarURL and it will be reflected in all of their tweets, past and future, something you wouldn't get for free in a denormalized world.

However, in order to present a tweet to the user, we must load the tweet itself, look up (via a join) the user to get their name and avatar URL, and then load the associated data from the URLs table in order to show a preview of any links. At scale, this becomes difficult because all three tables of data might well be physically separated from each other, which means lots of things need to happen in order to build up this complete picture.

Consider what a denormalized design would look like instead:

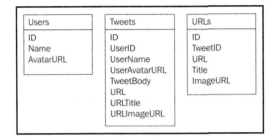

We still have the same three buckets of data, except that now our tweet contains everything it needs in order to render to the user without having to look up data from anywhere else. The hardcore relational database designers out there are realizing what this means by now, and it is no doubt making them feel uneasy.

Following this approach means that:

- Data is repeated âøø `AvatarURL` in User is repeated as `UserAvatarURL` in the tweet (waste of space, right?)
- If the user changes their `AvatarURL`, `UserAvatarURL` in the tweet will be out of date

Database design, at the end of the day, comes down to physics. We are deciding that our tweet is going to be read far more times than it is going to be written, so we'd rather take the pain upfront and take a hit in storage. There's nothing wrong with repeated data as long as there is an understanding about which set is the master set and which is duplicated for speed.

Changing data is an interesting topic in itself, but let's think about a few reasons why we might be OK with the trade-offs.

Firstly, the speed benefit to reading tweets is probably worth the unexpected behavior of changes to master data not being reflected in historical documents; it would be perfectly acceptable to decide to live with this emerged functionality for that reason.

Secondly, we might decide that it makes sense to keep a snapshot of data at a specific moment in time. For example, imagine if someone tweets asking whether people like their profile picture. If the picture changed, the tweet context would be lost. For a more serious example, consider what might happen if you were pointing to a row in an Addresses table for an order delivery and the address later changed. Suddenly, the order might look like it was shipped to a different place.

Finally, storage is becoming increasingly cheaper, so the need for normalizing data to save space is lessened. Twitter even goes as far as copying the entire tweet document for each of your followers. 100 followers on Twitter means that your tweet will be copied at least 100 times, maybe more for redundancy. This sounds like madness to relational database enthusiasts, but Twitter is making smart trade-offs based on its user experience; they'll happily spend a lot of time writing a tweet and storing it many times to ensure that when you refresh your feed, you don't have to wait very long to get updates.

If you want to get a sense of the scale of this, check out the Twitter API and look at what a tweet document consists of. It's a lot of data. Then, go and look at how many followers Lady Gaga has. This has become known in some circles as "the Lady Gaga problem" and is addressed by a variety of different technologies and techniques that are out of the scope of this chapter.

Now that we have an understanding of good NoSQL design practices, let's implement the types, functions, and methods required to drive the data part of our API.

Entities and data access

To persist data in Google Cloud Datastore, we need a struct to represent each entity. These entity structures will be serialized and deserialized when we save and load data through the `datastore` API. We can add helper methods to perform the interactions with the data store, which is a nice way to keep such functionality physically close to the entities themselves. For example, we will model an answer with a struct called `Answer` and add a `Create` method that in turn calls the appropriate function from the `datastore` package. This prevents us from bloating our HTTP handlers with lots of data access code and allows us to keep them clean and simple instead.

One of the foundation blocks of our application is the concept of a question. A question can be asked by a user and answered by many. It will have a unique ID so that it is addressable (referable in a URL), and we'll store a timestamp of when it was created.

Create a new file inside `answersapp` called `questions.go` and add the following `struct` function:

```
type Question struct {
    Key *datastore.Key `json:"id" datastore:"-"`
    CTime time.Time `json:"created"`
    Question string `json:"question"`
    User UserCard `json:"user"`
    AnswersCount int `json:"answers_count"`
```

```
}
```

The structure describes a question in our application. Most of it will seem quite obvious, as we've done similar things in the previous chapters. The `UserCard` struct represents a denormalized `User` entity, both of which we'll add later.

 You can import the `datastore` package in your Go project using this:
`import "google.golang.org/appengine/datastore"`

It's worth spending a little time understanding the `datastore.Key` type.

Keys in Google Cloud Datastore

Every entity in Datastore has a key, which uniquely identifies it. They can be made up of either a string or an integer depending on what makes sense for your case. You are free to decide the keys for yourself or let Datastore automatically assign them for you; again, your use case will usually decide which is the best approach to take and we'll explore both in this chapter.

Keys are created using the `datastore.NewKey` and `datastore.NewIncompleteKey` functions and are used to put and get data into and out of Datastore via the `datastore.Get` and `datastore.Put` functions.

In Datastore, keys and entity bodies are distinct, unlike in MongoDB or SQL technologies, where it is just another field in the document or record. This is why we are excluding `Key` from our `Question` struct with the `datastore:"-"` field tag. Like the `json` tags, this indicates that we want Datastore to ignore the `Key` field altogether when it is getting and putting data.

Keys may optionally have parents, which is a nice way of grouping associated data together and Datastore makes certain assurances about such groups of entities, which you can read more about in the Google Cloud Datastore documentation online.

Putting data into Google Cloud Datastore

Before we save data into Datastore, we want to ensure that our question is valid. Add the following method underneath the Question struct definition:

```go
func (q Question) OK() error {
  if len(q.Question) < 10 {
    return errors.New("question is too short")
  }
  return nil
}
```

The OK function will return an error if something is wrong with the question, or else it will return nil. In this case, we just check to make sure the question has at least 10 characters.

To persist this data in the data store, we are going to add a method to the Question struct itself. At the bottom of questions.go, add the following code:

```go
func (q *Question) Create(ctx context.Context) error {
  log.Debugf(ctx, "Saving question: %s", q.Question)
  if q.Key == nil {
    q.Key = datastore.NewIncompleteKey(ctx, "Question", nil)
  }
  user, err := UserFromAEUser(ctx)
  if err != nil {
    return err
  }
  q.User = user.Card()
  q.CTime = time.Now()
  q.Key, err = datastore.Put(ctx, q.Key, q)
  if err != nil {
    return err
  }
  return nil
}
```

The Create method takes a pointer to Question as the receiver, which is important because we want to make changes to the fields.

 If the receiver was (q Question) without *, we would get a copy of the question rather than a pointer to it, and any changes we made to it would only affect our local copy and not the original Question struct itself.

The first thing we do is use `log` (from the `https://godoc.org/google.golang.org/appen gine/log` package) to write a debug statement saying we are saving the question. When you run your code in a development environment, you will see this appear in the terminal; in production, it goes into a dedicated logging service provided by Google Cloud Platform.

If the key is `nil` (that means this is a new question), we assign an incomplete key to the field, which informs Datastore that we want it to generate a key for us. The three arguments we pass are `context.Context` (which we must pass to all datastore functions and methods), a string describing the kind of entity, and the parent key; in our case, this is `nil`.

Once we know there is a key in place, we call a method (which we will add later) to get or create `User` from an App Engine user and set it to the question and then set the `CTime` field (created time) to `time.Now`, timestamping the point at which the question was asked.

One we have our `Question` function in good shape, we call `datastore.Put` to actually place it inside the data store. As usual, the first argument is `context.Context`, followed by the question key and the question entity itself.

Since Google Cloud Datastore treats keys as separate and distinct from entities, we have to do a little extra work if we want to keep them together in our own code. The `datastore.Put` method returns two arguments: the complete key and `error`. The key argument is actually useful because we're sending in an incomplete key and asking the data store to create one for us, which it does during the put operation. If successful, it returns a new `datastore.Key` object to us, representing the completed key, which we then store in our `Key` field in the `Question` object.

If all is well, we return `nil`.

Add another helper to update an existing question:

```
func (q *Question) Update(ctx context.Context) error {
  if q.Key == nil {
    q.Key = datastore.NewIncompleteKey(ctx, "Question", nil)
  }
  var err error
  q.Key, err = datastore.Put(ctx, q.Key, q)
  if err != nil {
    return err
  }
  return nil
}
```

This method is very similar except that it doesn't set the `CTime` or `User` fields, as they will already have been set.

Reading data from Google Cloud Datastore

Reading data is as simple as putting it with the `datastore.Get` method, but since we want to maintain keys in our entities (and `datastore` methods don't work like that), it's common to add a helper function like the one we are going to add to `questions.go`:

```
func GetQuestion(ctx context.Context, key *datastore.Key)
(*Question, error) {
  var q Question
  err := datastore.Get(ctx, key, &q)
  if err != nil {
    return nil, err
  }
  q.Key = key
  return &q, nil
}
```

The `GetQuestion` function takes `context.Context` and the `datastore.Key` method of the question to get. It then does the simple task of calling `datastore.Get` and assigning the key to the entity before returning it. Of course, errors are handled in the usual way.

This is a nice pattern to follow so that users of your code know that they never have to interact with `datastore.Get` and `datastore.Put` directly but rather use the helpers that can ensure the entities are properly populated with the keys (along with any other tweaks that they might want to do before saving or after loading).

Google App Engine users

Another service we are going to make use of is the Google App Engine Users API, which provides the authentication of Google accounts (and Google Apps accounts).

Create a new file called `users.go` and add the following code:

```
type User struct {
  Key *datastore.Key `json:"id" datastore:"-"`
  UserID string `json:"-"`
  DisplayName string `json:"display_name"`
  AvatarURL string `json:"avatar_url"`
  Score int `json:"score"`
}
```

Similar to the `Question` struct, we have `Key` and a few fields that make up the `User` entity. This struct represents an object that belongs to our application that describes a user; we will have one for every authenticated user in our system, but this isn't the same user object that we'll get from the Users API.

Importing the `https://godoc.org/google.golang.org/appengine/user` package and calling the `user.Current(context.Context)` function will return either nil (if no user is authenticated) or a `user.User` object. This object belongs to the Users API and isn't suitable for our data store, so we need to write a helper function that will translate the App Engine user into our `User`.

Watch out that `goimports` doesn't automatically import `os/user` instead; sometimes it's best if you handle imports manually.

Add the following code to `users.go`:

```go
func UserFromAEUser(ctx context.Context) (*User, error) {
  aeuser := user.Current(ctx)
  if aeuser == nil {
    return nil, errors.New("not logged in")
  }
  var appUser User
  appUser.Key = datastore.NewKey(ctx, "User", aeuser.ID, 0, nil)
  err := datastore.Get(ctx, appUser.Key, &appUser)
  if err != nil && err != datastore.ErrNoSuchEntity {
    return nil, err
  }
  if err == nil {
    return &appUser, nil
  }
  appUser.UserID = aeuser.ID
  appUser.DisplayName = aeuser.String()
  appUser.AvatarURL = gravatarURL(aeuser.Email)
  log.Infof(ctx, "saving new user: %s", aeuser.String())
  appUser.Key, err = datastore.Put(ctx, appUser.Key, &appUser)
  if err != nil {
    return nil, err
  }
  return &appUser, nil
}
```

We get the currently authenticated user by calling `user.Current`, and if it is `nil`, we return with an error. This means that the user is not logged in and the operation cannot complete. Our web package will be checking and ensuring that users are logged in for us, so by the time they hit an API endpoint, we'll expect them to be authenticated.

We then create a new `appUser` variable (which is of our `User` type) and set `datastore.Key`. This time, we aren't making an incomplete key; instead, we are using `datastore.NewKey` and specifying a string ID, matching the User API ID. This key predictability means that not only will there only be one `User` entity per authenticated user in our application, but it also allows us to load a `User` entity without having to use a query.

If we had the App Engine User ID as a field instead, we would need to do a query to find the record we are interested in. Querying is a more expensive operation compared to a direct `Get` method, so this approach is always preferred if you can do it.

We then call `datastore.Get` to attempt to load the `User` entity. If this is the first time the user has logged in, there will be no entity and the returned error will be the special `datastore.ErrNoSuchEntity` variable. If that's the case, we set the appropriate fields and use `datastore.Put` to save it. Otherwise, we just return the loaded `User`.

Note that we are checking for early returns in this function. This is to ensure that it is easy to read the execution flow of our code without having to follow it in and out of indented blocks. I call this the line of sight of code and have written about it on my blog at `https://medium.com/@matryer`.

For now, we'll use Gravatar again for avatar pictures, so add the following helper function to the bottom of `users.go`:

```
func gravatarURL(email string) string {
  m := md5.New()
  io.WriteString(m, strings.ToLower(email))
  return fmt.Sprintf("//www.gravatar.com/avatar/%x", m.Sum(nil))
}
```

Embedding denormalized data

If you recall, our Question type doesn't take the author as `User`; rather, the type was `UserCard`. When we embed denormalized data into other entities, sometimes we will want them to look slightly different from the master entity. In our case, since we do not store the key in the `User` entity (remember the `Key` fields have `datastore:"-"`), we need to have a new type that stores the key.

At the bottom of `users.go`, add the `UserCard` struct and the associated helper method for `User`:

```
type UserCard struct {
  Key         *datastore.Key `json:"id"`
  DisplayName string         `json:"display_name"`
  AvatarURL   string         `json:"avatar_url"`
}
func (u User) Card() UserCard {
  return UserCard{
    Key:         u.Key,
    DisplayName: u.DisplayName,
    AvatarURL:   u.AvatarURL,
  }
}
```

Note that `UserCard` doesn't specify a `datastore` tag, so the `Key` field will indeed be persisted in the data store. Our `Card()` helper function just builds and returns `UserCard` by copying the values of each field. This seems wasteful but offers great control, especially if you want embedded data to look very different from its original entity.

Transactions in Google Cloud Datastore

Transactions allow you to specify a series of changes to the data store and commit them as one. If any of the individual operations fails, the whole transaction will not be applied. This is extremely useful if you want to maintain counters or have multiple entities that depend on each other's state. During a transaction in Google Cloud Datastore, all entities that are read are locked (other code is prevented from making changes) until the transaction is complete, providing an additional sense of security and preventing data races.

If you were building a bank (it seems crazy, but the guys at Monzo in London are indeed building a bank using Go), you might represent user accounts as an entity called `Account`. To transfer money from one account to another, you'd need to make sure the money was deducted from account A and deposited into account B as a single transaction. If either fails, people aren't going to be happy (to be fair, if the deduction operation failed, the owner of account A would probably be happy because B would get the money without it costing A anything).

To see where we are going to use transactions, let's first add model answers to the questions.

Create a new file called `answers.go` and add the following struct and validation method:

```
type Answer struct {
   Key    *datastore.Key `json:"id" datastore:"-"`
   Answer string         `json:"answer"`
   CTime  time.Time      `json:"created"`
   User   UserCard       `json:"user"`
   Score  int            `json:"score"`
}
func (a Answer) OK() error {
   if len(a.Answer) < 10 {
     return errors.New("answer is too short")
   }
   return nil
}
```

`Answer` is similar to a question, has `datastore.Key` (which will not be persisted), has `CTime` to capture the timestamp, and embeds `UserCard` (representing the person answering the question). It also has a `Score` integer field, which will go up and down as users vote on the answers.

Using transactions to maintain counters

Our `Question` struct has a field called `AnswerCount`, where we intend to store an integer that represents the number of answers that a question has solicited.

First, let's look at what can happen if we don't use a transaction to keep track of the `AnswerCount` field by tracking the concurrent activity of answers 4 and 5 of a question:

Step	Answer 4	Answer 5	Question.AnswerCount
1	Load question	Load question	3
2	AnswerCount=3	AnswerCount=3	3
3	AnswerCount++	AnswerCount++	3
4	AnswerCount=4	AnswerCount=4	3
5	Save the answer and question	Save the answer and question	4

You can see from the table that without locking Question, AnswerCount would end up being 4 instead of 5 if the answers came in at the same time. Locking with a transaction will look more like this:

Step	Answer 4	Answer 5	Question.AnswerCount
1	Lock the question	Lock the question	3
2	AnswerCount=3	Waiting for unlock	3
3	AnswerCount++	Waiting for unlock	3
4	Save the answer and question	Waiting for unlock	4
5	Release lock	Waiting for unlock	4
6	Finished	Lock the question	4
7		AnswerCount=4	4
8		AnswerCount++	4
9		Save the answer and question	5

In this case, whichever answer obtains the lock first will perform its operation, and the other operation will wait before continuing. This is likely to slow down the operation (since it has to wait for the other one to finish), but that's a price worth paying in order to get the numbers right.

It's best to keep the amount of work inside a transaction as small as possible because you are essentially blocking other people while the transaction is underway. Outside of transactions, Google Cloud Datastore is extremely fast because it isn't making the same kinds of guarantees.

In code, we use the `datastore.RunInTransaction` function. Add the following to `answers.go`:

```go
func (a *Answer) Create(ctx context.Context, questionKey *datastore.Key)
error {
  a.Key = datastore.NewIncompleteKey(ctx, "Answer", questionKey)
  user, err := UserFromAEUser(ctx)
  if err != nil {
    return err
  }
  a.User = user.Card()
  a.CTime = time.Now()
  err = datastore.RunInTransaction(ctx, func(ctx context.Context) error {
    q, err := GetQuestion(ctx, questionKey)
    if err != nil {
```

```
    return err
  }
  err = a.Put(ctx)
  if err != nil {
    return err
  }
  q.AnswersCount++
  err = q.Update(ctx)
  if err != nil {
    return err
  }
  return nil
}, &datastore.TransactionOptions{XG: true})
if err != nil {
  return err
}
return nil
}
```

We first create a new incomplete key (using the `Answer` kind) and set the parent as the question key. This will mean that the question will become the ancestor to all these answers.

> Ancestor keys are special in Google Cloud Datastore, and it is recommended that you read about the nuances behind them in the documentation on the Google Cloud Platform website.

Using our `UserFromAEUser` function, we get the user who is answering the question and set `UserCard` inside `Answer` before setting `CTime` to the current time, as done earlier.

Then, we start our transaction by calling the `datastore.RunInTransaction` function that takes a context as well as a function where the transactional code will go. There is a third argument, which is a set of `datastore.TransactionOptions` that we need to use in order to set `XG` to `true`, which informs the data store that we'll be performing a transaction across entity groups (both `Answer` and `Question` kinds).

> When it comes to writing your own functions and designing your own APIs, it is highly recommended that you place any function arguments at the end; otherwise, inline function blocks such as the ones in the preceding code obscure the fact that there is another argument afterwards. It's quite difficult to realize that the `TransactionOptions` object is an argument being passed into the `RunInTransaction` function, and I suspect somebody on the Google team regrets this decision.

Transactions work by providing a new context for us to use, which means that code inside the transaction function looks the same, as if it weren't in a transaction. This is a nice piece of API design (and it means that we can forgive the function for not being the final argument).

Inside the transaction function, we use our GetQuestion helper to load the question. Loading data inside the transaction function is what obtains a lock on it. We then put the answer to save it, update the AnswerCount integer, and update the question. If all is well (provided none of these steps returns an error), the answer will be saved and AnswerCount will increase by one.

If we do return an error from our transaction function, the other operations are canceled and the error is returned. If that happens, we'll just return that error from our Answer.Create method and let the user try again.

Next, we are going to add our GetAnswer helper, which is similar to our GetQuestion function:

```
func GetAnswer(ctx context.Context, answerKey *datastore.Key)
(*Answer, error) {
  var answer Answer
  err := datastore.Get(ctx, answerKey, &answer)
  if err != nil {
    return nil, err
  }
  answer.Key = answerKey
  return &answer, nil
}
```

Now we are going to add our Put helper method in answers.go:

```
func (a *Answer) Put(ctx context.Context) error {
  var err error
  a.Key, err = datastore.Put(ctx, a.Key, a)
  if err != nil {
    return err
  }
  return nil
}
```

These two functions are very similar to the GetQuestion and Question.Put methods, but let's resist the temptation of abstracting it and drying up the code for now.

Avoiding early abstraction

Copying and pasting is generally seen by programmers as a bad thing because it is usually possible to abstract the general idea and **DRY (Don't repeat yourself)** up the code. However, it is worth resisting the temptation to do this right away because it is very easy to design a bad abstraction, which you are then stuck with since your code will start to depend on it. It is better to duplicate the code in a few places first and later revisit them to see whether a sensible abstraction is lurking there.

Querying in Google Cloud Datastore

So far, we have only been putting and getting single objects into and out of Google Cloud Datastore. When we display a list of answers to a question, we want to load all of these answers in a single operation, which we can do with datastore.Query.

The querying interface is a fluent API, where each method returns the same object or a modified object, allowing you to chain calls together. You can use it to build up a query consisting of ordering, limits, ancestors, filters, and so on. We will use it to write a function that will load all the answers for a given question, showing the most popular (those with a higher Score value) first.

Add the following function to answers.go:

```
func GetAnswers(ctx context.Context, questionKey *datastore.Key)
([]*Answer, error) {
  var answers []*Answer
  answerKeys, err := datastore.NewQuery("Answer").
    Ancestor(questionKey).
    Order("-Score").
    Order("-CTime").
    GetAll(ctx, &answers)
  for i, answer := range answers {
    answer.Key = answerKeys[i]
  }
  if err != nil {
    return nil, err
  }
  return answers, nil
}
```

We first create an empty slice of pointers to `Answer` and use `datastore.NewQuery` to start building a query. The `Ancestor` method indicates that we're looking only for answers that belong to the specific question, where the `Order` method calls specify that we want to first order by descending `Score` and then by the newest first. The `GetAll` method performs the operation, which takes in a pointer to our slice (where the results will go) and returns a new slice containing all the keys.

> The order of the keys returned will match the order of the entities in the slice. This is how we know which key corresponds to each item.

Since we are keeping keys and the entity fields together, we range over the answers and assign `answer.Key` to the corresponding `datastore.Key` argument returned from `GetAll`.

> We are keeping our API simple for the first version by not implementing paging, but ideally you would need to; otherwise, as the number of questions and answers grows, you will end up trying to deliver everything in a single request, which would overwhelm the user and maybe the servers.

If we had a step in our application of authorizing the answer (to protect it from spam or inappropriate content), we might want to add an additional filter for `Authorized` to be `true`, in which case we could do this:

```
datastore.NewQuery("Answer").
  Filter("Authorized =", true)
```

> For more information on querying and filtering, consult the Google Cloud Datastore API documentation online.

Another place where we need to query data is when we show the top questions on the home page of our app. Our first version of top questions will just show those questions that have the most answers; we consider them to be the most interesting, but you could change this functionality in the future without breaking the API to order by score or even question views.

We will build `Query` on the `Question` kind and use the `Order` method to first order by the number of answers (with the highest first), followed by time (also, highest/latest first). We will also use the `Limit` method to make sure we only select the top 25 questions for this API. Later, if we implement paging, we can even make this dynamic.

In `questions.go`, add the `TopQuestions` function:

```
func TopQuestions(ctx context.Context) ([]*Question, error) {
  var questions []*Question
  questionKeys, err := datastore.NewQuery("Question").
    Order("-AnswersCount").
    Order("-CTime").
    Limit(25).
    GetAll(ctx, &questions)
  if err != nil {
    return nil, err
  }
  for i := range questions {
    questions[i].Key = questionKeys[i]
  }
  return questions, nil
}
```

This code is similar to loading the answers, and we end up returning a slice of `Question` objects or an error.

Votes

Now that we have modeled questions and answers in our application, it's time to think about how voting might work.

Let's design it a little:

- Users vote answers up and down based on their opinion of them
- Answers are ordered by their score so the best ones appear first
- Each person is allowed one vote per answer
- If a user votes again, they should replace their previous vote

We will make use of a few things we have learned so far in this chapter; transactions will help us ensure the correct score is calculated for answers, and we'll use predictable keys again to ensure that each person gets only one vote per answer.

We will first build a structure to represent each vote and use field tags to be a little more specific about how we want the data store to index our data.

Indexing

Reads from Google Cloud Datastore are extremely fast due to the extensive use of indexes. By default, every field in our structure is indexed. Queries that attempt to filter on fields that aren't indexed will fail (the method will return an error); the data store doesn't fall back to scanning like some other technologies do because it's considered too slow. If one query filters two or more fields, an additional index must be added that is composed of all fields.

A structure with 10 fields would perform multiple write operations when you put it: one for the entity itself and one for each index that needs to be updated. So it is sensible to turn off indexing for fields that are you not planning to query on.

In `questions.go`, add the `datastore` field tags to the `Question` structure:

```
type Question struct {
  Key *datastore.Key `json:"id" datastore:"-"`
  CTime time.Time `json:"created" datastore:",noindex"`
  Question string `json:"question" datastore:",noindex"`
  User UserCard `json:"user"`
  AnswersCount int `json:"answers_count"`
}
```

The addition of the `datastore:",noindex"` field tags will tell the data store not to index these fields.

> The `,noindex` value beginning with a comma is a little confusing. The value is essentially a list of comma-separated arguments, the first being the name we want the data store to use when storing each field (just like it does for the `json` tag). Since we don't want to say anything about the name we want the data store to use the real field name we are omitting it; so the first argument is empty, and the second argument is `noindex`.

Do this for fields that we do not want indexed in the `Answer` structure:

```
type Answer struct {
  Key *datastore.Key `json:"id" datastore:"-"`
  Answer string `json:"answer" datastore:",noindex"`
  CTime time.Time `json:"created"`
  User UserCard `json:"user" datastore:",noindex"`
  Score int `json:"score"`
}
```

And for the `Vote` structure, do this:

```
type Vote struct {
  Key *datastore.Key `json:"id" datastore:"-"`
  MTime time.Time `json:"last_modified" datastore:",noindex"`
  Question QuestionCard `json:"question" datastore:",noindex"`
  Answer AnswerCard `json:"answer" datastore:",noindex"`
  User UserCard `json:"user" datastore:",noindex"`
  Score int `json:"score" datastore:",noindex"`
}
```

You can also add a `noindex` declaration to all fields inside our card types: `AnswerCard`, `UserCard`, and `QuestionCard`.

 The fields we have left without `noindex` will be used in queries, and we need to make sure Google Cloud Datastore does indeed maintain indexes on these fields.

Embedding a different view of entities

Now it's time to create our `Vote` structure, which we'll do inside a new file called `votes.go`:

```
type Vote struct {
  Key *datastore.Key `json:"id" datastore:"-"`
  MTime time.Time `json:"last_modified" datastore:",noindex"`
  Question QuestionCard `json:"question" datastore:",noindex"`
  Answer AnswerCard `json:"answer" datastore:",noindex"`
  User UserCard `json:"user" datastore:",noindex"`
  Score int `json:"score" datastore:",noindex"`
}
```

A `Vote` structure contains many of our embeddable card types representing `Question`, `Answer` and `User` casting the vote. It also contains a `Score` integer, which will be either 1 or −1 (depending on whether they voted up or down). We will also keep track of when they cast their vote (or last changed it) with the `MTimetime.Time` field.

You can use pointers to the `*Card` types in the `Vote` struct if you like. This would save additional copies being made when if you pass the `Vote` object in and out of functions, but that would mean that any changes made inside these functions would affect the original data rather than just their local copy. In most situations, there isn't much of a performance benefit to using pointers and it might be considered simpler to omit them. This book deliberately mixes both approaches to show you how they work, but you should understand the implications before making a decision.

Like our `UserCard` method, we are going to add appropriate versions for questions and answers, but this time we are going to be more selective about which fields should be included and which should be left out.

In `questions.go`, add the `QuestionCard` type and the associated helper method:

```
type QuestionCard struct {
  Key *datastore.Key `json:"id" datastore:",noindex"`
  Question string `json:"question" datastore:",noindex"`
  User     UserCard `json:"user" datastore:",noindex"`
}
func (q Question) Card() QuestionCard {
  return QuestionCard{
    Key:      q.Key,
    Question: q.Question,
    User:     q.User,
  }
}
```

The `QuestionCard` type captures the `Question` string and who asked it (our `UserCard` method, again), but we are leaving out the `CTime` and `AnswersCount` fields.

Let's add `AnswerCard` to `answers.go` next:

```
type AnswerCard struct {
  Key     *datastore.Key `json:"id" datastore:",noindex"`
  Answer string          `json:"answer" datastore:",noindex"`
  User    UserCard        `json:"user" datastore:",noindex"`
}

func (a Answer) Card() AnswerCard {
```

```
    return AnswerCard{
      Key:     a.Key,
      Answer:  a.Answer,
      User:    a.User,
    }
  }
```

Similarly, we are only capturing the `Answer` string and `User` and excluding `CTime` and `Score`.

Deciding which fields to capture and which to omit is entirely dependent on the user experience you wish to provide. We might decide that when we show a vote, we want to show the score of `Answer` at the time, or we might want to show the current score of `Answer` regardless of what it was at the time the vote was cast. Perhaps we want to send a push notification to the user who wrote the answer saying something like "Blanca has up-voted your answer to Ernesto's question it now has a score of 15", in which case we would need to grab the `Score` field too.

Casting a vote

Before our API is a complete feature, we need to add the ability for users to cast votes. We'll break this piece into two functions in order to increase the readability of our code.

Inside `votes.go`, add the following function:

```
func CastVote(ctx context.Context, answerKey *datastore.Key, score int)
(*Vote, error) {
  question, err := GetQuestion(ctx, answerKey.Parent())
  if err != nil {
    return nil, err
  }
  user, err := UserFromAEUser(ctx)
  if err != nil {
    return nil, err
  }
  var vote Vote
  err = datastore.RunInTransaction(ctx, func(ctx context.Context) error {
    var err error
    vote, err = castVoteInTransaction(ctx, answerKey, question, user,
     score)
    if err != nil {
      return err
    }
    return nil
```

```
  }, &datastore.TransactionOptions{XG: true})
  if err != nil {
    return nil, err
  }
  return &vote, nil
}
```

The `CastVote` function takes (along with the obligatory `Context`) `datastore.Key` for the answer that is being voted for and a score integer. It loads the question and the current user, starts a data store transaction, and passes execution off to the `castVoteInTransaction` function.

Accessing parents via datastore.Key

Our `CastVote` function could require that we know `datastore.Key` for `Question` so that we can load it. But one nice feature about ancestor keys is that from the key alone, you can access the parent key. This is because the hierarchy of keys is maintained in the key itself, a bit like a path.

Three answers to question 1 might have these keys:

- Question,1/Answer,1
- Question,1/Answer,2
- Question,1/Answer,3

The actual details of how keys work under the hood are kept internal to the datastore package and could change at any time. So it is smart to only rely on things that the API guarantees such as being able to access the parent via the `Parent` method.

Line of sight in code

The cost of writing a function is relatively low compared to the cost of maintaining it, especially in successful, long-running projects. So it is worth taking the time to ensure the code is readable by our future selves and others.

Code can be said to have a good line of sight if it is easy to glance at and if it understands the usual, expected flow of the statements (the happy path). In Go, we can achieve this by following a few simple rules when we write code:

- Align the happy path to the left edge so that you can scan down a single column and see the expected flow of execution
- Don't hide the happy path logic inside a nest of indented braces
- Exit early from your function
- Indent only to handle errors or edge cases
- Extract functions and methods to keep bodies small and readable

 There are a few more details to writing good line of sight code, which are outlined and maintained at `http://bit.ly/lineofsightincode`.

In order to prevent our `CastVote` function from becoming too big and difficult to follow, we have broken out the core functionality into its own function, which we will now add to `votes.go`:

```go
func castVoteInTransaction(ctx context.Context, answerKey *datastore.Key,
question *Question, user *User, score int) (Vote, error) {
  var vote Vote
  answer, err := GetAnswer(ctx, answerKey)
  if err != nil {
    return vote, err
  }
  voteKeyStr := fmt.Sprintf("%s:%s", answerKey.Encode(), user.Key.Encode())
  voteKey := datastore.NewKey(ctx, "Vote", voteKeyStr, 0, nil)
  var delta int // delta describes the change to answer score
  err = datastore.Get(ctx, voteKey, &vote)
  if err != nil && err != datastore.ErrNoSuchEntity {
    return vote, err
  }
  if err == datastore.ErrNoSuchEntity {
    vote = Vote{
      Key:      voteKey,
      User:     user.Card(),
      Answer:   answer.Card(),
      Question: question.Card(),
      Score:    score,
    }
  } else {
    // they have already voted - so we will be changing
    // this vote
```

```
      delta = vote.Score * -1
    }
    delta += score
    answer.Score += delta
    err = answer.Put(ctx)
    if err != nil {
      return vote, err
    }
    vote.Key = voteKey
    vote.Score = score
    vote.MTime = time.Now()
    err = vote.Put(ctx)
    if err != nil {
      return vote, err
    }
    return vote, nil
  }
```

While this function is long, its line of sight isn't too bad. The happy path flows down the left edge, and we only indent to return early in case of errors and the case where we create a new Vote object. This means that we can easily track what it is doing.

We take in the answer key, the related question, the user casting the vote and the score, and return a Vote object, or else an error if something goes wrong.

First, we get the answer which, since we're inside a transaction, will lock it until the transaction is complete (or stops due to an error).

We then build the key for this vote, which is made up of the keys of both the answer and the user encoded into a single string. This means that only one Vote entity will exist in the data store for each user/answer pair; so a user may only have one vote per answer as per our design.

We then use the vote key to attempt to load the Vote entity from the data store. Of course, the first time a user votes on a question, no entity will exist, which we can check by seeing whether the error returned from datastore.Get is the special datastore.ErrNoSuchEntity value or not. If it is, we create the new Vote object, setting the appropriate fields.

We are maintaining a score `delta` integer, which will represent the number that needs to be added to the answer score after the vote has happened. When it's the first time a user has voted on a question, the delta will be either 1 or −1. If they are changing their vote from down to up (−1 to 1), the delta will be 2, which cancels out the previous vote and adds the new one. We multiply the delta by −1 to undo the previous vote if there was one (if `err !=` `datastore.ErrNoSuchEntity`). This has the nice effect of also not making any difference (`delta` will be 0) if they happen to cast the same vote twice in either direction.

Finally, we change the score on the answer and put it back into the data store before updating the final fields in our `Vote` object and putting that in too. We then return and our `CastVote` function exits the `datastore.RunInTransaction` function block, thus releasing Answer and letting others cast their votes on it too.

Exposing data operations over HTTP

Now that we have built all of our entities and the data access methods that operate on them, it's time to wire them up to an HTTP API. This will feel more familiar as we have already done this kind of thing a few times in the book.

Optional features with type assertions

When you use interface types in Go, you can perform type assertions to see whether the objects implement other interfaces, and since you can write interfaces inline, it is possible to very easily find out whether an object implements a specific function.

If `v` is `interface{}`, we can see whether it has the `OK` method using this pattern:

```
if obj, ok := v.(interface{ OK() error }); ok {
  // v has OK() method
} else {
  // v does not have OK() method
}
```

If the `v` object implements the method described in the interface, `ok` will be `true` and `obj` will be an object on which the OK method can be called. Otherwise, `ok` will be false.

One problem with this approach is that it hides the secret functionality from users of the code, so you must either document the function very well in order to make it clear or perhaps promote the method to its own first-class interface and insist that all objects implement it. Remember that we must always seek clear code over clever code. As a side exercise, see whether you can add the interface and use it in the decode signature instead.

We are going to add a function that will help us decode JSON request bodies and, optionally, validate the input. Create a new file called `http.go` and add the following code:

```
func decode(r *http.Request, v interface{}) error {
  err := json.NewDecoder(r.Body).Decode(v)
  if err != nil {
    return err
  }
  if valid, ok := v.(interface {
    OK() error
  }); ok {
    err = valid.OK()
    if err != nil {
      return err
    }
  }
  return nil
}
```

The decode function takes `http.Request` and a destination value called v, which is where the data from the JSON will go. We check whether the OK method is implemented, and if it is, we call it. We expect OK to return nil if the object looks good; otherwise, we expect it to return an error that explains what is wrong. If we get an error, we'll return it and let the calling code deal with it.

If all is well, we return nil at the bottom of the function.

Response helpers

We are going to add a pair of helper functions that will make responding to API requests easy. Add the `respond` function to `http.go`:

```
func respond(ctx context.Context, w http.ResponseWriter,
  r *http.Request, v interface{}, code int) {
  var buf bytes.Buffer
  err := json.NewEncoder(&buf).Encode(v)
```

```
  if err != nil {
    respondErr(ctx, w, r, err, http.StatusInternalServerError)
    return
  }
  w.Header().Set("Content-Type",
   "application/json; charset=utf-8")
  w.WriteHeader(code)
  _, err = buf.WriteTo(w)
  if err != nil {
    log.Errorf(ctx, "respond: %s", err)
  }
}
```

The respond method contains a `context`, `ResponseWriter`, `Request`, the object to respond with, and a status code. It encodes `v` into an internal buffer before setting the appropriate headers and writing the response.

We are using a buffer here because it's possible that the encoding might fail. If it does so but has already started writing the response, the 200 OK header will be sent to the client, which is misleading. Instead, encoding to a buffer lets us be sure that completes without issue before deciding what status code to respond with.

Now add the `respondErr` function at the bottom of `http.go`:

```
func respondErr(ctx context.Context, w http.ResponseWriter,
 r *http.Request, err error, code int) {
  errObj := struct {
    Error string `json:"error"`
  }{ Error: err.Error() }
  w.Header().Set("Content-Type", "application/json; charset=utf-8")
  w.WriteHeader(code)
  err = json.NewEncoder(w).Encode(errObj)
  if err != nil {
    log.Errorf(ctx, "respondErr: %s", err)
  }
}
```

This function writes `error` wrapped in a struct that embeds the error string as a field called `error`.

Parsing path parameters

Some of our API endpoints will need to pull IDs out of the path string, but we don't want to add any dependencies to our project (such as an external router package); instead, we are going to write a simple function that will parse path parameters for us.

Let's first write a test that will explain how we want our path parsing to work. Create a file called http_test.go and add the following unit test:

```go
func TestPathParams(t *testing.T) {
  r, err := http.NewRequest("GET", "1/2/3/4/5", nil)
  if err != nil {
    t.Errorf("NewRequest: %s", err)
  }
  params := pathParams(r, "one/two/three/four")
  if len(params) != 4 {
    t.Errorf("expected 4 params but got %d: %v", len(params), params)
  }
  for k, v := range map[string]string{
    "one":   "1",
    "two":   "2",
    "three": "3",
    "four":  "4",
  } {
    if params[k] != v {
      t.Errorf("%s: %s != %s", k, params[k], v)
    }
  }
  params = pathParams(r, "one/two/three/four/five/six")
  if len(params) != 5 {
    t.Errorf("expected 5 params but got %d: %v", len(params), params)
  }
  for k, v := range map[string]string{
    "one":   "1",
    "two":   "2",
    "three": "3",
    "four":  "4",
    "five":  "5",
  } {
    if params[k] != v {
      t.Errorf("%s: %s != %s", k, params[k], v)
    }
  }
}
```

We expect to be able to pass in a pattern and have a map returned that discovers the values from the path in http.Request.

Run the test (with go test -v) and note that it fails.

At the bottom of `http.go`, add the following implementation to make the test pass:

```
func pathParams(r *http.Request,pattern string) map[string]string{
  params := map[string]string{}
  pathSegs := strings.Split(strings.Trim(r.URL.Path, "/"), "/")
  for i, seg := range strings.Split(strings.Trim(pattern, "/"), "/") {
    if i > len(pathSegs)-1 {
      return params
    }
    params[seg] = pathSegs[i]
  }
  return params
}
```

The function breaks the path from the specific `http.Request` and builds a map of the values with keys taken from breaking the pattern path. So for a pattern of `/questions/id` and a path of `/questions/123`, it would return the following map:

```
questions: questions
id:        123
```

Of course, we'd ignore the `questions` key, but `id` will be useful.

Exposing functionality via an HTTP API

Now we have all the tools we need in order to put together our API: helper functions to encode and decode data payloads in JSON, path parsing functions, and all the entities and data access functionality to persist and query data in Google Cloud Datastore.

HTTP routing in Go

The three endpoints we are going to add in order to handle questions are outlined in the following table:

HTTP request	Description
POST /questions	Ask a new question
GET /questions/{id}	Get the question with the specific ID
GET /questions	Get the top questions

Since our API design is relatively simple, there is no need to bloat out our project with an additional dependency to solve routing for us. Instead, we'll roll our own very simple adhoc routing using normal Go code. We can use a simple `switch` statement to detect which HTTP method was used and our `pathParams` helper function to see whether an ID was specified before passing execution to the appropriate place.

Create a new file called `handle_questions.go` and add the following `http.HandlerFunc` function:

```go
func handleQuestions(w http.ResponseWriter, r *http.Request) {
  switch r.Method {
  case "POST":
    handleQuestionCreate(w, r)
  case "GET":
    params := pathParams(r, "/api/questions/:id")
    questionID, ok := params[":id"]
    if ok { // GET /api/questions/ID
      handleQuestionGet(w, r, questionID)
      return
    }
    handleTopQuestions(w, r) // GET /api/questions/
  default:
    http.NotFound(w, r)
  }
}
```

If the HTTP method is POST, then we'll call `handleQuestionCreate`. If it's GET, then we'll see whether we can extract the ID from the path and call `handleQuestionGet` if we can, or `handleTopQuestions` if we cannot.

Context in Google App Engine

If you remember, all of our calls to App Engine functions took a `context.Context` object as the first parameter, but what is that and how do we create one?

`Context` is actually an interface that provides cancelation signals, execution deadlines, and request-scoped data throughout a stack of function calls across many components and API boundaries. The Google App Engine SDK for Go uses it throughout its APIs, the details of which are kept internal to the package, which means that we (as users of the SDK) don't have to worry about it. This is a good goal for when you use Context in your own packages; ideally, the complexity should be kept internal and hidden.

You can, and should, learn more about `Context` through various online resources, starting with the *Go Concurrency Patterns: Context* blog post at `ht tps://blog.golang.org/context`.

To create a context suitable for App Engine calls, you use the `appengine.NewContext` function, which takes `http.Request` as an argument to which the context will belong.

Underneath the routing code we just added, let's add the handler that will be responsible for creating a question, and we can see how we will create a new context for each request:

```go
func handleQuestionCreate(w http.ResponseWriter, r *http.Request) {
  ctx := appengine.NewContext(r)
  var q Question
  err := decode(r, &q)
  if err != nil {
    respondErr(ctx, w, r, err, http.StatusBadRequest)
    return
  }
  err = q.Create(ctx)
  if err != nil {
    respondErr(ctx, w, r, err, http.StatusInternalServerError)
    return
  }
  respond(ctx, w, r, q, http.StatusCreated)
}
```

We create `Context` and store it in the `ctx` variable, which has become somewhat an accepted pattern throughout the Go community. We then decode our Question (which, due to the `OK` method, will also validate it for us) before calling the `Create` helper method that we wrote earlier. Every step of the way, we pass our context along.

If anything goes wrong, we make a call out to our `respondErr` function, which will write out the response to the client before returning and exiting early from the function.

If all is well, we respond with `Question` and a `http.StatusCreated` status code (201).

Decoding key strings

Since we are exposing the `datastore.Key` objects as the `id` field in our objects (via the `json` field tags), we expect users of our API to pass back these same ID strings when referring to specific objects. This means that we need to decode these strings and turn them back into `datastore.Key` objects. Luckily, the `datastore` package provides the answer in the form of the `datastore.DecodeKey` function.

At the bottom of `handle_questions.go`, add the following handle function to get a single question:

```
func handleQuestionGet(w http.ResponseWriter, r *http.Request,
  questionID string) {
  ctx := appengine.NewContext(r)
  questionKey, err := datastore.DecodeKey(questionID)
  if err != nil {
    respondErr(ctx, w, r, err, http.StatusBadRequest)
    return
  }
  question, err := GetQuestion(ctx, questionKey)
  if err != nil {
    if err == datastore.ErrNoSuchEntity {
      respondErr(ctx, w, r, datastore.ErrNoSuchEntity,
       http.StatusNotFound)
      return
    }
    respondErr(ctx, w, r, err, http.StatusInternalServerError)
    return
  }
  respond(ctx, w, r, question, http.StatusOK)
}
```

After we create Context again, we decode the `question ID` argument to turn the string back into a `datastore.Key` object. The `question ID` string is passed in from our routing handler code, which we added at the top of the file.

Assuming `question ID` is a valid key and the SDK was successfully able to turn it into `datastore.Key`, we call our `GetQuestion` helper function to load `Question`. If we get the `datastore.ErrNoSuchEntity` error, then we respond with a 404 (not found) status; otherwise, we'll report the error with a `http.StatusInternalServerError` code.

 When writing APIs, check out the HTTP status codes and other HTTP standards and see whether you can make use of them. Developers are used to them and your API will feel more natural if it speaks the same language.

If we are able to load the question, we call `respond` and send it back to the client as JSON.

Next, we are going to expose the functionality related to answers via a similar API to the one we used for questions:

HTTP request	Description
POST /answers	Submit an answer
GET /answers	Get the answers with the specified question ID

Create a new file called `handle_answers.go` and add the routing `http.HandlerFunc` function:

```
func handleAnswers(w http.ResponseWriter, r *http.Request) {
  switch r.Method {
  case "GET":
    handleAnswersGet(w, r)
  case "POST":
    handleAnswerCreate(w, r)
  default:
    http.NotFound(w, r)
  }
}
```

For GET requests, we call `handleAnswersGet`; for POST requests, we call `handleAnswerCreate`. By default, we'll respond with a `404 Not Found` response.

Using query parameters

As an alternative to parsing the path, you can just take query parameters from the URL in the request, which we will do when we add the handler that reads answers:

```
func handleAnswersGet(w http.ResponseWriter, r *http.Request) {
  ctx := appengine.NewContext(r)
  q := r.URL.Query()
  questionIDStr := q.Get("question_id")
  questionKey, err := datastore.DecodeKey(questionIDStr)
  if err != nil {
    respondErr(ctx, w, r, err, http.StatusBadRequest)
    return
  }
  answers, err := GetAnswers(ctx, questionKey)
  if err != nil {
    respondErr(ctx, w, r, err, http.StatusInternalServerError)
    return
  }
  respond(ctx, w, r, answers, http.StatusOK)
}
```

Here, we use `r.URL.Query()` to get the `http.Values` that contains the query parameters and use the Get method to pull out `question_id`. So, the API call will look like this:

```
/api/answers?question_id=abc123
```

> You should be consistent in your API in the real world. We have used a mix of path parameters and query parameters to show off the differences, but it is recommended that you pick one style and stick to it.

Anonymous structs for request data

The API for answering a question is to post to `/api/answers` with a body that contains the answer details as well as the question ID string. This structure is not the same as our internal representation of `Answer` because the question ID string would need to be decoded into `datastore.Key`. We could leave the field in and indicate with field tags that it should be omitted from both the JSON and the data store, but there is a cleaner approach.

We can specify an inline, anonymous structure to hold the new answer, and the best place to do this is inside the handler function that deals with that data this means that we don't need to add a new type to our API, but we can still represent the request data we are expecting.

At the bottom of `handle_answers.go`, add the `handleAnswerCreate` function:

```go
func handleAnswerCreate(w http.ResponseWriter, r *http.Request) {
  ctx := appengine.NewContext(r)
  var newAnswer struct {
    Answer
    QuestionID string `json:"question_id"`
  }
  err := decode(r, &newAnswer)
  if err != nil {
    respondErr(ctx, w, r, err, http.StatusBadRequest)
    return
  }
  questionKey, err := datastore.DecodeKey(newAnswer.QuestionID)
  if err != nil {
    respondErr(ctx, w, r, err, http.StatusBadRequest)
    return
  }
  err = newAnswer.OK()
  if err != nil {
    respondErr(ctx, w, r, err, http.StatusBadRequest)
    return
```

```
  }
  answer := newAnswer.Answer
  user, err := UserFromAEUser(ctx)
  if err != nil {
    respondErr(ctx, w, r, err, http.StatusBadRequest)
    return
  }
  answer.User = user.Card()
  err = answer.Create(ctx, questionKey)
  if err != nil {
    respondErr(ctx, w, r, err, http.StatusInternalServerError)
    return
  }
  respond(ctx, w, r, answer, http.StatusCreated)
}
```

Look at the somewhat unusual `var newAnswer struct` line. We are declaring a new variable called `newAnswer`, which has a type of an anonymous struct (it has no name) that contains `QuestionID string` and embeds `Answer`. We can decode the request body into this type, and we will capture any specific `Answer` fields as well as `QuestionID`. We then decode the question ID into `datastore.Key` as we did earlier, validate the answer, and set the `User` (`UserCard`) field by getting the currently authenticated user and calling the `Card` helper method.

If all is well, we call `Create`, which will do the work to save the answer to the question.

Finally, we need to expose the voting functionality in our API.

Writing self-similar code

Our voting API has only a single endpoint, a post to `/votes`. So, of course, there is no need to do any routing on this method (we could just check the method in the handler itself), but there is something to be said for writing code that is familiar and similar to other code in the same package. In our case, omitting a router might jar a little if somebody else is looking at our code and expects one after seeing the routers for questions and answers.

So let's add a simple router handler to a new file called `handle_votes.go`:

```
func handleVotes(w http.ResponseWriter, r *http.Request) {
  if r.Method != "POST" {
    http.NotFound(w, r)
    return
  }
  handleVote(w, r)
}
```

Our router just checks the method and exits early if it's not POST, before calling the handleVote function, which we will add next.

Validation methods that return an error

The OK method that we added to some of our objects is a nice way to add validation methods to our code.

We want to ensure that the incoming score value is valid (in our case, either −1 or 1), so we could write a function like this:

```
func validScore(score int) bool {
  return score == -1 || score == 1
}
```

If we used this function in a few places, we would have to keep repeating the code that explained that the score was not valid. If, however, the function returns an error, you can encapsulate that in one place.

To votes.go, add the following validScore function:

```
func validScore(score int) error {
  if score != -1 && score != 1 {
    return errors.New("invalid score")
  }
  return nil
}
```

In this version, we return nil if the score is valid; otherwise, we return an error that explains what is wrong.

We will make use of this validation function when we add our handleVote function to handle_votes.go:

```
func handleVote(w http.ResponseWriter, r *http.Request) {
  ctx := appengine.NewContext(r)
  var newVote struct {
    AnswerID string `json:"answer_id"`
    Score    int    `json:"score"`
  }
  err := decode(r, &newVote)
  if err != nil {
    respondErr(ctx, w, r, err, http.StatusBadRequest)
    return
  }
```

```
    err = validScore(newVote.Score)
    if err != nil {
      respondErr(ctx, w, r, err, http.StatusBadRequest)
      return
    }
    answerKey, err := datastore.DecodeKey(newVote.AnswerID)
    if err != nil {
      respondErr(ctx, w, r, errors.New("invalid answer_id"),
      http.StatusBadRequest)
      return
    }
    vote, err := CastVote(ctx, answerKey, newVote.Score)
    if err != nil {
      respondErr(ctx, w, r, err, http.StatusInternalServerError)
      return
    }
    respond(ctx, w, r, vote, http.StatusCreated)
}
```

This will look pretty familiar by now, which highlights why we put all the data access logic in a different place to our handlers; the handlers can then focus on HTTP tasks, such as decoding the request and writing the response, and leave the application specifics to the other objects.

We have also broken down the logic into distinct files, with a pattern of prefixing HTTP handler code with handle_, so we quickly know where to look when we want to work on a specific piece of the project.

Mapping the router handlers

Let's update our main.go file by changing the init function to map the real handlers to HTTP paths:

```
func init() {
  http.HandleFunc("/api/questions/", handleQuestions)
  http.HandleFunc("/api/answers/", handleAnswers)
  http.HandleFunc("/api/votes/", handleVotes)
}
```

You can also remove the now redundant handleHello handler function.

Running apps with multiple modules

For applications such as ours that have multiple modules, we need to list out all the YAML files for the `goapp` command.

To serve our new application, in a terminal, execute this:

```
goapp serve dispatch.yaml default/app.yaml api/app.yaml
  web/app.yaml
```

Starting with the dispatch file, we are listing all the associated configuration files. If you miss any, you will see an error when you try to serve your application. Here, you will notice that the output now lists that each module is being deployed on a different port:

```
● ● ●                          1. Python
echo:answersapp matryer$ goapp serve dispatch.yaml default/app.yaml api/app.yaml web/app.yaml
INFO      2016-10-07 14:09:25,977 devappserver2.py:769] Skipping SDK update check.
INFO      2016-10-07 14:09:26,005 api_server.py:205] Starting API server at: http://localhost:52500
INFO      2016-10-07 14:09:26,006 dispatcher.py:185] Starting dispatcher running at: http://localhost:8080
INFO      2016-10-07 14:09:26,008 dispatcher.py:197] Starting module "default" running at: http://localhost:8081
INFO      2016-10-07 14:09:26,009 dispatcher.py:197] Starting module "api" running at: http://localhost:8082
INFO      2016-10-07 14:09:26,012 dispatcher.py:197] Starting module "web" running at: http://localhost:8083
INFO      2016-10-07 14:09:26,013 admin_server.py:116] Starting admin server at: http://localhost:8000
```

We can access modules directly by visiting each port, but luckily we have our dispatcher running on port `:8080`, which will do that for us based on the rules we specified in our `dispatch.yaml` configuration file.

Testing locally

Now that we have built our application, head over to `localhost:8080` to see it in action. Use the features of the application by performing the following steps:

1. Log in using your real e-mail address (that way, you'll see your Gravatar picture).
2. Ask a question.
3. Submit a couple of answers.
4. Vote the answers up and down and see the scores changing.
5. Open another browser and sign in as someone else to see what the application looks like from their point of view.

Using the admin console

The admin console is running alongside our application and is accessible at
`localhost:8000`:

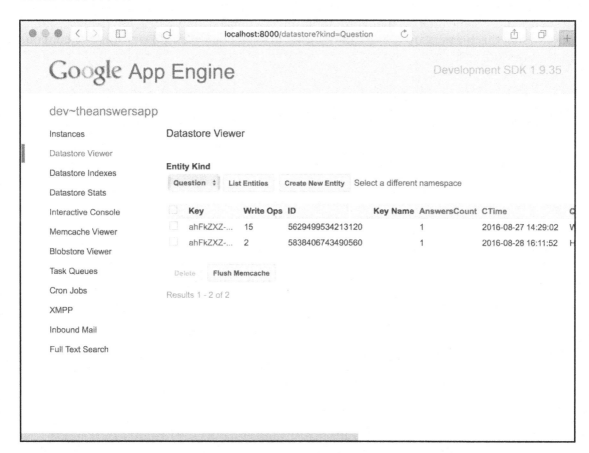

Datastore Viewer lets you inspect the data of your application. You can use it to see (and
even make changes to) the questions, answers, and votes data that are being generated as
you use the application.

Automatically generated indexes

You can also see which indexes have been automatically created by the development server in order to satisfy the queries your application makes. In fact, if you look in the default folder, you will notice that a new file called `index.yaml` has magically appeared. This file describes those same indexes that your application will need, and when you deploy your application, this file goes up to the cloud with it to tell Google Cloud Datastore to maintain these same indexes.

Deploying apps with multiple modules

Deploying the application is slightly more complicated with multiple modules, as the dispatcher and index files each require a dedicated deployment command.

Deploy the modules with the following:

```
goapp deploy default/app.yaml api/app.yaml web/app.yaml
```

Once the operation has finished, we can update the dispatcher using the `appcfg.py` command (which you must ensure is in your path you'll find it in the Google App Engine SDK for the Go folder we downloaded at the start of the chapter):

```
appcfg.py update_dispatch .
```

Once the dispatch has been updated, we can push the indexes to the cloud:

```
appcfg.py update_indexes —A YOUR_APPLICATION_ID_HERE ./default
```

Now that the application is deployed, we can see it in the wild by navigating to our *appspot* URL; `https://YOUR_APPLICATION_ID_HERE.appspot.com/`.

> You might get an error that says `The index for this query is not ready to serve`. This is because it takes Google Cloud Datastore a little time to prepare things on the server; usually, it doesn't take more than a few minutes, so go and have a cup of coffee and try again later.

An interesting aside is that if you hit the URL with HTTPS, Google's servers will serve it using HTTP/2.

Once your application is functional, ask an interesting question and send the link to your friends to solicit answers.

Summary

In this chapter, we built a fully functional question and answer application for Google App Engine.

We learned how to use the Google App Engine SDK for Go to build and test our application locally before deploying it to the cloud, ready for our friends and family to use. The application is ready to scale if it suddenly starts getting a lot of traffic, and we can rely on the healthy quota to satisfy early traffic.

We explored how to model data in Go code, keep track of keys, and persist and query data in Google Cloud Datastore. We also explored strategies to denormalize such data in order to make it quicker to read back at scale. We saw how transactions can guarantee data integrity by ensuring that only one operation occurs at a particular point in time, allowing us to build reliable counters for the score of our answers. We used predictable data store keys to ensure that our users can only have one vote per answer, and we used incomplete keys when we wanted the data store to generate the keys for us.

A lot of the techniques explored in this chapter would apply to any kind of application that persists data and interacts over a RESTful JSON API so the skills are highly transferrable.

In the next chapter, we are going to explore modern software architecture by building a real micro-service using the Go Kit framework. There are a lot of benefits to building solutions using micro-services, and so they have become a very popular choice for large, distributed systems. Lots of companies are already running such architectures (mostly written in Go) in production, and we will look at how they do it.

10
Micro-services in Go with the Go kit Framework

Micro-services are discrete components working together to provide functionality and business logic for a larger application, usually communicating over a network protocol (such as HTTP/2 or some other binary transport) and distributed across many physical machines. Each component is isolated from the others, and they take in well-defined inputs and yield well-defined outputs. Multiple instances of the same service can run across many servers and traffic can be load balanced between them. If designed correctly, it is possible for an individual instance to fail without bringing down the whole system and for new instances to be spun up during runtime to help handle load spikes.

Go kit (refer to `https://gokit.io`) is a distributed programming toolkit for the building of applications with a micro-service architecture founded by Peter Bourgon (`@peterbourgon` on Twitter) and now maintained by a slice of Gophers in the open. It aims to solve many of the foundational (and sometimes boring) aspects of building such systems as well as encouraging good design patterns, allowing you to focus on the business logic that makes up your product or service.

Go kit doesn't try to solve every problem from scratch; rather, it integrates with many popular related services to solve **SOA (service-oriented architecture)** problems, such as service discovery, metrics, monitoring, logging, load balancing, circuit breaking, and many other important aspects of correctly running micro-services at scale. As we build our service by hand using Go kit, you will notice that we will write a lot of boilerplate or scaffold code in order to get things working.

For smaller products and services with a small team of developers, you may well decide it is easier to just expose a simple JSON endpoint, but Go kit really shines for larger teams, building substantial systems with many different services, each being run tens or hundreds of times within the architecture. Having consistent logging, instrumentation, distributed tracing, and each item being similar to the next means running and maintaining such a system becomes significantly easier.

> *"Go kit is ultimately about encouraging good design practice within a service: SOLID design, or domain-driven-design, or the hexagonal architecture, etc. It's not dogmatically any of those, but tries to make good design/software engineering tractable."* â✎✎ÂÂPeter Bourgon

In this chapter, we are going to build some micro-services that address various security challenges (in a project called `vault`) â✇✇upon which we would be able to build further functionality. The business logic will be kept very simple, allowing us to focus on learning the principles around building micro-service systems.

There are some alternatives to Go kit as a technology choice; most of them have a similar approach but with different priorities, syntax, and patterns. Ensure that you look around at other options before embarking on a project, but the principles you learn in this chapter will apply across the board.

Specifically, in this chapter, you will learn:

- How to hand code a micro-service using Go kit
- What gRPC is and how to use it to build servers and clients
- How to use Google's protocol buffers and associated tools to describe services and communicate in a highly efficient binary format
- How endpoints in Go kit allow us to write a single service implementation and have it exposed via multiple transport protocols
- How Go kits-included subpackages help us solve lots of common problems
- How Middleware lets us wrap endpoints to adapt their behavior without touching the implementation itself
- How to describe method calls as requests and response messages
- How to rate limit our services to protect from surges in traffic
- A few other idiomatic Go tips and tricks

Some lines of code in this chapter stretch over many lines; they are written with the overflowing content right-aligned on the next line, as shown in this example:

```
func veryLongFunctionWithLotsOfArguments(one string, two int, three
  http.Handler, four string) (bool, error) {
    log.Println("first line of the function")
}
```

The first three lines in the preceding snippet should be written as one line. Don't worry; the Go compiler will be kind enough to point out if you get this wrong.

Introducing gRPC

There are many options when it comes to how our services will communicate with each other and how clients will communicate with the services, and Go kit doesn't care (rather, it doesn't mindâ◎◎it cares enough to provide implementations of many popular mechanisms). In fact, we are able to add multiple options for our users and let them decide which one they want to use. We will add support the familiar JSON over HTTP, but we are also going to introduce a new technology choice for APIs.

gRPC, short for Google's **Remote Procedure Call**, is an open source mechanism used to call code that is running remotely over a network. It uses HTTP/2 for transport and protocol buffers to represent the data that makes up services and messages.

An RPC service differs from RESTful web services because rather than making changes to data using well-defined HTTP standards, as you do with REST (POST to create something, PUT to update something, DELETE to delete something, and so on), you are triggering a remote function or method instead, passing in expected arguments and getting back one or more pieces of data in response.

To highlight the difference, imagine that we are creating a new user. In a RESTful world, we could make a request like this:

```
POST /users
{
  "name": "Mat",
  "twitter": "@matryer"
}
```

And we might get a response like this:

```
201 Created
{
  "id": 1,
  "name": "Mat",
  "twitter": "@matryer"
}
```

RESTful calls represent queries or changes to the state of resources. In an RPC world, we would use generated code instead in order to make binary serialized procedure calls that feel much more like normal methods or functions in Go.

The only other key difference between a RESTful service and a gPRC service is that rather than JSON or XML, gPRC speaks a special format called **protocol buffers**.

Protocol buffers

Protocol buffers (called `protobuf` in code) are a binary serialization format that is very small and extremely quick to encode and decode. You describe data structures in an abstract way using a declarative mini language, and generate source code (in a variety of languages) to make reading and writing the data easy for users.

You can think of protocol buffers as a modern alternative to XML, except that the definition of the data structure is separated from the content, and the content is in a binary format rather than text.

It's clear to see the benefits when you look at a real example. If we wanted to represent a person with a name in XML, we could write this:

```
<person>
  <name>MAT</name>
</person>
```

This takes up about 30 bytes (discounting whitespace). Let's see how it would look in JSON:

```
{"name":"MAT"}
```

Now we're down to 14 bytes, but the structure is still embedded in the content (the name field is spelled out along with the value).

The equivalent content in protocol buffers would only take five bytes. The following table shows each byte, along with the first five bytes of the XML and JSON representations for comparison. The **Description** row explains the meaning of the bytes in the **Content** row, which shows the protocol buffer bytes:

Byte	1	2	3	4	5
Content	0a	03	4d	61	72
Description	Type (string)	Length (3)	M	A	T
XML	<	p	e	r	s
JSON	{	"	n	a	m

The structure definition lives in a special `.proto` file, separate from the data.

There are still plenty of cases where XML or JSON would be a better choice than protocol buffers, and file size isn't the only measure when deciding a data format to use, but for fixed schema structures and remote procedure calls or for applications running at a truly massive scale, it's a popular choice for good reasons.

Installing protocol buffers

There are some tools to compile and generate source code for protocol buffers, which you can grab from the GitHub home page of the project at `https://github.com/google/protobuf/releases`. Once you've downloaded the file, unpack it and place the `protoc` file from the bin folder into an appropriate folder on your machine: one that is mentioned in your `$PATH` environment variable.

Once the protoc command is ready, we'll need to add a plugin that will allow us to work with Go code. In a terminal, execute this:

```
go get -u github.com/golang/protobuf/{proto,protoc-gen-go}
```

This will install two packages that we'll make use of later.

Protocol buffers language

To define our data structure, we are going to use the third version of the protocol buffers language, known as `proto3`.

Create a new folder in your $GOPATH called vault, and a subfolder called pb inside that. The pb package is where our protocol buffer definition and the generated source code will live.

We are going to define a service called Vault, which has two methods, Hash and Validate:

Method	Description
Hash	Generate a secure hash for a given password. The hash can be stored instead of storing the password in plain text.
Validate	Given a password and a previously generated hash, the Validate method will check to ensure that the password is correct.

Each service call has a request and response pair, which we will define as well. Inside pb, insert the following code into a new file called vault.proto:

```
syntax = "proto3";
package pb;
service Vault {
    rpc Hash(HashRequest) returns (HashResponse) {}
    rpc Validate(ValidateRequest) returns (ValidateResponse) {}
}
message HashRequest {
    string password = 1;
}
message HashResponse {
    string hash = 1;
    string err = 2;
}
message ValidateRequest {
    string password = 1;
    string hash = 2;
}
message ValidateResponse {
    bool valid = 1;
}
```

Vertical whitespace has been removed to save paper, but you are free to add spaces between each block if you think it improves readability.

The first things we specify in our file are that we are using the `proto3` syntax and the name of the package for the generated source code is `pb`.

The `service` block defines `Vault` and the two methods-with `HashRequest`, `HashResponse`, `ValidateRequest`, and `ValidateResponse` messages defined underneath. The lines beginning with `rpc` inside the service block indicate that our service consists of two remote procedure calls: `Hash` and `Validate`.

The fields inside a message take the following format:

```
type name = position;
```

The `type` is a string that describes the scalar value type, such as `string`, `bool`, `double`, `float`, `int32`, `int64`, and so on. The `name` is a human-readable string that describes the field, such as `hash` and `password`. The position is an integer that indicates where in the data stream that field appears. This is important because the content is a stream of bytes, and lining up the content to the definition is vital to being able to use the format. Additionally, if we were to add (or even rename) fields later (one of the key design features of protocol buffers), we could do so without breaking components that expect certain fields in a specific order; they would continue to work untouched, ignoring new data and just transparently passing it along.

 For a complete list of the supported types as well as a deep dive into the entire language, check out the documentation at `https://developers.go ogle.com/protocol-buffers/docs/proto3`.

Note that each method call has an associated request and response pair. These are the messages that will be sent over the network when the remote method is called.

Since the Hash method takes a single password string argument, the `HashRequest` object contains a single password string field. Like normal Go functions, the responses may contain an error, which is why both `HashResponse` and `ValidateResponse` have two fields. There is no dedicated `error` interface in proto3 like there is in Go, so we are going to turn the error into a string instead.

Generating Go code

Go doesn't understand proto3 code, but luckily the protocol buffer compiler and Go plugin we installed earlier can translate it into something Go does understand: Go code.

In a terminal, navigate to the pb folder and run the following:

```
protoc vault.proto --go_out=plugins=grpc:.
```

This will generate a new file called vault.pb.go. Open the file and inspect its contents. It has done a lot of work for us, including defining the messages and even creating VaultClient and VaultServer types for us to use, which will allow us to consume and expose the service, respectively.

> You are free to decode the rest of the generated code (the file descriptor looks especially interesting) if you are interested in the details. For now, we're going to trust that it works and use the pb package to build our service implementation.

Building the service

At the end of the day, whatever other dark magic is going on in our architecture, it will come down to some Go method being called, doing some work, and returning a result. So the next thing we are going to do is define and implement the Vault service itself.

Inside the vault folder, add the following code to a new service.go file:

```
// Service provides password hashing capabilities.
type Service interface {
  Hash(ctx context.Context, password string) (string,
    error)
  Validate(ctx context.Context, password, hash string)
    (bool, error)
}
```

This interface defines the service.

> You might think that VaultService would be a better name than just Service, but remember that since this is a Go package, it will been seen externally as vault.Service, which reads nicely.

We define our two methods: Hash and Validate. Each takes context.Context as the first argument, followed by normal string arguments. The responses are normal Go types as well: string, bool, and error.

Some libraries may still require the old context dependency, `golang.org/x/net/context`, rather than the `context` package that was made available first in Go 1.7. Watch out for errors complaining about mixed use and make sure you're importing the right one.

Part of designing micro-services is being careful about where state is stored. Even though you will implement the methods of a service in a single file, with access to global variables, you should never use them to store the per-request or even per-service state. It's important to remember that each service is likely to be running on many physical machines multiple times, each with no access to the others' global variables.

In this spirit, we are going to implement our service using an empty `struct`, essentially a neat idiomatic Go trick to group methods together in order to implement an interface without storing any state in the object itself. To `service.go`, add the following `struct`:

```
type vaultService struct{}
```

If the implementation did require any dependencies (such as a database connection or a configuration object), you could store them inside the struct and use the method receivers in your function bodies.

Starting with tests

Where possible, starting by writing test code has many advantages that usually end up increasing the quality and maintainability of your code. We are going to write a unit test that will use our new service to hash and then validate a password.

Create a new file called `service_test.go` and add the following code:

```
package vault
import (
  "testing"
  "golang.org/x/net/context"
)
func TestHasherService(t *testing.T) {
  srv := NewService()
  ctx := context.Background()
  h, err := srv.Hash(ctx, "password")
  if err != nil {
    t.Errorf("Hash: %s", err)
  }
  ok, err := srv.Validate(ctx, "password", h)
  if err != nil {
```

```
      t.Errorf("Valid: %s", err)
    }
    if !ok {
      t.Error("expected true from Valid")
    }
    ok, err = srv.Validate(ctx, "wrong password", h)
    if err != nil {
      t.Errorf("Valid: %s", err)
    }
    if ok {
      t.Error("expected false from Valid")
    }
  }
```

We will create a new service via the `NewService` method and then use it to call the `Hash` and `Validate` methods. We even test an unhappy case, where we get the password wrong and ensure that `Validate` returns `false`—otherwise, it wouldn't be very secure at all.

Constructors in Go

A **constructor** in other object-oriented languages is a special kind of function that creates instances of classes. It performs any initialization and takes in required arguments such as dependencies, among others. It is usually the only way to create an object in these languages, but it often has weird syntax or relies on naming conventions (such as the function name being the same as the class, for example).

Go doesn't have constructors; it's much simpler and just has functions, and since functions can return arguments, a constructor would just be a global function that returns a usable instance of a struct. The Go philosophy of simplicity drives these kinds of decisions for the language designers; rather than forcing people to have to learn about a new concept of constructing objects, developers only have to learn how functions work and they can build constructors with them.

Even if we aren't doing any special work in the construction of an object (such as initializing fields, validating dependencies, and so on), it is sometimes worth adding a construction function anyway. In our case, we do not want to bloat the API by exposing the `vaultService` type since we already have our `Service` interface type exposed and are hiding it inside a constructor is a nice way to achieve this.

Underneath the `vaultService` struct definition, add the `NewService` function:

```
// NewService makes a new Service.
func NewService() Service {
  return vaultService{}
```

```
}
```

Not only does this prevent us from needing to expose our internals, but if in the future we do need to do more work to prepare the `vaultService` for use, we can also do it without changing the API and, therefore, without requiring the users of our package to change anything on their end, which is a big win for API design.

Hashing and validating passwords with bcrypt

The first method we will implement in our service is `Hash`. It will take a password and generate a hash. The resulting hash can then be passed (along with a password) to the `Validate` method later, which will either confirm or deny that the password is correct.

> To learn more about the correct way to store passwords in applications, check out the Coda Hale blog post on the subject at `https://codahale.co m/how-to-safely-store-a-password/`.

The point of our service is to ensure that passwords never need to be stored in a database, since that's a security risk if anyone is ever able to get unauthorized access to the database. Instead, you can generate a one-way hash (it cannot be decoded) that can safely be stored, and when users attempt to authenticate, you can perform a check to see whether the password generates the same hash or not. If the hashes match, the passwords are the same; otherwise, they are not.

The `bcrypt` package provides methods that do this work for us in a secure and trustworthy way.

To `service.go`, add the `Hash` method:

```
func (vaultService) Hash(ctx context.Context, password
  string) (string, error) {
  hash, err :=
    bcrypt.GenerateFromPassword([]byte(password),
    bcrypt.DefaultCost)
  if err != nil {
    return "", err
  }
  return string(hash), nil
}
```

Ensure that you import the appropriate `bcrypt` package (try `golang.org/x/crypto/bcrypt`). We are essentially wrapping the `GenerateFromPassword` function to generate the hash, which we then return provided no errors occurred.

Note that the receiver in the `Hash` method is just `(vaultService)`; we don't capture the variable because there is no way we can store state on an empty `struct`.

Next up, let's add the `Validate` method:

```
func (vaultService) Validate(ctx context.Context,
  password, hash string) (bool, error) {
  err := bcrypt.CompareHashAndPassword([]byte(hash),
    []byte(password))
  if err != nil {
    return false, nil
  }
  return true, nil
}
```

Similar to `Hash`, we are calling `bcrypt.CompareHashAndPassword` to determine (in a secure way) whether the password is correct or not. If an error is returned, it means that something is amiss and we return `false` indicating that. Otherwise, we return `true` when the password is valid.

Modeling method calls with requests and responses

Since our service will be exposed through various transport protocols, we will need a way to model the requests and responses in and out of our service. We will do this by adding a `struct` for each type of message our service will accept or return.

In order for somebody to call the `Hash` method and then receive the hashed password as a response, we'll need to add the following two structures to `service.go`:

```
type hashRequest struct {
  Password string `json:"password"`
}
type hashResponse struct {
  Hash string `json:"hash"`
  Err  string `json:"err,omitempty"`
}
```

The `hashRequest` type contains a single field, the password, and the `hashResponse` has the resulting hash and an `Err` string field in case something goes wrong.

> To model remote method calls, you essentially create a `struct` for the incoming arguments and a `struct` for the return arguments.

Before continuing, see whether you can model the same request/response pair for the `Validate` method. Look at the signature in the `Service` interface, examine the arguments it accepts, and think about what kind of responses it will need to make.

We are going to add a helper method (of type `http.DecodeRequestFunc` from Go kit) that will be able to decode the JSON body of `http.Request` to `service.go`:

```
func decodeHashRequest(ctx context.Context, r
 *http.Request) (interface{}, error) {
  var req hashRequest
  err := json.NewDecoder(r.Body).Decode(&req)
  if err != nil {
    return nil, err
  }
  return req, nil
}
```

The signature for `decodeHashRequest` is dictated by Go kit because it will later use it to decode HTTP requests on our behalf. In this function, we just use `json.Decoder` to unmarshal the JSON into our `hashRequest` type.

Next, we will add the request and response structures as well as a decode helper function for the `Validate` method:

```
type validateRequest struct {
  Password string `json:"password"`
  Hash     string `json:"hash"`
}
type validateResponse struct {
  Valid bool   `json:"valid"`
  Err   string `json:"err,omitempty"`
}
func decodeValidateRequest(ctx context.Context,
 r *http.Request) (interface{}, error) {
  var req validateRequest
  err := json.NewDecoder(r.Body).Decode(&req)
  if err != nil {
    return nil, err
```

```
    }
    return req, nil
  }
```

Here, the `validateRequest` struct takes both `Password` and `Hash` strings, since the signature has two input arguments and returns a response containing a `bool` datatype called `Valid` or `Err`.

The final thing we need to do is encode the response. In this case, we can write a single method to encode both the `hashResponse` and `validateResponse` objects.

Add the following code to `service.go`:

```
func encodeResponse(ctx context.Context,
  w http.ResponseWriter, response interface{})
error {
  return json.NewEncoder(w).Encode(response)
}
```

Our `encodeResponse` method just asks `json.Encoder` to do the work for us. Note again that the signature is general since the `response` type is `interface{}`; this is because it's a Go kit mechanism for decoding to `http.ResponseWriter`.

Endpoints in Go kit

Endpoints are a special function type in Go kit that represent a single RPC method. The definition is inside the `endpoint` package:

```
type Endpoint func(ctx context.Context, request
  interface{})
(response interface{}, err error)
```

An endpoint function takes `context.Context` and `request`, and it returns `response` or `error`. The `request` and `response` types are `interface{}`, which tells us that it is up to the implementation code to deal with the actual types when building endpoints.

Endpoints are powerful because, like `http.Handler` (and `http.HandlerFunc`), you can wrap them with generalized middleware to solve a myriad of common issues that arise when building micro-services: logging, tracing, rate limiting, error handling, and more.

Go kit solves transporting over various protocols and uses endpoints as a general way to jump from their code to ours. For example, the gRPC server will listen on a port, and when it receives the appropriate message, it will call the corresponding `Endpoint` function. Thanks to Go kit, this will all be transparent to us, as we only need to deal in Go code with our `Service` interface.

Making endpoints for service methods

In order to turn our service methods into `endpoint.Endpoint` functions, we're going to write a function that handles the incoming `hashRequest`, calls the `Hash` service method, and depending on the response, builds and returns an appropriate `hashResponse` object.

To `service.go`, add the `MakeHashEndpoint` function:

```
func MakeHashEndpoint(srv Service) endpoint.Endpoint {
  return func(ctx context.Context, request interface{})
  (interface{}, error) {
    req := request.(hashRequest)
    v, err := srv.Hash(ctx, req.Password)
    if err != nil {
      return hashResponse{v, err.Error()}, nil
    }
    return hashResponse{v, ""}, nil
  }
}
```

This function takes `Service` as an argument, which means that we can generate an endpoint from any implementation of our `Service` interface. We then use a type assertion to specify that the request argument should, in fact, be of type `hashRequest`. We call the `Hash` method, passing in the context and `Password`, which we get from `hashRequest`. If all is well, we build `hashResponse` with the value we got back from the `Hash` method and return it.

Let's do the same for the `Validate` method:

```
func MakeValidateEndpoint(srv Service) endpoint.Endpoint {
  return func(ctx context.Context, request interface{})
  (interface{}, error) {
    req := request.(validateRequest)
    v, err := srv.Validate(ctx, req.Password, req.Hash)
    if err != nil {
      return validateResponse{false, err.Error()}, nil
    }
    return validateResponse{v, ""}, nil
```

```
        }
    }
```

Here, we are doing the same: taking the request and using it to call the method before building a response. Note that we never return an error from the Endpoint function.

Different levels of error

There are two main types of errors in Go kit: transport errors (network failure, timeouts, dropped connection, and so on) and business logic errors (where the infrastructure of making the request and responding was successful, but something in the logic or data wasn't correct).

If the Hash method returns an error, we are not going to return it as the second argument; instead, we are going to build hashResponse, which contains the error string (accessible via the Error method). This is because the error returned from an endpoint is intended to indicate a transport error, and perhaps Go kit will be configured to retry the call a few times by some middleware. If our service methods return an error, it is considered a business logic error and will probably always return the same error for the same input, so it's not worth retrying. This is why we wrap the error into the response and return it to the client so that they can deal with it.

Wrapping endpoints into a Service implementation

Another very useful trick when dealing with endpoints in Go kit is to write an implementation of our vault.Service interface, which just makes the necessary calls to the underlying endpoints.

To service.go, add the following structure:

```
type Endpoints struct {
    HashEndpoint     endpoint.Endpoint
    ValidateEndpoint endpoint.Endpoint
}
```

In order to implement the vault.Service interface, we are going to add the two methods to our Endpoints structure, which will build a request object, make the request, and parse the resulting response object into the normal arguments to be returned.

Add the following `Hash` method:

```
func (e Endpoints) Hash(ctx context.Context, password
  string) (string, error) {
  req := hashRequest{Password: password}
  resp, err := e.HashEndpoint(ctx, req)
  if err != nil {
    return "", err
  }
  hashResp := resp.(hashResponse)
  if hashResp.Err != "" {
    return "", errors.New(hashResp.Err)
  }
  return hashResp.Hash, nil
}
```

We are calling `HashEndpoint` with `hashRequest`, which we create using the password argument before caching the general response to `hashResponse` and returning the Hash value from it or an error.

We will do this for the Validate method:

```
func (e Endpoints) Validate(ctx context.Context, password,
  hash string) (bool, error) {
  req := validateRequest{Password: password, Hash: hash}
  resp, err := e.ValidateEndpoint(ctx, req)
  if err != nil {
    return false, err
  }
  validateResp := resp.(validateResponse)
  if validateResp.Err != "" {
    return false, errors.New(validateResp.Err)
  }
  return validateResp.Valid, nil
}
```

These two methods will allow us to treat the endpoints we have created as though they are normal Go methods; very useful for when we actually consume our service later in this chapter.

An HTTP server in Go kit

The true value of Go kit becomes apparent when we create an HTTP server for our endpoints to hash and validate.

Create a new file called `server_http.go` and add the following code:

```
package vault
import (
  "net/http"
  httptransport "github.com/go-kit/kit/transport/http"
  "golang.org/x/net/context"
)
func NewHTTPServer(ctx context.Context, endpoints
 Endpoints) http.Handler {
  m := http.NewServeMux()
  m.Handle("/hash", httptransport.NewServer(
    ctx,
    endpoints.HashEndpoint,
    decodeHashRequest,
    encodeResponse,
  ))
  m.Handle("/validate", httptransport.NewServer(
    ctx,
    endpoints.ValidateEndpoint,
    decodeValidateRequest,
    encodeResponse,
  ))
  return m
}
```

We are importing the `github.com/go-kit/kit/transport/http` package and (since we're also importing the `net/http` package) telling Go that we're going to explicitly refer to this package as `httptransport`.

We are using the `NewServeMux` function from the standard library to build `http.Handler` interface with simple routing and mapping the `/hash` and `/validate` paths. We take the `Endpoints` object since we want our HTTP server to serve these endpoints, including any middleware that we will add later. Calling `httptransport.NewServer` is how we get Go kit to give us an HTTP handler for each endpoint. Like most functions, we pass in `context.Context` as the first argument, which will form the base context for each request. We also pass in the endpoint as well as the decoding and encoding functions that we wrote earlier so that the server knows how to unmarshal and marshal the JSON messages.

A gRPC server in Go kit

Adding a gPRC server using Go kit is almost as easy as adding a JSON/HTTP server, like we did in the last section. In our generated code (in the pb folder), we were given the following pb.VaultServer type:

```
type VaultServer interface {
  Hash(context.Context, *HashRequest)
    (*HashResponse, error)
  Validate(context.Context, *ValidateRequest)
    (*ValidateResponse, error)
}
```

This type is very similar to our own Service interface, except that it takes in generated request and response classes rather than raw arguments.

We'll start by defining a type that will implement the preceding interface. Add the following code to a new file called server_grpc.go:

```
package vault
import (
  "golang.org/x/net/context"
  grpctransport "github.com/go-kit/kit/transport/grpc"
)
type grpcServer struct {
  hash     grpctransport.Handler
  validate grpctransport.Handler
}
func (s *grpcServer) Hash(ctx context.Context,
 r *pb.HashRequest) (*pb.HashResponse, error) {
  _, resp, err := s.hash.ServeGRPC(ctx, r)
  if err != nil {
    return nil, err
  }
  return resp.(*pb.HashResponse), nil
}
func (s *grpcServer) Validate(ctx context.Context,
 r *pb.ValidateRequest) (*pb.ValidateResponse, error) {
  _, resp, err := s.validate.ServeGRPC(ctx, r)
  if err != nil {
    return nil, err
  }
  return resp.(*pb.ValidateResponse), nil
}
```

Note that you'll need to import `github.com/go-kit/kit/transport/grpc` as `grpctransport`, along with the generated `pb` package.

The `grpcServer` struct contains a field for each of the service endpoints, this time of type `grpctransport.Handler`. Then, we implement the methods of the interface, calling the `ServeGRPC` method on the appropriate handler. This method will actually serve requests by first decoding them, calling the appropriate endpoint function, getting the response, and encoding it and sending it back to the client who made the request.

Translating from protocol buffer types to our types

You'll notice that we're using the request and response objects from the `pb` package, but remember that our own endpoints use the structures we added to `service.go` earlier. We are going to need a method for each type in order to translate to and from our own types.

 There's a lot of repetitive typing coming up; feel free to copy and paste this from the GitHub repository at `https://github.com/matryer/gobluepri nts` to save your fingers. We're hand coding this manually because it's important to understand all the pieces that make up the service.

To `server_grpc.go`, add the following function:

```
func EncodeGRPCHashRequest(ctx context.Context,
    r interface{}) (interface{}, error) {
    req := r.(hashRequest)
    return &pb.HashRequest{Password: req.Password}, nil
}
```

This function is an `EncodeRequestFunc` function defined by Go kit, and it is used to translate our own `hashRequest` type into a protocol buffer type that can be used to communicate with the client. It uses `interface{}` types because it's general, but in our case, we can be sure about the types so we cast the incoming request to `hashRequest` (our own type) and then build a new `pb.HashRequest` object using the appropriate fields.

We are going to do this for both encoding and decoding requests and responses for both hash and validate endpoints. Add the following code to `server_grpc.go`:

```
func DecodeGRPCHashRequest(ctx context.Context,
    r interface{}) (interface{}, error) {
    req := r.(*pb.HashRequest)
    return hashRequest{Password: req.Password}, nil
```

```
}
func EncodeGRPCHashResponse(ctx context.Context,
 r interface{}) (interface{}, error) {
  res := r.(hashResponse)
  return &pb.HashResponse{Hash: res.Hash, Err: res.Err},
    nil
}
func DecodeGRPCHashResponse(ctx context.Context,
 r interface{}) (interface{}, error) {
  res := r.(*pb.HashResponse)
  return hashResponse{Hash: res.Hash, Err: res.Err}, nil
}
func EncodeGRPCValidateRequest(ctx context.Context,
 r interface{}) (interface{}, error) {
  req := r.(validateRequest)
  return &pb.ValidateRequest{Password: req.Password,
    Hash: req.Hash}, nil
}
func DecodeGRPCValidateRequest(ctx context.Context,
 r interface{}) (interface{}, error) {
  req := r.(*pb.ValidateRequest)
  return validateRequest{Password: req.Password,
    Hash: req.Hash}, nil
}
func EncodeGRPCValidateResponse(ctx context.Context,
 r interface{}) (interface{}, error) {
  res := r.(validateResponse)
  return &pb.ValidateResponse{Valid: res.Valid}, nil
}
func DecodeGRPCValidateResponse(ctx context.Context,
 r interface{}) (interface{}, error) {
  res := r.(*pb.ValidateResponse)
  return validateResponse{Valid: res.Valid}, nil
}
```

As you can see, there is a lot of boilerplate coding to do in order to get things working.

 Code generation (not covered here) would have great application here, since the code is very predictable and self-similar.

The final thing to do in order to get our gRPC server working is to provide a helper function to create an instance of our `grpcServer` structure. Underneath the `grpcServer` struct, add the following code:

```
func NewGRPCServer(ctx context.Context, endpoints
Endpoints) pb.VaultServer {
  return &grpcServer{
    hash: grpctransport.NewServer(
      ctx,
      endpoints.HashEndpoint,
      DecodeGRPCHashRequest,
      EncodeGRPCHashResponse,
    ),
    validate: grpctransport.NewServer(
      ctx,
      endpoints.ValidateEndpoint,
      DecodeGRPCValidateRequest,
      EncodeGRPCValidateResponse,
    ),
  }
}
```

Like our HTTP server, we take in a base context and the actual `Endpoints` implementation that we are exposing via the gRPC server. We create and return a new instance of our `grpcServer` type, setting the handlers for both `hash` and `validate` by calling `grpctransport.NewServer`. We use our `endpoint.Endpoint` functions for our service and tell the service which of our encoding/decoding functions to use for each case.

Creating a server command

So far, all of our service code lives inside the `vault` package. We are now going to use this package to create a new tool to expose the server functionality.

Create a new folder in `vault` called `cmd`, and inside it create another called `vaultd`. We are going to put our command code inside the `vaultd` folder because even though the code will be in the `main` package, the name of the tool will be `vaultd` by default. If we just put the command in the `cmd` folder, the tool would be built into a binary called `cmd`-which is pretty confusing.

 In Go projects, if the primary use of the package is to be imported into other programs (such as Go kit), then the root level files should make up the package and will have an appropriate package name (not `main`). If the primary purpose is a command-line tool, such as the Drop command (htt ps://github.com/matryer/drop), then the root files will be in the `main` package.

The rationale for this comes down to usability; when importing a package, you want the string the user has to type to be the shortest it can be. Similarly, when using `go install`, you want the path to be short and sweet.

The tool we are going to build (suffixed with `d`, indicating that it is a daemon or a background task) will spin up both our gRPC and JSON/HTTP servers. Each will run in their own goroutine, and we will trap any termination signals or errors from the servers, which will cause the termination of our program.

In Go kit, main functions end up being quite large, which is by design; there is a single function that contains the entirety of your micro-service; from there, you can dig down into the details, but it provides an at-a-glance view of each component.

We will build up the `main` function piece by piece inside a new `main.go` file in the `vaultd` folder, starting with the fairly big list of imports:

```go
import (
    "flag"
    "fmt"
    "log"
    "net"
    "net/http"
    "os"
    "os/signal"
    "syscall"
    "your/path/to/vault"
    "your/path/to/vault/pb"
    "golang.org/x/net/context"
    "google.golang.org/grpc"
)
```

The `your/path/to` prefixes should be replaced with the actual route from `$GOPATH` to where your project is. Pay attention to the context import too; it's quite possible that you just need to type context rather than the import listed here depending on when Go kit transitions to Go 1.7. Finally, the `grpc` package from Google provides everything we need in order to expose gRPC capabilities over the network.

Now, we will put together our `main` function; remember that all the sections following this one go inside the body of the `main` function:

```
func main() {
  var (
    httpAddr = flag.String("http", ":8080",
      "http listen address")
    gRPCAddr = flag.String("grpc", ":8081",
      "gRPC listen address")
  )
  flag.Parse()
  ctx := context.Background()
  srv := vault.NewService()
  errChan := make(chan error)
```

We use flags to allow the ops team to decide which endpoints we will listen on when exposing the service on the network, but provide sensible defaults of :8080 for the JSON/HTTP server and :8081 for the gRPC server.

We then create a new context using the `context.Background()` function, which returns a non-nil, empty context that has no cancelation or deadline specified and contains no values, perfect for the base context of all of our services. Requests and middleware are free to create new context objects from this one in order to add request-scoped data or deadlines.

Next, we use our `NewService` constructor to make a new `Service` type for us and make a zero-buffer channel, which can take an error should one occur.

We will now add the code that traps termination signals (such as *Ctrl + C*) and sends an error down `errChan`:

```
go func() {
  c := make(chan os.Signal, 1)
  signal.Notify(c, syscall.SIGINT, syscall.SIGTERM)
  errChan <- fmt.Errorf("%s", <-c)
}()
```

Here, in a new goroutine, we ask `signal.Notify` to tell us when we receive the SIGINT or SIGTERM signals. When that happens, the signal will be sent down the c channel, at which point we'll format it as a string (its `String()` method will be called), and we turn that into an error, which we'll send down `errChan`, resulting in the termination of the program.

Using Go kit endpoints

It is time to create one of our endpoints instances that we can pass to our servers. Add the following code to the main function body:

```
hashEndpoint := vault.MakeHashEndpoint(srv)
validateEndpoint := vault.MakeValidateEndpoint(srv)
endpoints := vault.Endpoints{
  HashEndpoint:     hashEndpoint,
  ValidateEndpoint: validateEndpoint,
}
```

We are assigning the fields to the output of our endpoint helper functions for both the hash and validate methods. We are passing in the same service for both, so the `endpoints` variable essentially ends up being a wrapper around our `srv` service.

> You may be tempted to neaten up this code by removing the assignment to the variables altogether and just set the return of the helper functions to the fields in the struct initialization, but when we come to add middleware later, you'll be thankful for this approach.

We are now ready to start up our JSON/HTTP and gRPC servers using these endpoints.

Running the HTTP server

Now we will add the goroutine to make and run the JSON/HTTP server to the main function body:

```
// HTTP transport
go func() {
  log.Println("http:", *httpAddr)
  handler := vault.NewHTTPServer(ctx, endpoints)
  errChan <- http.ListenAndServe(*httpAddr, handler)
}()
```

All the heavy lifting has already been done for us in our package code by Go kit, so we are left with simply calling the `NewHTTPServer` function, passing in the background context and the service endpoints we wish for it to expose, before calling the standard library's `http.ListenAndServe`, which exposes the handler functionality in the specified `httpAddr`. If an error occurs, we send it down the error channel.

Running the gRPC server

There is a little more work to do in order to run the gRPC server, but it is still pretty simple. We must create a low-level TCP network listener and serve the gRPC server over that. Add the following code to the main function body:

```
go func() {
  listener, err := net.Listen("tcp", *gRPCAddr)
  if err != nil {
    errChan <- err
    return
  }
  log.Println("grpc:", *gRPCAddr)
  handler := vault.NewGRPCServer(ctx, endpoints)
  gRPCServer := grpc.NewServer()
  pb.RegisterVaultServer(gRPCServer, handler)
  errChan <- gRPCServer.Serve(listener)
}()
```

We make the TCP listener on the `gRPCAddr` endpoint specified, sending any errors down the `errChan` error channel. We use `vault.NewGRPCServer` to create the handler, again passing in the background context and the instance of `Endpoints` we are exposing.

> Note how both the JSON/HTTP server and the gRPC server are actually exposing the same service—literally the same instance.

We then create a new gRPC server from Google's `grpc` package and register it using our own generated `pb` package via the `RegisterVaultServer` function.

> The `RegisterVaultService` function just calls `RegisterService` on our `grpcServer` but hides the internals of the service description that was automatically generated. If you look in `vault.pb.go` and search for the `RegisterVaultServer` function, you will see that it makes a reference to something like `&_Vault_serviceDesc`, which is the description of the service. Feel free to dig around the generated code; the metadata is especially interesting, but out of scope for this book.

We then ask the server to `Serve` itself, throwing any errors down the same error channel if they occur.

> It's out of scope for this chapter, but it is recommended that every service be delivered with **Transport Layer Security** (**TLS**), especially the ones dealing with passwords.

Preventing a main function from terminating immediately

If we closed our main function here, it would immediately exit and terminate all of our servers. This is because everything we're doing that would prevent this is inside its own goroutine. To prevent this, we need a way to block the function at the end to wait until something tells the program to terminate.

Since we are using the `errChan` error channel for errors, this is a perfect candidate. We can just listen on this channel, which (while nothing has been sent down it) will block and allow the other goroutines to do their work. If something goes wrong (or if a termination signal is received), the `<-errChan` call will unblock and exit and all goroutines will be stopped.

At the bottom of the main function, add the final statement and closing block:

```
    log.Fatalln(<-errChan)
}
```

When an error occurs, we'll just log it and exit with a nonzero code.

Consuming the service over HTTP

Now that we have wired everything up, we can test the HTTP server using the `curl` commandâ©©or any tool that lets us make JSON/HTTP requests.

In a terminal, let's start by running our servers. Head over to the `vault/cmd/vaultd` folder and start the program:

```
go run main.go
```

Once the server is running, you'll see something like this:

```
http: :8080
grpc: :8081
```

Now, open another terminal and issue the following HTTP request using `curl`:

```
curl -XPOST -d '{"password":"hernandez"}'
http://localhost:8080/hash
```

We are making a POST request to the hash endpoint with a JSON body that contains the password we want for hashing. Then, we get something like this:

```
{"hash":"$2a$10$IXYT10DuK3Hu.
  NZQsyNafF1tyxe5QkYZKM5by/5Ren"}
```

The hash in this example won't match yoursâ⊚⊚there are many acceptable hashes and there's no way to know which one you'll get. Ensure that you copy and paste your actual hash (everything inside the double quotes).

The resulting hash is what we would store in our data store given the specified password. Then, when the user tries to log in again, we will make a request with the password they entered, along with this hash, to the validate endpoint:

```
curl -XPOST -d
 '{"password":"hernandez",
   "hash":"PASTE_YOUR_HASH_HERE"}'
http://localhost:8080/validate
```

Make this request by copying and pasting the correct hash and entering the same `hernandez` password, and you will see this result:

```
{"valid":true}
```

Now, change the password (this is equivalent to the user getting it wrong) and you will see this:

```
{"valid":false}
```

You can see that the JSON/HTTP micro-service exposure for our vault service is complete and working.

Next, we will look at how we can consume the gRPC version.

Building a gRPC client

Unlike JSON/HTTP services, gRPC services aren't easy for humans to interact with. They're really intended as machine-to-machine protocols, and so we must write a program if we wish to use them.

To help us do this, we are first going to add a new package inside our vault service called
`vault/client/grpc`. It will, given a gRPC client connection object that we get from
Google's `grpc` package, provide an object that performs the appropriate calls, encoding and
decoding, for us, all hidden behind our own `vault.Service` interface. So, we will be able
to use the object as though it is just another implementation of our interface.

Create new folders inside vault so that you have the path of `vault/client/grpc`. You can
imagine adding other clients if you so wish, so this seems a good pattern to establish.

Add the following code to a new `client.go` file:

```
func New(conn *grpc.ClientConn) vault.Service {
  var hashEndpoint = grpctransport.NewClient(
    conn, "Vault", "Hash",
    vault.EncodeGRPCHashRequest,
    vault.DecodeGRPCHashResponse,
    pb.HashResponse{},
  ).Endpoint()
  var validateEndpoint = grpctransport.NewClient(
    conn, "Vault", "Validate",
    vault.EncodeGRPCValidateRequest,
    vault.DecodeGRPCValidateResponse,
    pb.ValidateResponse{},
  ).Endpoint()
  return vault.Endpoints{
    HashEndpoint:     hashEndpoint,
    ValidateEndpoint: validateEndpoint,
  }
}
```

The `grpctransport` package is referring to `github.com/go-kit/kit/transport/grpc`.
This might feel familiar by now; we are making two new endpoints based on the specified
connection, this time being explicit about the `Vault` service name and the endpoint names
`Hash` and `Validate`. We pass in appropriate encoders and decoders from our vault
package and empty response objects before wrapping them both in our `vault.Endpoints`
structure that we added-the one that implements the `vault.Service` interface that just
triggers the specified endpoints for us.

A command-line tool to consume the service

In this section, we are going to write a command-line tool (or CLI-command-line interface), which will allow us to communicate with our service through the gRPC protocol. If we were writing another service in Go, we would use the vault client package in the same way as we will when we write our CLI tool.

Our tool will let you access the services in a fluent way on the command line by separating commands and arguments with spaces such that we can hash a password like this:

```
vaultcli hash MyPassword
```

We will be able to validate a password with a hash like this:

```
vaultcli hash MyPassword HASH_GOES_HERE
```

In the cmd folder, create a new folder called vaultcli. Add a main.go file and insert the following main function:

```
func main() {
  var (
    grpcAddr = flag.String("addr", ":8081",
      "gRPC address")
  )
  flag.Parse()
  ctx := context.Background()
  conn, err := grpc.Dial(*grpcAddr, grpc.WithInsecure(),
  grpc.WithTimeout(1*time.Second))
  if err != nil {
    log.Fatalln("gRPC dial:", err)
  }
  defer conn.Close()
  vaultService := grpcclient.New(conn)
  args := flag.Args()
  var cmd string
  cmd, args = pop(args)
  switch cmd {
  case "hash":
    var password string
    password, args = pop(args)
    hash(ctx, vaultService, password)
  case "validate":
    var password, hash string
    password, args = pop(args)
    hash, args = pop(args)
    validate(ctx, vaultService, password, hash)
  default:
```

```
        log.Fatalln("unknown command", cmd)
    }
}
```

Ensure that you import the `vault/client/grpc` package as `grpcclient` and `google.golang.org/grpc` as `grpc`. You'll also need to import the `vault` package.

We parse the flags and get a background context as usual before dialing the gRPC endpoint to establish a connection. If all is well, we defer the closing of the connection and create our vault service client using that connection. Remember that this object implements our `vault.Service` interface, so we can just call the methods as though they were normal Go methods, without worrying about the fact that communication is taking place over a network protocol.

Then, we start parsing the command-line arguments in order to decide which execution flow to take.

Parsing arguments in CLIs

Parsing arguments in command-line tools is very common, and there is a neat idiomatic way to do it in Go. The arguments are all available via the `os.Args` slice, or if you're using flags, the `flags.Args()` method (which gets arguments with flags stripped). We want to take each argument off the slice (from the beginning) and consume them in an order, which will help us decide which execution flow to take through the program. We're going to add a helper function called `pop`, which will return the first item, and the slice with the first item trimmed.

We'll write a quick unit test to ensure that our `pop` function is working as expected. If you would like to try and write the pop function yourself, then you should do that once the test is in place. Remember that you can run tests by navigating to the appropriate folder in a terminal and executing this:

```
go test
```

Create a new file inside `vaultcli` called `main_test.go` and add the following test function:

```
func TestPop(t *testing.T) {
  args := []string{"one", "two", "three"}
  var s string
  s, args = pop(args)
  if s != "one" {
    t.Errorf("unexpected "%s"", s)
```

```
    }
    s, args = pop(args)
    if s != "two" {
      t.Errorf("unexpected "%s"", s)
    }
    s, args = pop(args)
    if s != "three" {
      t.Errorf("unexpected "%s"", s)
    }
    s, args = pop(args)
    if s != "" {
      t.Errorf("unexpected "%s"", s)
    }
}
```

We expect each call to pop to yield the next item in the slice and empty arguments once the slice is empty.

At the bottom of main.go, add the pop function:

```
func pop(s []string) (string, []string) {
  if len(s) == 0 {
    return "", s
  }
  return s[0], s[1:]
}
```

Maintaining good line of sight by extracting case bodies

The only thing that remains for us to do is implement the hash and validate methods referred to in the switch statement shown earlier.

We could have embedded this code inside the switch statement itself, but that would make the main function very difficult to read and also hide happy path execution at different indentation levels, something we should try to avoid.

Instead, it is a good practice to have the cases inside the switch statement jump out to a dedicated function, taking in any arguments it needs. Underneath the main function, add the following hash and validate functions:

```
func hash(ctx context.Context, service vault.Service,
  password string) {
  h, err := service.Hash(ctx, password)
  if err != nil {
```

```
      log.Fatalln(err.Error())
   }
   fmt.Println(h)
}
func validate(ctx context.Context, service vault.Service,
   password, hash string) {
   valid, err := service.Validate(ctx, password, hash)
   if err != nil {
      log.Fatalln(err.Error())
   }
   if !valid {
      fmt.Println("invalid")
      os.Exit(1)
   }
   fmt.Println("valid")
}
```

These functions simply call the appropriate method on the service, and depending on the result, log or print the results to the console. If the validate method returns false, the program will exit with an exit code of 1, since nonzero means an error.

Installing tools from the Go source code

To install the tool, we just have to navigate to the `vaultcli` folder in a terminal and type this:

```
go install
```

Provided there are no errors, the package will be built and deployed to the `$GOPATH/bin` folder, which should already be listed in your `$PATH` environment variable. This means that the tool is ready for use just like a normal command in your terminal.

The name of the binary that is deployed will match the folder name, and this is why we have an additional folder inside the `cmd` folder even if we are only building a single command.

Once you have installed the command, we can use it to test the gRPC server.

Head over to `cmd/vaultd` and start the server (if it isn't already running) by typing the following:

```
go run main.go
```

In another terminal, let's hash a password by typing this:

```
vaultcli hash blanca
```

Note that the hash is returned. Now let's validate this hash:

```
vaultcli validate blanca PASTE_HASH_HERE
```

The hash may contain special characters that interfere with your terminal, so you should escape the string with quotes if required.
On a Mac, format the argument with $'PASTE_HASH_HERE' to properly escape it.
On Windows, try surrounding the argument with exclamation points: !PASTE_HASH_HERE!.

If you get the password right, you'll notice that you see the word valid; otherwise, you'll see invalid.

Rate limiting with service middleware

Now that we have built a complete service, we are going to see how easy it is to add middleware to our endpoints in order to extend the service without touching the actual implementations themselves.

In real-world services, it is sensible to limit the number of requests it will attempt to handle so that the service doesn't get overwhelmed. This can happen if the process needs more memory than is available, or we might notice performance degradation if it eats up too much of the CPU. In a micro-service architecture, the strategy to solving these problems is to add another node and spread the load, which means that we want each individual instance to be rate limited.

Since we are providing the client, we should add rate limiting there, which would prevent too many requests from getting on the network. But it is also sensible to add rate limiting to the server in case many clients are trying to access the same services at the same time. Luckily, endpoints in Go kit are used for both the client and server, so we can use the same code to add middleware in both places.

We are going to add a **Token Bucket**-based rate limiter, which you can read more about at h ttps://en.wikipedia.org/wiki/Token_bucket. The guys at Juju have written a Go implementation that we can use by importing github.com/juju/ratelimit, and Go kit has middleware built for this very implementation, which will save us a lot of time and effort.

The general idea is that we have a bucket of tokens, and each request will need a token in order to do its work. If there are no tokens in the bucket, we have reached our limit and the request cannot be completed. Buckets refill over time at a specific interval.

Import github.com/juju/ratelimit and before we create our hashEndpoint, insert the following code:

```
rlbucket := ratelimit.NewBucket(1*time.Second, 5)
```

The NewBucket function creates a new rate limiting bucket that will refill at a rate of one token per second, up to a maximum of five tokens. These numbers are pretty silly for our case, but we want to be able to reach our limits manually during the development.

Since the Go kit ratelimit package has the same name as the Juju one, we are going to need to import it with a different name:

```
import ratelimitkit "github.com/go-kit/kit/ratelimit"
```

Middleware in Go kit

Endpoint middleware in Go kit is specified by the endpoint.Middleware function type:

```
type Middleware func(Endpoint) Endpoint
```

A piece of middleware is simply a function that takes Endpoint and returns Endpoint. Remember that Endpoint is also a function:

```
type Endpoint func(ctx context.Context, request
   interface{}) (response interface{}, err error)
```

This gets a little confusing, but they are the same as the wrappers we built for http.HandlerFunc. A middleware function returns an Endpoint function that does something before and/or after calling the Endpoint being wrapped. The arguments passed into the function that returns the Middleware are closured in, which means that they are available to the inner code (via closures) without the state having to be stored anywhere else.

We are going to use the `NewTokenBucketLimiter` middleware from Go kit's `ratelimit` package, and if we take a look at the code, we'll see how it uses closures and returns functions to inject a call to the token bucket's `TakeAvailable` method before passing execution to the `next` endpoint:

```
func NewTokenBucketLimiter(tb *ratelimit.Bucket)
  endpoint.Middleware {
  return func(next endpoint.Endpoint) endpoint.Endpoint {
    return func(ctx context.Context, request interface{})
    (interface{}, error) {
      if tb.TakeAvailable(1) == 0 {
        return nil, ErrLimited
      }
      return next(ctx, request)
    }
  }
}
```

A pattern has emerged within Go kit where you obtain the endpoint and then put all middleware adaptations inside their own block immediately afterwards. The returned function is given the endpoint when it is called, and the same variable is overwritten with the result.

For a simple example, consider this code:

```
e := getEndpoint(srv)
{
  e = getSomeMiddleware()(e)
  e = getLoggingMiddleware(logger)(e)
  e = getAnotherMiddleware(something)(e)
}
```

We will now do this for our endpoints; update the code inside the main function to add the rate limiting middleware:

```
hashEndpoint := vault.MakeHashEndpoint(srv)
{
  hashEndpoint = ratelimitkit.NewTokenBucketLimiter
    (rlbucket)(hashEndpoint)
}
validateEndpoint := vault.MakeValidateEndpoint(srv)
{
  validateEndpoint = ratelimitkit.NewTokenBucketLimiter
    (rlbucket)(validateEndpoint)
}
endpoints := vault.Endpoints{
  HashEndpoint:     hashEndpoint,
```

```
ValidateEndpoint: validateEndpoint,
}
```

There's nothing much to change here; we're just updating the `hashEndpoint` and `validateEndpoint` variables before assigning them to the `vault.Endpoints` struct.

Manually testing the rate limiter

To see whether our rate limiter is working, and since we set such low thresholds, we can test it just using our command-line tool.

First, restart the server (so the new code runs) by hitting *Ctrl + C* in the terminal window running the server. This signal will be trapped by our code, and an error will be sent down `errChan`, causing the program to quit. Once it has terminated, restart it:

```
go run main.go
```

Now, in another window, let's hash some passwords:

```
vaultcli hash bourgon
```

Repeat this command a few timesâ©©in most terminals, you can press the up arrow key and return. You'll notice that the first few requests succeed because it's within the limits, but if you get a little more aggressive and issue more than five requests in a second, you'll notice that we get errors:

```
$ vaultcli hash bourgon
$2a$10$q3NTkjG0YFZhTG6gBU2WpenFmNzdN74oX0MDSTryiAqRXJ7RVw9sy
$ vaultcli hash bourgon
$2a$10$CdEEtxSDUyJEIFaykbMMl.EikxvV5921gs/./7If6VOdh2x0Q1oLW
$ vaultcli hash bourgon
$2a$10$1DSqQJJGCmVOptwIx6rrSOZwLlOhjHNC83OPVE8SdQ9q73Li5x2le
$ vaultcli hash bourgon
Invoke: rpc error: code = 2 desc = rate limit exceeded
$ vaultcli hash bourgon
Invoke: rpc error: code = 2 desc = rate limit exceeded
$ vaultcli hash bourgon
Invoke: rpc error: code = 2 desc = rate limit exceeded
$ vaultcli hash bourgon
$2a$10$kriTDXdyT6J4IrqZLwgBde663nLhoG3innhCNuf8H2nHf7kxnmSza
```

This shows that our rate limiter is working. We see errors until the token bucket fills back up, where our requests are fulfilled again.

Graceful rate limiting

Rather than returning an error (which is a pretty harsh response), perhaps we would prefer the server to just hold onto our request and fulfill it when it can-called throttling. For this case, Go kit provides the `NewTokenBucketThrottler` middleware.

Update the middleware code to use this middleware function instead:

```
hashEndpoint := vault.MakeHashEndpoint(srv)
{
  hashEndpoint = ratelimitkit.NewTokenBucketThrottler(rlbucket,
    time.Sleep)(hashEndpoint)
}
validateEndpoint := vault.MakeValidateEndpoint(srv)
{
  validateEndpoint = ratelimitkit.NewTokenBucketThrottler(rlbucket,
    time.Sleep)(validateEndpoint)
}
endpoints := vault.Endpoints{
  HashEndpoint:      hashEndpoint,
  ValidateEndpoint: validateEndpoint,
}
```

The first argument to `NewTokenBucketThrottler` is the same endpoint as earlier, but now we have added a second argument of `time.Sleep`.

 Go kit allows us to customize the behavior by specifying what should happen when the delay needs to take place. In our case, we're passing `time.Sleep`, which is a function that will ask execution to pause for the specified amount of time. You could write your own function here if you wanted to do something different, but this works for now.

Now repeat the test from earlier, but this time, note that we never get an error-instead, the terminal will hang for a second until the request can be fulfilled.

Summary

We covered a lot through this chapter as we put together a real example of a micro-service. There is a lot of work involved without code generation, but the benefits for large teams and big micro-service architectures pay for the investment as you build self-similar, discrete components that make up the system.

We learned how gRPC and protocol buffers give us highly efficient transport communications between clients and servers. Using the `proto3` language, we defined our service, including messages, and used the tools to generate a Go package that provided the client and server code for us.

We explored the fundamentals of Go kit and how we can use endpoints to describe the methods of our services. We let Go kit do the heavy lifting for us when it came to building HTTP and gRPC servers by making use of the packages included in the project. We saw how middleware functions let us easily adapt our endpoints to, among other things, rate limit the amount of traffic the server will have to handle.

We also learned about constructors in Go, a neat trick to parse incoming command-line arguments, and how to hash and validate passwords using the `bcrypt` package, which is a sensible approach that helps us avoid storing passwords at all.

There is a lot more to building micro-services, and it is recommended that you head over to the Go kit website at `https://gokit.io` or join the conversation on the `#go-kit` slack channel at gophers.slack.com to learn more.

Now that we have built our Vault service, we need to think about our options in order to deploy it into the wild. In the next chapter, we'll package our micro-service into a Docker container and deploy it to Digital Ocean's cloud.

11
Deploying Go Applications Using Docker

Docker is an open source ecosystem (technology and range of associated services) that allows you to package applications into containers that are simple, lightweight, and portable; they will run in the same way regardless of which environment they run on. This is useful when you consider that our development environment (perhaps a Mac) is different from a production environment (such as a Linux server or even a cloud service) and that there is a large number of different places that we might want to deploy the same application.

Most cloud platforms already support Docker, which makes it a great option to deploy our apps into the wild.

In Chapter 9, *Building a Q&A Application for Google App Engine*, we built an application for Google App Engine. We would need to make significant changes to our code if we decided that we wanted to run our application on a different platform even if we forget about our use of Google Cloud Datastore. Building applications with a mind to deploying them within Docker containers gives us an additional level of flexibility.

 Did you know that Docker itself was written in Go? See for yourself by browsing the source code at https://github.com/docker/docker.

In this chapter, you will learn:

- How to write a simple Dockerfile to describe an application
- How to use the docker command to build the container
- How to run Docker containers locally and terminate them

- How to deploy Docker containers to Digital Ocean
- How to use the features in Digital Ocean to spin up instances that already have Docker preconfigured

We are going to put the Vault service we created in `Chapter 10`, *Micro-services in Go with the Go kit Framework*, into a Docker image and deploy it to the cloud.

Using Docker locally

Before we can deploy our code to the cloud, we must use the Docker tools on our development machine to build and push the image to Docker Hub.

Installing Docker tools

In order to build and run containers, you need to install Docker on your development machine. Head over to `https://www.docker.com/products/docker` and download the appropriate installer for your computer.

Docker and its ecosystem are evolving rapidly, so it is a good idea to make sure you're up to date with the latest release. Similarly, it is possible that some details will change in this chapter; if you get stuck, visit the project home page at `https://github.com/matryer/goblueprints` for some helpful tips.

Dockerfile

A Docker image is like a mini virtual machine. It contains everything that's needed to run an application: the operating system the code will run on, any dependencies that our code might have (such as Go kit in the case of our Vault service), and the binaries of our application itself.

An image is described with `Dockerfile`; a text file containing a list of special commands that instruct Docker how to build the image. They are usually based on another container, which saves you from building up everything that might be needed in order to build and run Go applications.

Inside the `vault` folder from the code we wrote in `Chapter 10`, *Micro-services in Go with the Go kit Framework*, add a file called `Dockerfile` (note that this filename has no extension), containing the following code:

```
FROM scratch
MAINTAINER Your Name <your@email.address>
ADD vaultd vaultd
EXPOSE 8080 8081
ENTRYPOINT ["/vaultd"]
```

Each line in a `Dockerfile` file represents a different command that is run while the image is being built. The following table describes each of the commands we have used:

Command	Description
FROM	The name of the image that this image will be based on. Single words, such as scratch, represent official Docker images hosted on Docker Hub. For more information on the scratch image, refer to `https://hub.docker.com/_/scratch/`.
ADD	Copies files into the container. We are copying our `vaultd` binary and calling it `vaultd`.
EXPOSE	Exposes the list of ports; in our case, the Vault service binds to `:8080` and `:8081`.
ENTRYPOINT	The binary to run when the container is executed in our case, the `vaultd` binary, which will be put there by the previous call to go install.
MAINTAINER	Name and email of the person responsible for maintaining the Docker image.

For a complete list of the supported commands, consult the online Docker documentation at `https://docs.docker.com/engine/reference/builder/#dockerfile-reference`.

Building Go binaries for different architectures

Go supports cross-complication, a mechanism by which we can build a binary on one machine (say, our Mac) targeted for a different operating system (such as Linux or Windows) and architecture. Docker containers are Linux-based; so, in order to deliver a binary that can run in that environment, we must first build one.

In a terminal, navigate to the vault folder and run the following command:

```
CGO_ENABLED=0 GOOS=linux go build -a ./cmd/vaultd/
```

We are essentially calling go build here but with a few extra bits and pieces to control the build process. CGO_ENABLED and GOOS are environment variables that go build will pay attention to, -a is a flag, and ./cmd/vaultd/ is the location of the command we want to build (in our case, the vaultd command we built in the previous chapter).

- The CGO_ENABLED=0 indicates that we do not want cgo to be enabled. Since we are not binding to any C dependencies, we can reduce the size of our build by disabling this.
- GOOS is short for Go Operating System and lets us specify which OS we are targeting, in our case, Linux. For a complete list of the available options, you can look directly in the Go source code by visiting https://github.com/golang/go/blob/master/src/go/build/syslist.go.

After a short while, you'll notice that a new binary has appeared, called vaultd. If you're on a non-Linux machine, you won't be able to directly execute this but don't worry; it'll run inside our Docker container just fine.

Building a Docker image

To build the image, in a terminal, navigate to Dockerfile and run the following command:

```
docker build -t vaultd
```

We are using the docker command to build the image. The final dot indicates that we want to build Dockerfile from the current directory. The -t flag specifies that we want to give our image the name of vaultd. This will allow us to refer to it by name rather than a hash that Docker will assign to it.

If this is the first time you've used Docker, and in particular the scratch base image, then it will take some time to download the required dependencies from Docker Hub depending on your Internet connection. Once that's finished, you will see output similar to the following:

```
Step 1 : FROM scratch
 --->
Step 2 : MAINTAINER Your Name <your@email.address>
 ---> Using cache
 ---> a8667f8f0881
Step 3 : ADD vaultd vaultd
```

```
  ---> 0561c999c1e3
Removing intermediate container 4b75fde507df
Step 4 : EXPOSE 8080 8081
  ---> Running in 8f169f5b3b44
  ---> 1d7758c20b3a
Removing intermediate container 8f169f5b3b44
Step 5 : ENTRYPOINT /vaultd
  ---> Running in b5d55d6429be
  ---> b7178985dddf
Removing intermediate container b5d55d6429be
Successfully built b7178985dddf
```

For each command, a new image is created (you can see the intermediate containers being disposed of along the way) until we end up with the final image.

Since we are building our binary on our local machine and copying it into the container (with the ADD command), our Docker image ends up being only about 7 MB: pretty small when you consider that it contains everything it needs to run our services.

Running a Docker image locally

Now that our image is built, we can test it by running it with the following command:

```
docker run -p 6060:8080 -p 6061:8081 --name localtest --rm vaultd
```

The docker run command will spin up an instance of the vaultd image.

The -p flags specify a pair of ports to be exposed, the first value is the host port and the second value (following the colon) is the port within the image. In our case, we are saying that we want port 8080 to be exposed onto port 6060 and port 8081 exposed via port 6061.

We are giving the running instance a name of localtest with the --name flag, which will help us to identify it when inspecting and stopping it. The --rm flag indicates that we want the image to be removed once we have stopped it.

If this is successful, you will notice that the Vault service has indeed begun because it is telling us the ports to which it is bound:

```
2016/09/20 15:56:17 grpc: :8081
2016/09/20 15:56:17 http: :8080
```

These are the internal ports; remember that we have mapped these to different external ports instead. This seems confusing but ends up being very powerful, since the person responsible for spinning up the instances of the service gets to decide which ports are right for their environment, and the Vault service itself doesn't have to worry about it.

To see this running, open another terminal and use the `curl` command to access the JSON endpoint of our password hashing service:

```
curl -XPOST -d '{"password":"monkey"}' localhost:6060/hash
```

You will see something that resembles the output from the running service:

```
{"hash":"$2a$0$wk4qc74ougOkbkt/TWuRQHSg03i1ataNupbDADBwpe"}
```

Inspecting Docker processes

To see what Docker instances are running, we can use the `docker ps` command. In the terminal, type the following:

```
docker ps
```

You'll get a text table outlining the following properties:

CONTAINER ID	0b5e35dca7cc
IMAGE	vaultd
COMMAND	/bin/sh -c /go/bin/vaultd
CREATED	3 seconds ago
STATUS	Up 2 seconds
PORTS	0.0.0.0:6060->8080/tcp, 0.0.0.0:6061->8081/tcp
NAMES	localtest

The details show you a high-level overview of the image we just started. Note that the **PORTS** sections shows you the mapping from external to internal.

Stopping a Docker instance

We are used to hitting *Ctrl + C* in the window running our code to stop it, but since it's running inside a container, that won't work. Instead, we need to use the `docker stop` command.

Since we gave our instance the name `localtest`, we can use this to stop it by typing this in an available terminal window:

```
docker stop localtest
```

After a few moments, you'll notice that the terminal that was running the image has now returned to the prompt.

Deploying Docker images

Now that we have contained our Vault service inside a Docker container, we are going to do some useful things with it.

The first thing we are going to do is push this to the Docker Hub so that other people may spin up their own instances or even build new images based on it.

Deploying to Docker Hub

Head over to Docker Hub at `https://hub.docker.com` and create an account by clicking on the **Log In** link in the top-right-hand corner and then clicking on **Create Account**. Of course, if you already have an account, just log in.

Now in a terminal, you are going to authenticate with this account by running Docker's `login` command:

```
docker login -u USERNAME -p PASSWORD https://index.docker.io/v1/
```

> If you see an error such as `WARNING: Error loading config, permission denied`, then try the command again with the `sudo` command prefix. This goes for all of Docker commands from this point onwards, since we're using a secured configuration.

Ensure that you replace USERNAME and PASSWORD with your actual username and password of the account you just created.

If successful, you'll see, **Login Succeeded**.

Next, back in the web browser, click on **Create Repository** and create a new repository called vault. The actual name for this image is going to be USERNAME/vault, so we're going to need to rebuild the image locally to match this.

 Note that for public consumption, we are calling the image vault rather than vaultd. This is a deliberate difference so that we can make sure we are dealing with the right image, but this is also a better name for users anyway.

In a terminal, build the new repository with the correct name:

```
docker build -t USERNAME/vault
```

This will build the image again, this time with the appropriate name. To deploy the image to the Docker Hub, we use Docker's push command:

```
docker push USERNAME/vault
```

After some time, the image and its dependencies will be pushed to Docker Hub:

```
f477b97e9e48: Pushed
384c907d1173: Pushed
80168d020f50: Pushed
0ceba54dae47: Pushed
4d7388e75674: Pushed
f042db76c15c: Pushing [====>                ] 21.08 MB/243.6 MB
d15a527c2ee1: Pushing [=====>               ] 15.77 MB/134 MB
751f5d9ad6db: Pushing [======>              ] 16.49 MB/122.6 MB
17587239b3df: Pushing [===================>] 17.01 MB/44.31 MB
9e63c5bce458: Pushing [==================> ] 65.58 MB/125.1 MB
```

Now head over to the Docker Hub to see the details of your image, or look at an example at https://hub.docker.com/r/matryer/vault/.

Deploying to Digital Ocean

Digital Ocean is a cloud service provider that offers competitive prices to host virtual machines. It makes deploying and serving Docker images very easy. In this section, we are going to deploy a droplet (Digital Ocean's terminology for a single machine) that runs our dockerized Vault service in the cloud.

Specifically, following are the steps to deploy Docker images to Digital Ocean:

1. Create a droplet.
2. Gain access to it via a web-based console.
3. Pull our `USERNAME/vault` container.
4. Run the container.
5. Access our hosted Vault service remotely via the `curl` command.

Digital Ocean is a **Platform as a Service (PaaS)** architecture, and as such, the user experience is likely to change from time to time, so the exact flow described here might not be entirely accurate by the time you come to perform these tasks. Usually, by looking around at the options, you will be able to figure out how to proceed, but screenshots have been included to help guide you.

This section also assumes that you have enabled any billing that might be required in order to create droplets.

Creating a droplet

Sign up or log in to Digital Ocean by visiting `https://www.digitalocean.com` in the browser. Ensure that you use a real e-mail address, as this is where they will send the root password for the droplet you are going to create.

Deploying Go Applications Using Docker

If you have no other droplets, you will be presented with a blank screen. Click on **Create Droplet**:

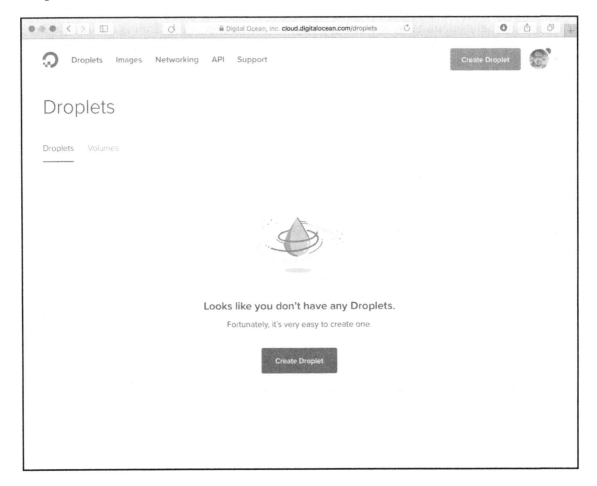

Inside the **One-click apps** tab, look for the latest Docker option; at the time of writing this, it is **Docker 1.12.1 on 16.04**, which means Docker version 1.12.1 is running on Ubuntu 16.04.

Scroll down the page to select the remaining options, including picking a size (the smallest size will do for now) and a location (pick the closest geographic location to you). We won't bother adding additional services (such as volumes, networking, or backups) for now just proceed with the simple droplet.

It might be a nice idea to give your droplet a meaningful hostname so that it's easy to find later, something like `vault-service-1` or similar; it doesn't really matter for now:

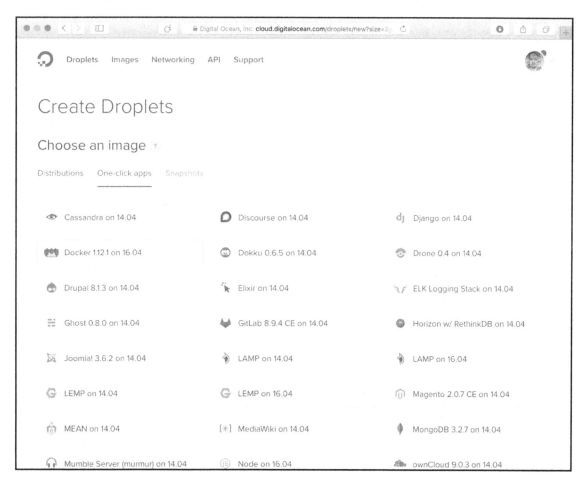

You can optionally add SSH keys for additional security, but for simplicity's sake, we are going to continue without it. For production, it is recommended that you always do this.

At the bottom of the page, click on **Create**:

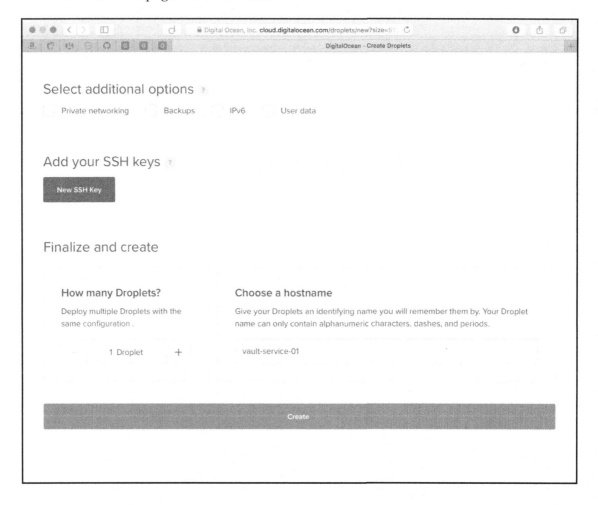

Accessing the droplet's console

Once your droplet has been created, select it from the **Droplets** list and look for the **Console** option (it may be written as `Access console`).

After a few moments, you will be presented with a web-based terminal. This is how we will control the droplet, but first, we must log in:

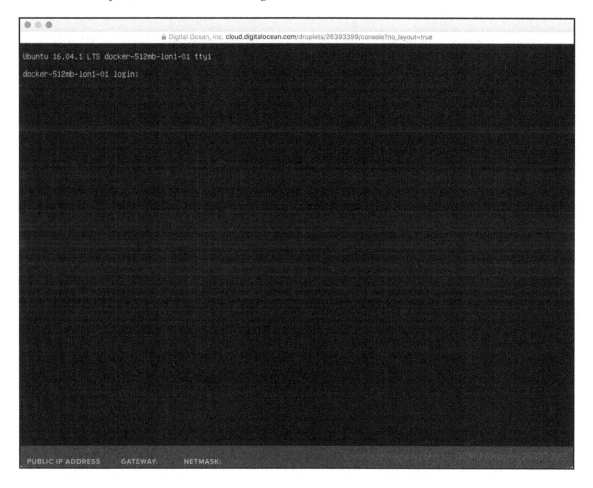

Enter the login username as `root`, and check your e-mail for the root password that Digital Ocean has sent you. At the time of writing this, you cannot copy and paste this, so be ready to carefully type out a long string as accurately as you can.

> The password might well be a lowercase hexadecimal string, which will help you know which characters are likely to appear. For example, everything that looks like an *O* is probably *zero*, and *1* is unlikely to be an *I* or *L*.

Once you've logged in for the first time, you'll be asked to change your password which involves typing the long generated password again! Security can be so inconvenient at times.

Pulling Docker images

Since we selected the Docker app as a starting point for our droplet, Digital Ocean has kindly configured Docker to already be running inside our instance, so we can just use the `docker` command to finish setting things up.

In the web-based terminal, pull your container with the following command, remembering to replace `USERNAME` with your Docker Hub username:

```
docker pull USERNAME/vault
```

> If, for whatever reason, this isn't working for you, you can try using the Docker image placed there by the author by typing this: `docker pull matryer/vault`

Docker will go and pull down everything it needs in order to run the image we created earlier:

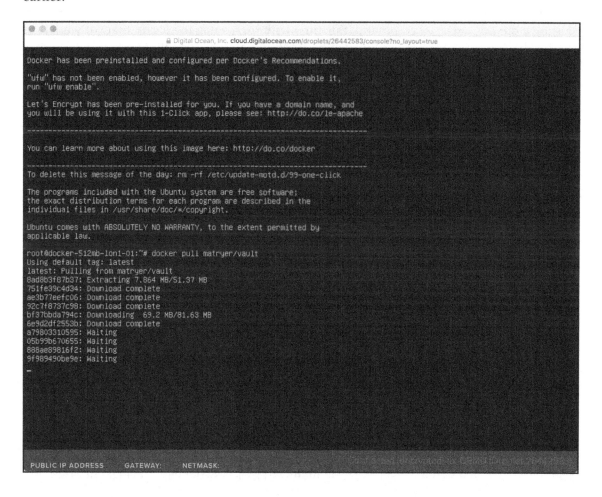

Running Docker images in the cloud

Once the image and its dependencies have successfully downloaded, we will be able to run it using a the `docker run` command, this time with the `-d` flag to specify that we want it to run as a background daemon. In the web-based terminal, type the following:

```
docker run -d -p 6060:8080 -p 6061:8081 --name vault USERNAME/vault
```

This is similar to the command we ran earlier, except that this time, we are giving it the name vault, and we have omitted the `--rm` flag, since it is not compatible (and doesn't make sense) with the background daemon mode.

The Docker image containing our Vault service will start running and is now ready to test.

Accessing Docker images in the cloud

Now that our Docker image is running in our droplet within Digital Ocean's platform, we can start using it.

In the Digital Ocean web control panel, select **Droplets** and look for the one we just created. We need to know the IP address so that we can access the services remotely. Once you have located the IP address of the droplet, click on it to copy it.

Open a local terminal on your computer (do not use the web-based terminal) and use the `curl` command (or equivalent) to make the following request:

```
curl -XPOST -d '{"password":"Monkey"}' http://IPADDRESS:6060/hash
```

Remember to replace IPADDRESS with the actual IP address you copied from Digital Ocean's web control panel.

You will notice that you have successfully managed to access the JSON/HTTP endpoint of our Vault service when you get a response similar to the following:

```
{"hash":"$2a$10$eGFGRZ2zMfsXss.6CgK6/N7TsmF.6MAv6i7Km4AHC"}
```

See whether you can modify the `curl` command to validate the hash that was provided using the `/validate` endpoint.

Summary

In this chapter, we built and deployed our Vault Go application using Docker to Digital Ocean's cloud.

After installing the Docker tools, we saw how easy it was to package up our Go application into a Docker image and push it to Docker Hub. We created our Digital Ocean droplet using the helpful Docker app that they provide and controlled it via a web-based console. Once inside, we were able to pull our Docker image from the Docker Hub and run it inside our droplet.

Using the public IP of the droplet, we were then able to remotely access the Vault service's JSON/HTTP endpoint to hash and validate passwords.

Good Practices for a Stable Go Environment

Writing Go code is a fun and enjoyable experience, where compile-time errors rather than being a pain actually guide you to write robust, high-quality code. However, every now and then, you will encounter environmental issues that start to get in the way and break your flow. While you can usually resolve these issues after some searching and a little tweaking, setting up your development environment correctly goes a long way in reducing problems, allowing you to focus on building useful applications.

In this chapter, we are going to install Go from scratch on a new machine and discuss some of the environmental options we have and the impact they might have in the future. We will also consider how collaboration might influence some of our decisions as well as what impact open sourcing our packages might have.

Specifically, we are going to:

- Install Go on your development machine
- Learn what the GOPATH environment variable is for and discuss a sensible approach for its use
- Learn about the Go tools and how to use them to keep the quality of our code high
- Learn how to use a tool to automatically manage our imports
- Think about on *save* operations for our .go files and how we can integrate the Go tools as part of our daily development
- Look at some popular code editor options to write Go code

Installing Go

The best way to install Go is to use one of the many installers available online at `https://golang.org/dl/`. Go to the Go website and click on **Download**, and then look for the latest 1.x version for your computer. The **Featured downloads** section at the top of the page contains links to the most popular versions, so yours will probably be in that list.

The code in this book has been tested with Go 1.7, but any 1.x release will work. For future versions of Go (2.0 and higher), you may need to tweak the code as major version releases may well contain breaking changes.

Configuring Go

Go is now installed, but in order to use the tools, we must ensure that it is properly configured. To make calling the tools easier, we need to add our `go/bin` path to the `PATH` environment variable.

On Unix systems, you should add export `PATH=$PATH:/opt/go/bin` (make sure it is the path you chose when installing Go) to your `.bashrc` file.
On Windows, open **System Properties** (try right-clicking on **My Computer**), and under **Advanced**, click on the **Environment Variables** button and use the UI to ensure that the `PATH` variable contains the path to your `go/bin` folder.

In a terminal (you may need to restart it for your changes to take effect), you can make sure this worked by printing the value of the `PATH` variable:

```
echo $PATH
```

Ensure that the value printed contains the correct path to your `go/bin` folder; for example, on my machine it prints as follows:

```
/usr/local/bin:/usr/bin:/bin:/opt/go/bin
```

The colons (semicolons on Windows) between the paths indicate that the `PATH` variable is actually a list of folders rather than just one folder. This indicates that each folder included will be searched when you enter commands in your terminal.

Now we can make sure the Go build we just made runs successfully:

```
go version
```

Executing the go command (which can be found in your go/bin location) like this will print out the current version for us. For example, for Go 1.77.1, you should see something similar to the following:

```
go version go1.77.1 darwin/amd64
```

Getting GOPATH right

GOPATH is another environment variable to a folder (such as PATH in the previous section) that is used to specify the location for the Go source code and the compiled binary packages. Using the import command in your Go programs will cause the compiler to look in the GOPATH location to find the packages you are referring to. When using go get and other commands, projects are downloaded into the GOPATH folder.

While the GOPATH location can contain a list of colon-separated folders, such as PATH and you can even have a different value for GOPATH depending on which project you are working in it is strongly recommended that you use a single GOPATH location for everything, and this is what we will assume you will do for the projects in this book.

Create a new folder called go, this time in your Users folder somewhere perhaps in a Work subfolder. This will be our GOPATH target and is where all the third-party code and binaries will end up as well as where we will write our Go programs and packages. Using the same technique you used when setting the PATH environment variable in the previous section, set the GOPATH variable to the new go folder. Let's open a terminal and use one of the newly installed commands to get a third-party package for us to use:

```
go get github.com/matryer/silk
```

Getting the silk library will actually cause this folder structure to be created: $GOPATH/src/github.com/matryer/silk. You can see that the path segments are important in how Go organizes things, which helps namespace projects and keeps them unique. For example, if you created your own package called silk, you wouldn't keep it in the GitHub repository of matryer, so the path would be different.

When we create projects in this book, you should consider a sensible GOPATH root for them. For example, I used github.com/matryer/goblueprints, and if you were to go get that, you would actually get a complete copy of all the source code for this book in your GOPATH folder!

Go tools

An early decision made by the Go core team was that all Go code should look familiar and obvious to everybody who speaks Go rather than each code base requiring additional learning in order for new programmers to understand it or work on it. This is an especially sensible approach when you consider open source projects, some of which have hundreds of contributors coming and going all the time.

There is a range of tools that can assist us in achieving the high standards set by the Go core team, and we will look at some of the tools in action in this section.

In your GOPATH location, create a new folder called `tooling` and create a new `main.go` file containing the following code verbatim:

```
package main
import (
  "fmt"
)
func main() {
  return
  var name string
  name = "Mat"
  fmt.Println("Hello ", name)
}
```

The tight spaces and lack of indentation are deliberate as we are going to look at a very cool utility that comes with Go.

In a terminal, navigate to your new folder and run this:

go fmt -w

At Gophercon 2014 in Denver, Colorado, most people learned that rather than pronouncing this little triad as *format* or *f, m, t*, it is actually pronounced as a word. Try saying it to yourself now: *fhumt*; it seems that computer programmers aren't weird enough without speaking an alien language to each other too!

You will notice that this little tool has actually tweaked our code file to ensure that the layout (or format) of our program matches Go standards. The new version is much easier to read:

```
package main
import (
  "fmt"
)
```

```
func main() {
  return
  var name string
  name = "Mat"
  fmt.Println("Hello ", name)
}
```

The `go fmt` command cares about indentation, code blocks, unnecessary whitespace, unnecessary extra line feeds, and more. Formatting your code in this way is a great practice to ensure that your Go code looks like all other Go code.

Next, we are going to vet our program to make sure that we haven't made any mistakes or decisions that might be confusing to our users; we can do this automatically with another great tool that we get for free:

```
go vet
```

The output for our little program points out an obvious and glaring mistake:

```
main.go:10: unreachable code
exit status 1
```

We are calling `return` at the top of our function and then trying to do other things. The `go vet` tool has noticed this and points out that we have unreachable code in our file.

It isn't just silly mistakes like this that `go vet` will catch; it will also look for subtler aspects of your program that will guide you toward writing the best Go code you can. For an up-to-date list of what the vet tool will report on, check out the documentation at `https://golang.org/cmd/vet/`.

The final tool we will play with is called `goimports`, and it was written by Brad Fitzpatrick to automatically fix (add or remove) `import` statements for Go files. It is an error in Go to import a package and not use it, and obviously, trying to use a package without importing it won't work either. The `goimports` tool will automatically rewrite our `import` statement based on the contents of our code file. First, let's install `goimports` with this familiar command:

```
go get golang.org/x/tools/cmd/goimports
```

Update your program to import some packages that we are not going to use and remove the `fmt` package:

```
import (
  "net/http"
  "sync"
)
```

When we try to run our program by calling `go run main.go`, we will see that we get some errors:

```
./main.go:4: imported and not used: "net/http"
./main.go:5: imported and not used: "sync"
./main.go:13: undefined: fmt
```

These errors tell us that we have imported packages that we are not using and missing the `fmt` package and that in order to continue, we need to make corrections. This is where `goimports` comes in:

```
goimports -w *.go
```

We are calling the `goimports` command with the `-w` write flag, which will save us the task of making corrections to all files ending with `.go`.

Have a look at your `main.go` file now, and note that the `net/http` and `sync` packages have been removed and the `fmt` package has been put back in.

You could argue that switching to a terminal to run these commands takes more time than just doing it manually, and you would probably be right in most cases, which is why it is highly recommended that you integrate the Go tools with your text editor.

Cleaning up, building, and running tests on save

Since the Go core team has provided us with such great tools as `fmt`, `vet`, `test`, and `goimports`, we are going to look at a development practice that has proven to be extremely useful. Whenever we save a `.go` file, we want to perform the following tasks automatically:

1. Use `goimports` and `fmt` to fix our imports and format the code.
2. Vet the code for any faux pas and tell us immediately.
3. Attempt to build the current package and output any build errors.
4. If the build is successful, run the tests for the package and output any failures.

Because Go code compiles so quickly (Rob Pike once actually said that it doesn't build quickly, but it's just not slow like everything else), we can comfortably build entire packages every time we save a file. This is also true for running tests to help us if we are developing in a TDD style, and the experience is great. Every time we make changes to our code, we can immediately see whether we have broken something or had an unexpected impact on some other part of our project. We'll never see package import errors again because our `import` statement will have been fixed for us, and our code will be correctly formatted right in front of our eyes.

Some editors are likely to not support running code in response to specific events, such as saving a file, which leaves you with two options: you can either switch to a better editor, or you can write your own script file that runs in response to filesystem changes. The latter solution is out of the scope of this book; instead, we will focus on how to implement this functionality in a couple of popular editor codes.

Integrated developer environments

The **Integrated Developer Environments (IDEs)** are essentially text editors with additional features that make writing code and building software easier. Text with special meaning, such as string literals, types, function names, and so on are often colored differently by syntax highlighting, or you may get autocomplete options as you're typing. Some editors even point out errors in your code before you've executed it.

There are many options to choose from, and mostly, it comes down to personal preference, but we will look at some of the more popular choices as well as how to set them up to build Go projects.

The most popular editors include the following:

- Sublime Text 3
- Visual Studio Code
- Atom
- Vim (with vim-go)

You can see a complete curated list of options at `https://github.com/golang/go/wiki/ID EsAndTextEditorPlugins`.

In this section, we are going to explore Sublime Text 3 and Visual Studio Code.

Sublime Text 3

Sublime Text 3 is an excellent editor to write Go code that runs on OS X, Linux, and Windows and has an extremely powerful expansion model, which makes it easy to customize and extend. You can download Sublime Text from `http://www.sublimetext.com/` and trial-use it for free before deciding whether you want to buy it or not.

Thanks to **DisposaBoy** (refer to `https://github.com/DisposaBoy`), there is already a Sublime expansion package for Go, which actually gives us a wealth of features and power that a lot of Go programmers actually miss out on. We are going to install this `GoSublime` package and then build upon it to add our desired on-save functionality.

Before we can install `GoSublime`, we need to install Package Control into Sublime Text. Head over to `https://sublime.wbond.net/` and click on the **Installation** link for instructions on how to install Package Control. At the time of writing this, it's simply a case of copying the single, albeit long, line command and pasting it into the Sublime console, which can be opened by navigating to **View | Show Console** from the menu.

Once this is complete, press *shift + command + P* and type `Package Control: Install Package` and press *return* when you have selected the option. After a short delay (where Package Control is updating its listings), a box will appear, allowing you to search for and install GoSublime just by typing it in, selecting it, and pressing *return*. If all is well, GoSublime will be installed and writing Go code will just become an order of magnitude easier.

Now that you have GoSublime installed, you can open a short help file containing the details of the package by pressing *command + .*, *command + 2* (the command key and period at the same time, followed by the command key and number 2).

For some additional help while saving, press *command + .*, *command + 5* to open the GoSublime settings and add the following entry to the object:

```
"on_save": [
  {
    "cmd": "gs9o_open",
    "args": {
      "run": ["sh", "go build . errors && go test -i && go test &&
      go vet && golint"],
      "focus_view": false
    }
  }
]
```

Note that the settings file is actually a JSON object, so ensure that you add the `on_save` property without corrupting the file. For example, if you have properties before and after, ensure the appropriate commas are in place.

The preceding setting will tell Sublime Text to build the code looking for errors, install test dependencies, run tests, and vet the code whenever we save the file. Save the settings file (don't close it just yet), and let's see this in action.

Navigate to **Choose File** | **Open...** from the menu and select a folder to open for now, let's open our `tooling` folder. The simple user interface of Sublime Text makes it clear that we only have one file in our project right now: `main.go`. Click on the file and add some extra linefeeds, and add and remove some indenting. Then, navigate to **File** | **Save** from the menu, or press *command* + *S*. Note that the code is immediately cleaned up, and provided that you haven't removed the oddly placed return statement from `main.go`, you will notice that the console has appeared and is reporting the issue thanks to go vet:

```
main.go:8: unreachable code
```

Holding down *command* + *shift* and double-clicking on the unreachable code line in the console will open the file and jump the cursor to the right line in question. You can see how helpful this feature is going to be as you continue to write Go code.

If you add an unwanted import to the file, you will notice that on using `on_save`, you are told about the problem, but it wasn't automatically fixed. This is because we have another tweak to make. In the same settings file as the one you added the `on_save` property to, add the following property:

```
"fmt_cmd": ["goimports"]
```

This tells GoSublime to use the `goimports` command instead of `go fmt`. Save this file again, and head back to `main.go`. Add `net/http` to the imports again, remove `fmt` import, and save the file. Note that the unused package was removed, and `fmt` was put back again.

Visual Studio Code

A surprise entry in the running for best Go IDE is Microsoft's Visual Studio Code, available for free at `https://code.visualstudio.com`.

Once you've downloaded it from the website, open a Go file (any file with a `.go` extension) and note that Visual Studio Code asks whether you'd like to install the recommended plugins to make working with Go files easier:

Click on **Show Recommendations** and click on **Install** next to the suggested Go plugin:

It may ask you to restart Visual Studio Code to enable the plugin, and it may also ask you to install some additional commands:

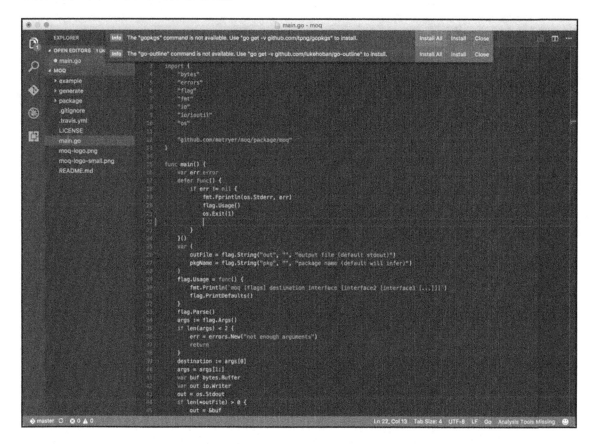

Click on **Install All** to install all the dependencies, being sure to wait for the previous installation process to finish before initiating others. After a short while, you will notice that a few tools were installed.

Write some messy code (or copy and paste some from https://github.com/matryer/goblueprints/blob/master/appendixA/messycode/main.go) into Visual Studio Code and hit save. You will notice that the imports were fixed and the code was nicely formatted as per the Go standard.

There are many more features that you can make use of, but we won't dig into them further here.

Summary

In this appendix, we installed Go and are now ready to start building real projects. We learned about the GOPATH environment variable and discovered a common practice of keeping one value for all projects. This approach dramatically simplifies working on Go projects, where you are likely to continue to encounter tricky failures otherwise.

We discovered how the Go toolset can really help us produce high-quality, community-standards-compliant code that any other programmer could pick up and work on with little to no additional learning. And more importantly, we looked at how automating the use of these tools means we can truly get down to the business of writing applications and solving problems, which is all developers really want to do.

We looked at a couple of options for code editors or IDEs and saw how easy it was to add plugins or extensions that help writing Go code easier.

Index

Made in the USA
Monee, IL
02 June 2021